From the Editor

The Computeractive Ultimate Guide:
Raspberry Pi for Kids

Contact us:
letters@computeractive.co.uk

Any parent or grandparent reading this will probably remember the 'golden age' of home computing back in the 1980s, when grown-ups and children alike experimented with devices such as the ZX Spectrum, the Acorn Electron and the BBC Micro, learning valuable skills in the process. These were the computers that brought families together, inspiring a generation of programmers, scientists and engineers.

Over the last couple of decades, Windows PCs, Apple Macs and tablets have changed the way we use computers altogether. With devices like these, you don't really need to understand much about how they work in order to use them. You certainly don't need to know anything about programming languages and you probably won't even pick up this type of knowledge by osmosis; this whole side of computing is carefully concealed behind colourful graphics and easy-to-use interfaces. To their credit, Microsoft and Apple have made computers much more accessible than they used to be. But modern PCs are not only expensive, they also lack the opportunity for creativity and excitement offered by earlier home computers.

The Raspberry Pi changes all that. It's cheap (from just £24) and easy to use, but offers the chance for people of all ages to re-engage with the true principles of computing and learn something of value, whilst having bags of fun in the process. Now is a great time to jump on-board, too. Earlier this year, Google and the Raspberry Pi Foundation joined forces, promising to donate 15,000 free Raspberry Pi computers to schools across the UK. Since then, the Secretary of State for Education has announced plans for some big changes to the national curriculum, which could potentially push computer science and related subjects right to the forefront of the classroom as soon as 2014.

The Raspberry Pi might be small but its potential is enormous. The aim of this guide is to tap into that by helping parents and children to get started with their Pi and work together on a wide range of fun projects that are both enjoyable and educational. Who knows – maybe computing is on the verge of a whole new golden age.

Jonathan Parkyn
Editor

Raspberry Pi for Kids

EDITORIAL
Editor: Jonathan Parkyn
Art Editor: Ian Jackson
Production Editor: Nigel Whitfield
Consulting Editor: Daniel Booth
Digital Production Manager: Nicky Baker

Contributors: James Bennett, Darien Graham-Smith, Kevin Partner, Tim Smith, Kelvyn Taylor, Nigel Whitfield, Wayne Williams

MANAGEMENT
MagBook Publisher: Dharmesh Mistry
Operations Director: Robin Ryan
MD of Advertising: Julian Lloyd-Evans
Newstrade Director: David Barker
MD of Enterprise: Martin Belson
Chief Operating Officer: Brett Reynolds
Group Finance Director: Ian Leggett
Chief Executive: James Tye
Chairman: Felix Dennis

The Computeractive Ultimate Guide: Raspberry Pi for Kids
ISBN 978-1-78106-214-2

LICENSING AND SYNDICATION
To license this product please contact Carlotta Serantoni on +44 (0) 20 7907 6550 or email carlotta_serantoni@dennis.co.uk
To syndicate content from this product please contact Anj Dosaj-Halai on +44 (0) 20 7907 6132 or email anj_dosaj-halai@dennis.co.uk

The paper used within this MagBook is produced from sustainable fibre, manufactured by mills with a valid chain of custody.

Printed at Polestar, Bicester.

Contents

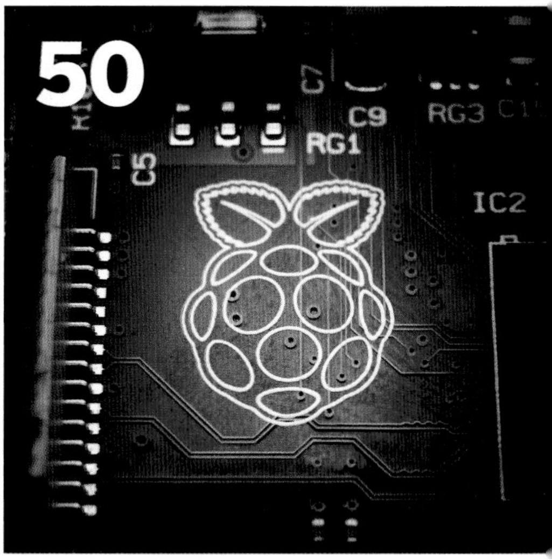

JARGON FREE! You'll notice we've highlighted all the technical terms used throughout this guide and you'll find a full glossary on page **130**

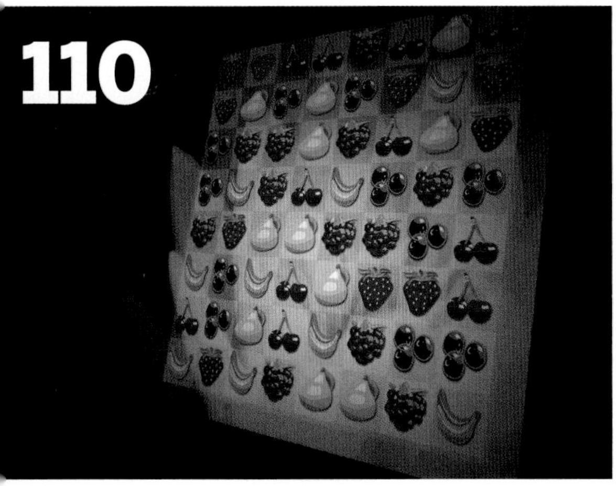

WORKSHOPS

25 pages of step-by-step guides, hints and tips

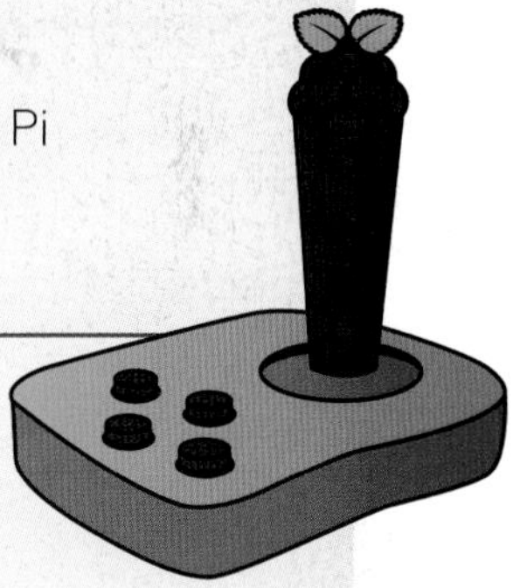

Meet the Raspberry Pi

Introducing the credit card-sized PC that has become a phenomenon

WHAT YOU'LL LEARN

- Find out exactly what the Raspberry Pi is
- Discover why the Pi was invented
- See what you can do with it

The Raspberry Pi is the sub-£30 computer that has proved more popular than anyone could have ever anticipated. In just over a year it has grown from being virtually unknown to becoming a product with enormous mass-market appeal. Demand has been so strong that, until recently, the Raspberry Pi Foundation (*www.raspberrypi.org*) and its official suppliers had been struggling to keep up. However, the Pi is now in mass production and it's easy to get hold of one. There are two slightly different models available but in both cases the possibilities offered by this cheap, unassuming little circuit board are almost limitless.

So what exactly is the Raspberry Pi? Where did it come from and how can you harness the computer's extraordinary potential for helping you with your studies and for having fun? These questions and more are among those we aim to answer over the course of this Ultimate Guide.

▼ **Small but perfectly formed, the Raspberry Pi is a great way to learn programming**

The Raspberry Pi story

Back in 2006, the Computer Laboratory at the University of Cambridge had a problem. Fewer and fewer students were applying to study computer science at the university, and the skill levels of those who did apply were declining year on year. Whereas, in the past, undergraduates had typically arrived at the university with some coding experience, by the mid-noughties most knew much more about PowerPoint than about programming.

This was partly due to a switch in emphasis at school towards teaching office applications and web design rather than how to program, but it was also because the earlier generation of home computers had been replaced by games consoles. Why did that matter? Because a ZX Spectrum, BBC Model B or Commodore 64 could be used both to play games and create software. The PlayStation 3 and Xbox, for all their technological superiority, are sealed units with no way for the average user to create their own games.

Perhaps the biggest problem, however, is caused by the way in which the internet has become part of everyday life. The average household now has at least one PC, often a laptop, which they use for everything from banking through online shopping to social networking and playing games. The idea of handing over this essential piece of kit to an inexperienced student of programming fills the rest of the family with fear – what if their experiments led to a problem with their internet banking or, worse, Facebook? What if the prospective programmer wanted to use it for hours at a time? What would they use for their Ocado shop?

There's another problem with modern laptops – they're simply over-the-top for learning to program on. Over-powered, distracting and complicated, today's operating systems are a million miles away from the blinking cursor of the classic home computer.

So, led by then-director of studies Eben Upton, the group that would one day become the Raspberry Pi Foundation set itself the target of encouraging 1,000 new computer science students across the UK. Since they couldn't re-write the syllabus taught in schools, they decided to focus on what they could do – so they began work on a new type of computer that would be easy to program and, critically, cheap to buy.

▲ Just add LEGO, and sixty three helping of Raspberry Pi, to make a supercomputer

Surprise hit

Fast-forward to February 2012 and component suppliers Farnell and RS Electronics opened their websites for pre-orders of the Raspberry Pi. Though the project had been started with the aim of producing 1,000 units per year, initial interest was such that 10,000 were planned for production in 2012. Within minutes of going live with their Raspberry Pi order pages, the initial allocation had disappeared in a wisp of smoke. A few days later, 100,000 pre-orders had been taken, with around a million units estimated to have shipped in 2012.

An education edition is due to be launched at a price that would allow a school to buy a dozen Raspberry Pis for the cost of one budget laptop and the foundation has also launched an even cheaper £24 version, called the Model A, with a lower specification. For the most part, this guide will focus on the more capable Model B, though our instructions can be used for either device.

The perfect platform for learning programming

The Pi has been designed to provide the ideal environment for learning programming – whether that's simply for the fun of it or as the start of a career. It's cheap, compact and rugged, and it comes with most of the tools you need to create your own programs built in.

It may not be as fast as the family laptop, but think about this; the computer controlling the Mars Curiosity rover currently trundling across the surface of the red planet is less powerful than a £30 Raspberry Pi. If NASA's chip can power a space probe, just imagine what you can do with your Pi. ca

▼ Use your Kindle as a screen for the Raspberry Pi, with KindleBerry Pi

THE POSSIBILITIES

Throughout this guide we will be demonstrating the many ways you can make use of your Raspberry Pi, from turning it into a security camera to spot trespassers in your bedroom to using it to program your own very first game. But it needn't stop there.
Here are just a few of the inspirational real-life projects that Raspberry Pi owners have carried out themselves.

The LEGO supercomputer
The University of Southampton used 64 Raspberry Pi computers and LEGO bricks to create the most powerful Pi – the 1TB Pi (the cumulative amount of memory provided by its SD cards). Iridis-Pi, as the computer is known, is named after the university's own supercomputer.
Find out how to make your own (or simply how it was done) at *www.snipca.com/9330*. Unfortunately, there is no bulk order discount for buying 64 Pi computers at once.

The first Pi in space
Dave Akerman has launched four Raspberry Pi computers high into the skies (*www.snipca.com/9297*). Fantastically, he uses a tiny Doctor Who Tardis to house the Pi and several hydrogen-filled weather balloons to transport the Pi into near space. The fourth launch, in March, sent the Pi 35km above Earth where a 3G link and onboard telemetry ensured plenty of stratospheric photos could be relayed back to 'mission control'.
Before the Pi travelled beyond 3G range, Pi fans were able to track the Pi Tardis via a live video stream. There's a video of the mission on the RasPi.TV website (*www.snipca.com/9270*).

Turning a Kindle into a mini Pi PC
If you're happy to 'jailbreak' your Kindle you can turn it into a mini computer. You'll need a powered USB hub, a small keyboard (for setup) and a terminal emulator for the Kindle. Details on setting up USB networking and how to enable multi-user screen mode are given on this blog post titled KindleBerry Pi (*www.snipca.com/9244*).

Adding Wi-Fi to a digital SLR camera
You can buy a camera to add directly to your Pi computer (*www.snipca.com/9296*), but some people prefer to hack their existing cameras and marry them with their Pi.
Linux developer David Hunt installed a Raspberry Pi in a camera grip and used its USB port to add a Wi-Fi dongle. This lets him back up his digital photos as he goes. He also suggests controlling the camera remotely over Wi-Fi. Instructions and a summary of what he did are available at *www.snipca.com/9295*.

SECTION 1

First steps

The Raspberry Pi works differently to most computers but there's no need to panic – we're here to help you get started

Despite its diminutive size, the Raspberry Pi can feel like a daunting prospect to begin with. The fact that it comes as a naked circuit board makes it look very technical. And, since it doesn't run Windows, the idea of learning a whole new interface can seem off-putting. In fact, one of the Pi's chief advantages is its simplicity. Anyone can learn how to use it, whatever your age and regardless of how much previous experience you've had. And in this section of our guide we explain all you need to know to get going, including what you'll need and how it all fits together.

IN THIS SECTION

What is the Raspberry Pi?

We examine the Pi up close to find out what makes it tick

WHAT YOU'LL LEARN

- Discover how the Pi works
- Understand the difference between the Model A and the Model B
- Find out the best place to buy one

Raspberry Pi computers were conceived to inspire young programmers to hone their coding talents and earn themselves a place on the computing degree course at Cambridge University. But when word got out about a tiny sub-£30 computer anyone could buy and write programs for, suddenly everyone wanted to get their hands on a slice of Pi.

When your Raspberry Pi arrives, the first thing you'll notice when you clap eyes on it is that it's very different to the type of computer you might be used to. For starters, it's tiny – the size of a credit card. It also has no case; it's simply a printed circuit board. Despite its diminutive size, low price and unglamorous appearance, however, the Pi is a fully functional computer. Let's take a closer look at the Pi's component parts and find out what types of tasks it's physically capable of.

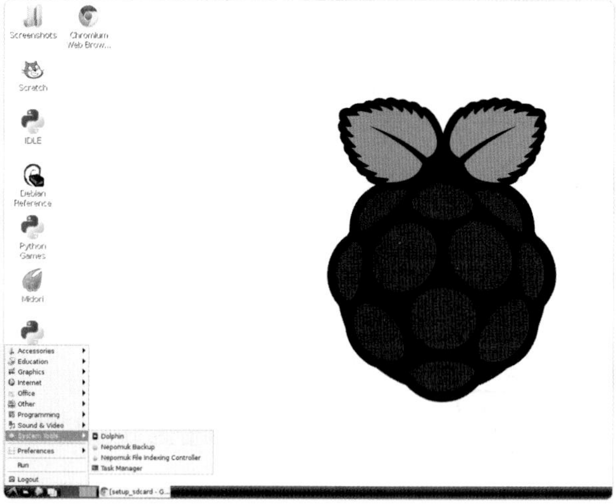

▲ Just like a PC, the Pi has a user-friendly, graphical interface

The brains

A single chip (1 on the diagram) contains **memory**, the **central processing unit** and graphics chip. The Raspberry Pi uses a chip designed by ARM – the same company that designs processors used in many smartphones and tablets. The version used in the Pi is slower than you'll find in an iPad, for example, but it's fast enough to do the job.

Unlike the relatively pedestrian **CPU**, the Graphics Processing Unit on the Pi is equivalent to a top-of-the-line mobile device. It can run 3D games and play **high-definition** video (indeed, one of the most common uses for the Pi is as a very cheap media centre). With the right software, a TV and a broadband link you can have iPlayer, YouTube and other internet video services at your fingertips.

The Pi comes with 512**MB** of Random Access Memory (**RAM**) – plenty for the uses we're going to put it to. It also comes with an **SD card** slot (2) – exactly the same as that used by many digital cameras – which takes the place of the hard disk found in most laptops. Programs are stored on the SD card and, once the Pi is powered on, these are copied into the much faster RAM until the computer is turned off, when the RAM is cleared. One great convenience of the Pi is that you can turn it from a media player to a desktop computer simply by swapping out the SD card – much easier than removing a laptop's hard disk!

Sound and vision

One of the design requirements for the Raspberry Pi was that it should be easy to hook up to existing equipment, so it includes an **HDMI** port (3) for connecting to a TV or computer monitor. HDMI

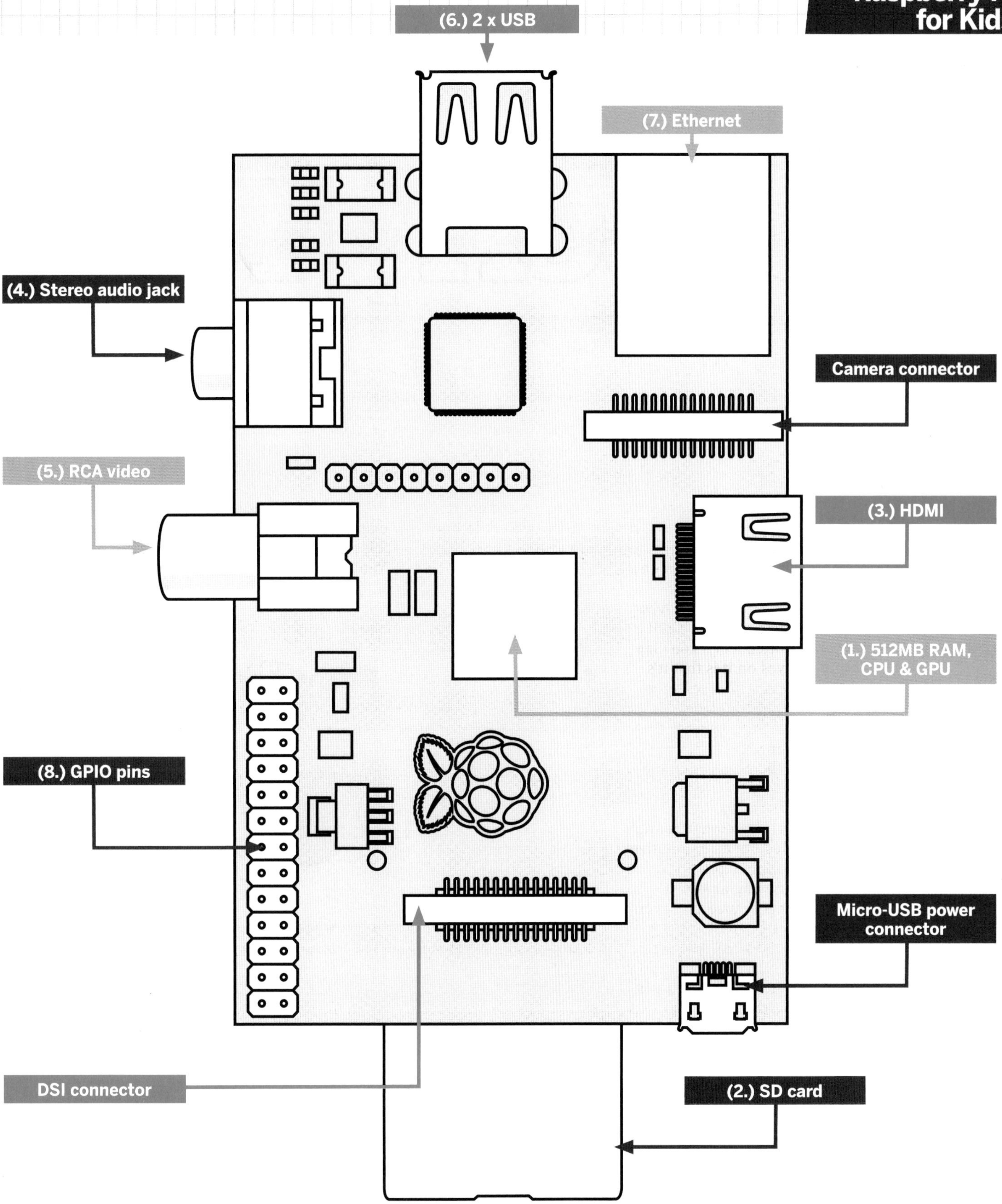
(6.) 2 x USB
(7.) Ethernet
(4.) Stereo audio jack
Camera connector
(5.) RCA video
(3.) HDMI
(1.) 512MB RAM, CPU & GPU
(8.) GPIO pins
Micro-USB power connector
DSI connector
(2.) SD card

> “ The Raspberry Pi is designed to plug into your TV. Just add a keyboard, mouse and power supply. ”

carries both picture and sound, so if you use a monitor without built-in speakers, you may need to plug a set of speakers into the stereo audio jack (4). If your monitor doesn't have an HDMI socket, you can buy a cheap adaptor to convert it to **DVI** – it's even possible to connect a **VGA**-only monitor with an adaptor and a bit of wrangling.

If you're really stuck, you can use the RCA video jack (5) to connect to the composite video input on an old-fashioned CRT TV. However, this was added mainly to allow the Pi to be used in the Third World where TVs are more common than monitors – the picture quality is poor.

Connections

The Raspberry Pi Model B comes with two **USB** ports (6) that you can use to connect a keyboard, mouse, Wi-Fi dongle or any compatible peripheral. You'll probably want to buy a USB hub to allow you to plug in multiple devices at once – just make sure it has a separate power adaptor; the Pi's ports supply only a low voltage.

You can connect the Raspberry Pi Model B directly to your router or a wired network via the standard **Ethernet** port (7) – this gives the fastest and most reliable connection to the internet. Note that the cheaper Model A Pi has a slightly different selection of sockets – see the box below for more details.

▼ Farnell is one of the official suppliers of the Raspberry Pi in the United Kingdom

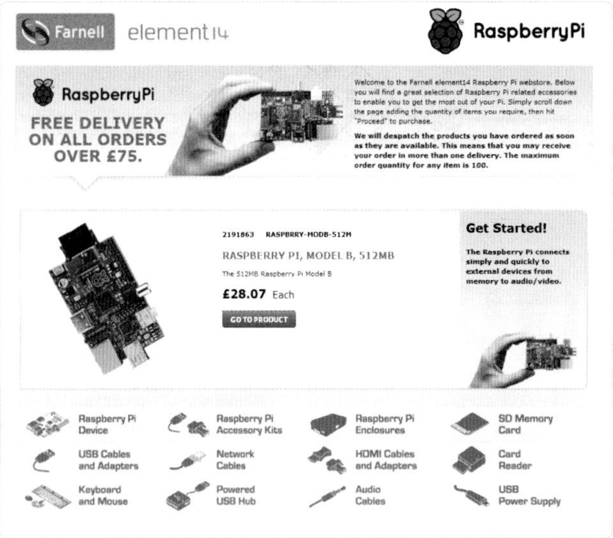

Pi Pins

So far, everything we've described (apart from the SD card) is pretty standard to all computers. However, the Pi has some extra capabilities not found on your common or garden laptop. The most important of these are the General Purpose Input Output (GPIO) pins (8), which offer various ways to control devices and receive input from sensors and such like. However, misusing these pins can bake your Pi so it's best to use one of the many add-on boards that allow you to experiment safely. We cover some of these options later on.

The Pi also includes a connector for a camera module and a DSI connector for connecting the Pi to certain specialist displays such as mobile phone screens. We'll be looking at some of the ways to expand and upgrade the Pi from page 120.

The software

There wouldn't be much point in a cheap computer if you had to install an expensive OS on it (such as Windows or Apple's OS X) to get it to work. This, and the fact that no version of Windows or OS X will work on the ARM chip in the Pi, means that the various OSes created for it are all based on the free and open-source **Linux**.

The foundation recommends Raspbian, a version of Debian that's a popular distribution of Linux. If this sounds like gobbledygook, don't worry – if you've used Windows, you'll find Raspbian pretty familiar.

You can even install Linux versions of many of the programs you're familiar with including LibreOffice for Microsoft-compatible word processing and spreadsheet work, and even the Chrome browser. We'll explain how to add software of all kinds from page 24. But before you do that you'll need to install Raspbian itself on your Pi first. Head to page 18 to find out how. ca

WHERE CAN I GET A PI?

If you haven't yet got a Raspberry Pi computer, head to Farnell (***http://uk.farnell.com***) or RS (***http://uk.rs-online.com***) to buy one. These official distributors are most likely to have the hard-to-find, cheaper Model A. You need to spend at least £24 per order at Farnell to pay using a debit or credit card (rather than setting up a business account). You can also buy a Pi through Amazon. However, it currently costs £25.16 plus shipping, compared to the £23.76 with free delivery that Farnell charges.

There isn't a big difference between the £24 256MB RAM Model A and the £34 512MB Model B. Both use a 700MHz Broadcom SoC (system on a chip) – the sort of processor that runs a smartphone and which includes a graphics chip as well as the main CPU. However, the Model A has a single USB port and doesn't have an Ethernet port, so you'll need to plug in a USB Wi-Fi dongle to get online. If you can afford the extra cash required to buy the Model B, then we recommend doing so, simply because of the added built-in connectivity options.

In addition to the Pi itself, you'll need a few other accessories before you can get started. Head to page 16 to find out what you'll need together with some important tips.

What do I need?

◀ The Pi will accept SD cards of up to 32GB in size

To get your Pi working, a few essential accessories are required. We explain what's needed and what your options are

WHAT YOU'LL LEARN

» Find out what you'll need to get started

» Discover how to get everything as cheaply as possible

» Learn how to control your Pi remotely

Although the Raspberry Pi is incredibly cheap considering what it can do, the barebones circuit board comes without many of the basic bits and pieces needed to turn it into a usable computer. While adding these can cost money, the good news is that in many cases you can use spare kit that you have lying around, or pick them up second-hand. Here we'll explain the must-have items, and also some optional accessories that can make the Raspberry Pi experience even more fun. Most accessories mentioned here are available from the official Pi partners, Farnell (*www.snipca.com/9715*) and RS Components (*www.snipca.com/9716*).

Storage

As the Raspberry Pi has no built-in storage, the most important extra you will need is an **SD card**. This stores the **operating system** along with your own files and projects. It must be at least 4GB in size and preferably a 'Class 4' speed grade or higher. The bigger the capacity the more room you'll have for your own stuff. Cards up to 32GB are supported - larger ones need some advanced tinkering to work. Cards are often bundled with the Pi itself for a couple of pounds extra, or a new 4GB SD card normally costs well under £7. Always buy branded cards from a reputable store to avoid fakes.

As the operating system is entirely contained on the SD card, there's nothing to stop you putting it on several cards and swapping them as needed - for example, you could have one card for programming projects and another configured to use your Raspberry Pi as a media player (see page 32).

Experienced users can connect **USB** hard disks or USB keys to add more file storage later if needed, but these can't easily be used for the operating system itself - the Pi can only start from an SD card. We'll be looking further into USB storage on page 28.

▼ Many micro-USB phone chargers are suitable for powering the Pi

Power supply

The Pi gets its power from a separate micro-USB power adapter, which can be bought very cheaply (CPC sells one for £3.54, *www.snipca.com/9717*). However, if you have a mobile phone charger with a micro-USB connector you might be able to use that instead.

The only requirement is that it can supply 5 volts and least 700 milliamps (mA) of current. Check the label on the power supply and look for the 'Output' figures. It should say '5V' and the milliamp rating - it doesn't matter how large the milliamp number is, as long as it's over 700mA. The more power it has, the less likely you are to have problems with USB devices.

Keyboard and mouse

To get up and running, a USB keyboard and mouse are essential. Any models are suitable, and no software or drivers are needed. Wireless sets are a good choice, as they only use one USB port. However, if the wireless adapter takes too much power, it can prevent the from Pi starting up. If this happens, it can be solved by using a powered USB hub instead (see opposite). CPC sells a basic wireless desktop set for £18.

◀ The Pi has HDMI (left) and composite (right) video connectors ▶

Display

The Pi offers two display connectors, **HDMI** and composite video. For best results use an HDMI cable (just over £1 on Amazon). Most HD TVs and some newer PC monitors have HDMI, but some older monitors only have **DVI** or **VGA** connectors. An HDMI to DVI cable costs around £5. If you already have an HDMI cable, a DVI adapter is a pound or so cheaper. HDMI to VGA converters sre more expensive at around £18, but still cheaper than a new monitor. Composite video cables (less than a pound) can be used with older CRT TVs.

Audio

The stereo minijack audio output on the Pi can be connected to headphones, powered speakers, or a standard hi-fi sound system. A 3.5mm minijack to dual-phono cable costing about a pound might be needed if the hi-fi has phono (also called RCA) connectors. If an HDMI cable is used to connect to a TV (or a monitor with built-in speakers), a separate audio cable isn't needed.

Network

To connect the Pi to the internet, a wired or Wi-Fi network connection to your home **router** is needed. The Model B Pi has a wired network port that takes a standard **Ethernet** network cable costing a couple of pounds. A USB Wi-Fi dongle can also be used, and CPC sells a compatible Dynamode 11n model for £7. If you already have a spare dongle it's worth trying, but not all work. No software is needed as the **drivers** are included in the operating system. For the Model A, you'll need a USB hub to connect dongle, keyboard and mouse at the same time. Head to page 26 to read more about using Wi-Fi.

▲ A USB Wi-Fi adapter is a handy way to network the Pi

Optional extras

One of the most useful accessories is a powered USB hub. This connects to one of the Pi's USB ports and allows several devices to be connected at once without draining power from the Pi. Hubs typically have four or seven ports, and a seven-port model from CPC costs just £10. Don't use unpowered hubs, as they could overload the Pi's power supply. A great addition to any Pi is a case to protect components. A basic plastic case costs £5.39 from CPC and comes in several colours.

There are loads of exciting new accessories appearing all the time, including a very cool Raspberry Pi camera board. We'll be looking at this and other upgrades and add-ons later on in our guide (from page 120). ca

SAVE MONEY WITH REMOTE DESKTOP

Thanks to a technology called remote desktop protocol (RDP), it is very easy to control a Pi via another computer, using the Remote Desktop feature found in all Windows PCs. This means that your Raspbian desktop will appear on the screen of a Windows computer and you'll be able to control it using the Windows PC's mouse and keyboard, rather than having to buy a dedicated keyboard, mouse or display. You'll still need to plug your Pi into a 'real' keyboard, mouse and display temporarily to get your Remote Desktop system up and running.

Remote Desktop isn't a suitable option for every purpose - for example if you want to use the Pi as a media player - but it is very handy for getting started. Setting up remote desktop is very easy (it needs a network connection, of course), with just one bit of extra software (xrdp) to be installed on the Pi by typing the command **sudo apt-get xrdp** in a terminal window. There are instructions at *www.snipca.com/9719* and on page 124

Install an operating system on your Pi

Find out how to set up your Raspberry Pi's OS the simple way

Once the jiffy bag containing your tiny new computer lands on your doormat, you have a little work to do before you can connect it to a display and boot it up, including installing an **operating system** (OS) – the software that provides an interface for the Pi and allows you to run other programs. The Raspberry Pi uses a standard **SD card** instead of the **hard disk** you'll find in most laptops, and your first job is to prepare the SD card and transfer a suitable operating system to it. Until recently, you had to use a special Windows program to 'burn' an OS image to your SD card; that option is still available should you wish to make use of it (see steps 5 and 6). However, the process of installing an operating system has been now been made a whole lot simpler thanks to something called NOOBS. It stands for New Out Of Box Software and makes setting up your Pi much simpler than before. Follow the steps to install the recommended operating system – Raspbian – on your Pi.

STEP 1 The Pi's Raspbian operating system runs from an SD card. Programs you install will also be stored and run from this card. You can use SD cards of up to 32GB, but a capacity of 4 or 8GB is plenty.
You can buy an SD card with the Raspbian operating system installed on it, such as the one for sale at *www.snipca.com/9314*. However, this Kingston-branded card is only a Class 4 SD card. We recommend buying a faster SD card (one with a higher class number), like the Class 10 card shown, and installing the free Raspbian OS yourself. You'll need a Windows-based computer (or a Mac) for this. If your computer doesn't have a built-in SD card slot you may need to attach a USB SD card reader. Many photo printers also have built-in SD card readers, so you could use this instead. ▼

STEP 2 You'll need to format the SD card first. Formatting will wipe the card's contents, so make sure it doesn't have anything you need stored on it. Windows has a built-in formatting tool but the Raspberry Pi Foundation recommends using the official SD Card Association Formatting Tool instead, as this is capable of formatting the entire card. PC users can download this tool free of charge from *www.snipca.com/9721* and if you're on a Mac, there's an OS X version of the tool (also free) at *www.snipca.com/9722*. We'll assume you're using Windows. Download the SDFormatter4 Zip file to your desktop, then right-click it and select Extract All, then Extract. Double-click the Setup.exe file in the extracted folder and follow the on-screen instructions to install the SD Formatter tool. ▼

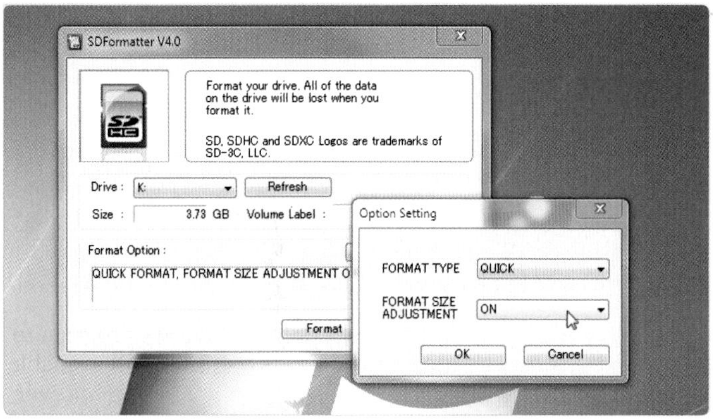

STEP 3 Insert your SD card into your PC, printer or card reader and launch SD Formatter. Under Drive, make absolutely sure that the drive letter selected is the one for your SD card; accidentally pick the wrong drive letter you could end up wiping another drive. Unplug any other external drives just to be safe and double-check by clicking on Start, then Computer that you have the correct drive selected. Now click Option and set Format Size Adjustment to On. Click OK then click Format and OK again twice. A summary will be displayed. Click OK and close the formatting tool. Now go to ***www.snipca.com/9319*** and download the NOOBS Zip file, using the Direct Download option. It's quite big (about **1GB**) so it might take a while to transfer to your PC. ▼

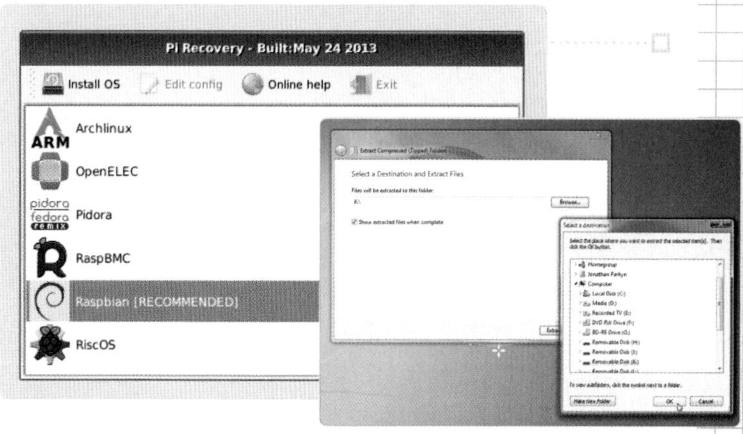

STEP 4 Right-click the Zip file and select Extract All. In the dialogue box, click the Browse button, navigate to the SD card and click OK then Extract. Now use the Safely Remove Hardware tool (in the Windows Notification Area) to eject the SD card and insert it into the Raspberry Pi. Set up the Pi as (see page 20) and switch it on. Your Pi will now boot into NOOBS and should automatically display a list of operating systems that you can install. If your screen remains blank, however, you can try manually selecting the correct display mode using the number keys on your keyboard. Tap 1 for **HDMI** mode, 2 for HDMI safe mode, 3 for Composite PAL (UK) mode and 4 for Composite NTSC (US) mode. Once you see the NOOBS dialogue, select Raspbian and click Install OS. ▼

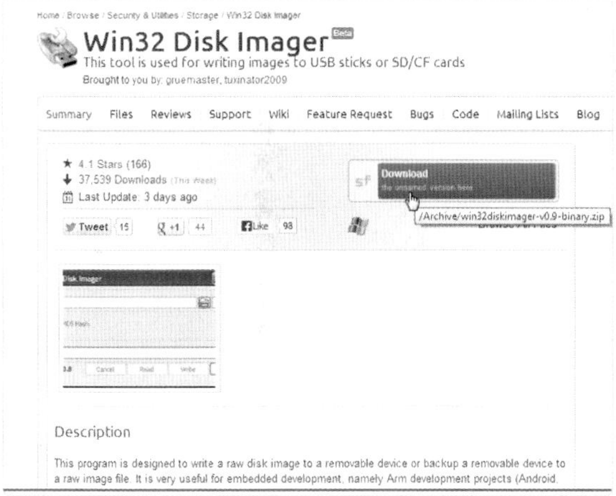

STEP 5 Though it is recommended that new users employ the NOOBS method, as described above, there is an alternative way of writing the Raspbian OS image to an SD card. You can use a utility called Image Writer for Windows to do this. Format the SD card as described in steps 1 to 3. Then, on a Windows PC, go to ***www.snipca.com/9723*** and download the most recent version of Image Writer. Make sure you get the Binary (win32diskimager-binary.zip), not the source version. Go to your Downloads folder, right-click on win32diskimager-binary.zip and select Extract All. You'll then be asked to pick a folder into which to copy the files it contains; do so then click Extract. ▼

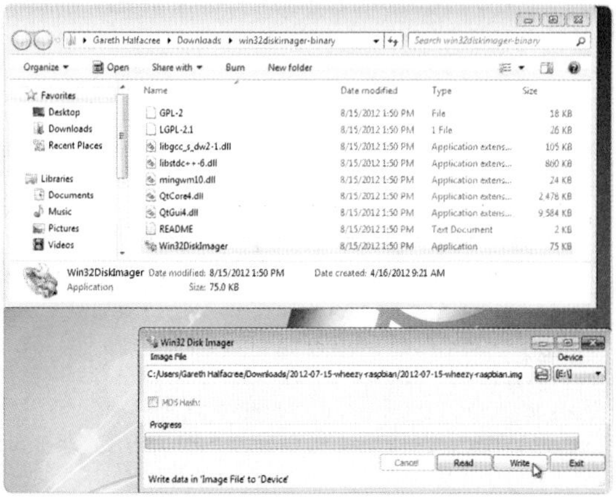

STEP 6 Now, go to the Raspberry Pi Foundation's download page at ***www.raspberrypi.org/downloads*** and look under the Raw Images section to find the Raspbian links – The 'wheezy' version is recommended for Raspberry Pi newcomers. Click the Direct Download link. Again, go to your Downloads folder, right-click and extract it. There will be only one file (it has the extension IMG). Double-click the Win32DiskImage.exe file you extracted in step 5. Click the blue folder icon and use the 'File open' box to find the IMG file you just extracted. Under Device, select your SD card from the list – be very careful to choose the correct drive letter for the SD card. Once you've checked this, click Write to transfer the image onto the card.●

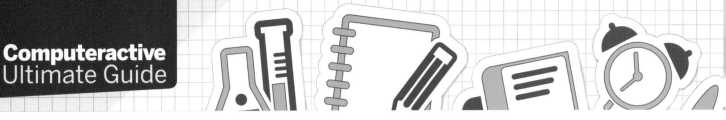

Set up your Raspberry Pi and switch it on

Find out how to put all the pieces of your Pi together and start it up for the very first time

If you followed the workshop on page 18, you should have an **SD card** ready with your Raspberry Pi's **operating system** installed. Now it's time to look at the hardware side of things. Thankfully, this part is straightforward. In most cases, there is only a single place for each cable to go and little chance of confusion with regards to what goes where. Because the Pi is supplied as a bare circuit board, care should be taken to discharge static electricity before handling it – so touch an earthed metal object (such as a radiator) or wear an anti-static wrist-strap. Here we're using a Model B, but we'll explain the differences for Model A owners. For more information on the cables and accessories required, refer back to page 16.

STEP 1 The SD card you prepared on page 18 slides into a wide, black slot that lies flush with the underside of the Raspberry Pi. The card should be inserted with the label facing away from the circuit board. The easiest way to insert the SD card is to flip the Pi onto its front, revealing the SD card slot. Push the SD card into the Pi with firm finger pressure. When fully inserted, the top of the card will be flush with the back of the slot, and the card itself will protrude from the edge of the Pi – it might look a little odd but this is how it should be. Don't try to force the SD card into the slot any further, as this could damage the slot itself. ▼

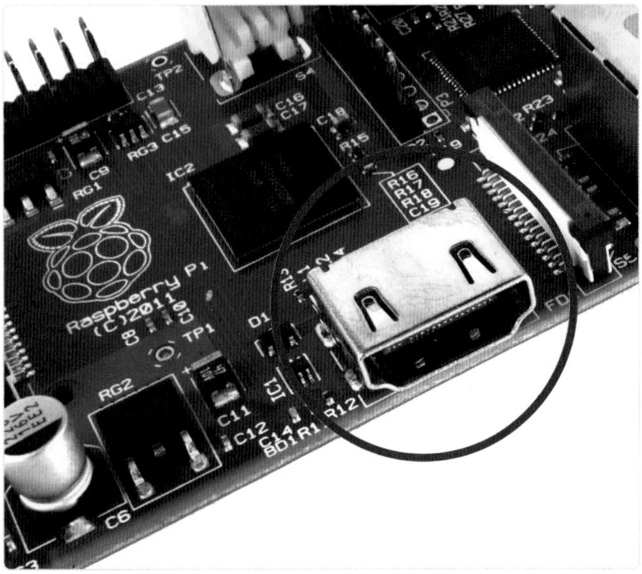

STEP 2 The Raspberry Pi is designed to be connected to either a television or a computer monitor. If connecting a Pi to a television, there are two methods; a digital connection via an **HDMI** cable (the same type of cable that the latest games consoles use) or analogue through a composite video cable (see step 3). For the best image quality, use the HDMI connection by connecting an HDMI lead from the port on the bottom of the Pi to your TV. You can connect to computer monitors that support HDMI in this way too. In both cases, the HDMI will also carry sound to the TV or monitor's built in speakers. If your monitor has a **DVI** input instead, buy an HDMI-to-DVI cable. Plug the DVI end into the monitor, and the HDMI end into the port on the bottom of the Pi. ▼

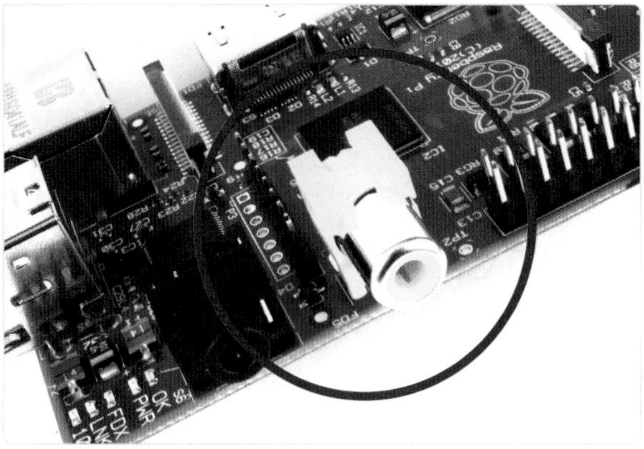

STEP 3 If you're using an older TV that lacks HDMI, connect a composite video cable from the yellow port on the top of the Pi to the TV's yellow composite socket. If the TV lacks a composite input but does have a Scart socket – the wide, flat connector type used by older video recorders – then composite-to-Scart adapters can be purchased at most electrical shops. If you're not connecting from HDMI-to-HDMI directly and you want to hear sound through your TV speakers, you will also need an audio cable with a 3.5mm jack and a pair of phono plugs. This should be connected to the black or light blue audio port on the top of the Pi, with the two plugs on the other end going into the TV's audio inputs or the Scart adapter. ▼

STEP 4 The Pi requires a keyboard and mouse that use **USB** connections; almost any modern devices will do. The Raspberry Pi Model B has two USB ports on its right-hand side. These sit proud of the other, Ethernet (network) port. Attach the keyboard and mouse, checking that the USB connectors are the right way up before pushing them in. Both the Pi's full-size USB ports will now be occupied. This doesn't matter in the short term but connecting additional USB devices later will require the purchase of a powered USB hub. Owners of Model A Raspberry Pi units will definitely need a hub, as this edition of the device only has a single USB port on it. See page 16 for more advice on USB hubs. ▼

STEP 5 The network connection needs to be made to the Pi in order to provide access to the internet. The Pi does not have built-in Wi-Fi connectivity, so this needs to be done using a traditional **Ethernet** network cable strung between the Pi and a **router** or modem. Push one end of the cable into the network port on the right-hand side of the Pi, making sure the small plastic lug is facing downwards. Once inserted far enough, the plug should make an audible click and resist being pulled out again. The other end of the cable should be connected to a router, **ADSL** modem or cable modem. It is also possible to add wireless network facilities; this is particularly useful for owners of the Model A Raspberry Pi, which doesn't have an Ethernet socket. Turn to page 26 for detailed instructions. ▼

STEP 6 Finally, the Pi needs power, from a mains adapter using a micro-USB cable. With all the cables connected, your Pi should look as shown. As soon as the Pi is connected to the power, it will switch on. Lots of text will scroll up the screen. The Raspi-config menu will appear; for now, these settings can be safely ignored (see page 22 for more on these), so just press the Tab key on the keyboard until the Finish option is selected then press Enter to leave the menu. A text screen will appear asking for a username. For the Raspbian operating system we installed on page 18, this is simply 'pi' – so type in **pi**, press the Enter key, then type **raspberry** as the password and press Enter again. ●

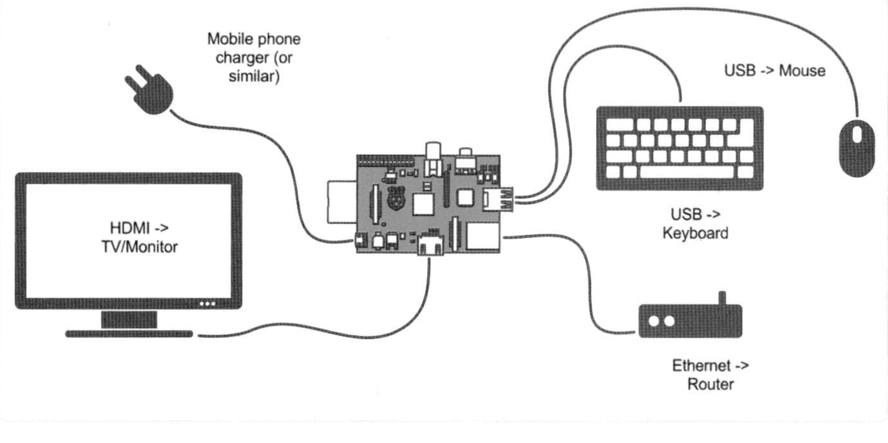

Configuring your Raspberry Pi

Explore the various configuration options available and find out how to optimise your Pi

Once the Raspbian operating system is installed on the Pi (see page 18) and it boots up for the first time, the first thing it does is run a special program called raspi-config. This allows you to configure many aspects of the Raspberry Pi's software and hardware. For example you can set the time zone, choose the correct keyboard, and even make the Pi run faster. It is a very easy program to use, but is essential for getting the best out of the Pi. Raspi-config can also be run at any time from the desktop or the command line. In this workshop we'll not only explain how to do this, but we'll also walk you through each of the main settings explaining what they do and how to make the right choices.

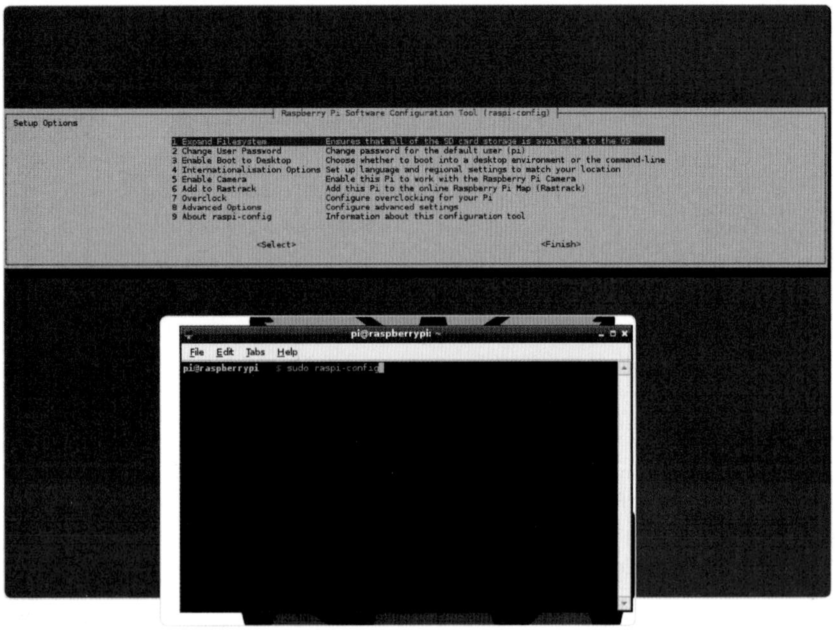

STEP 1 After installing the Raspbian operating system (see page 18), the Pi will restart and after a few moments of text scrolling down the screen, the raspi-config program screen will appear. It only does this automatically the first time Raspbian is started, but raspi-config can be started at any time. From the command line, just type **sudo raspi-config**. From the desktop, open the LXTerminal program and type the same command. Raspi-config is a simple text menu with nine options. Use the up and down arrow keys and the Tab key to navigate around the screen - the mouse will not work in this program. The first option on the screen (Expand Filesystem) isn't needed if you used the official NOOBS package to install Raspbian, we as explained in the workshop on page 18. ▼

STEP 2 The second option allows you to change the default password ('raspberry'), which is a good idea to help keep the Pi secure. Select this option, press Enter, then press Enter again. A command line appears asking for the new password. Type it, press Enter, type it again and press Enter again. When successful you will be returned to the main menu. The third option down is Enable Boot to Desktop, which saves you having to start the graphical desktop manually every time. Select this, press Enter, then choose Yes to go straight to the Desktop, or No if you prefer to start from the command line. Starting the Desktop from the command line is simply a matter of typing **startx** and pressing Enter. ▼

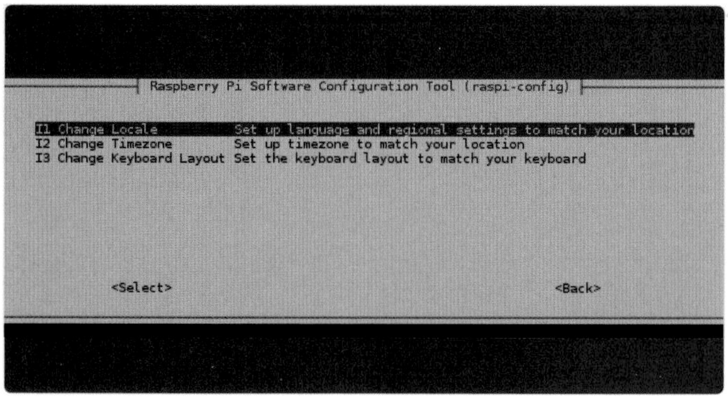

STEP 3 If a key on your keyboard produces the wrong letter, fix it with Internationalisation Options. Select this, press Enter, select Change Locale and press Enter. Choose 'All locales' from the list, select OK then press Enter. Select OK on the next screen, press Enter and wait until the main menu returns. Open the same menu again and choose Time Zone. Select Europe from the list, press Enter, select your nearest city and press Enter again. Finally, to set the keyboard layout, open Internationalisation Options again, choose Change Keyboard Layout then press Enter. Choose 'Generic 105-key (Intl) PC', press Enter, then 'English (UK)' and press Enter again. On the next three screens, we recommend keeping the default settings; press Enter until you return to the main menu. ▼

STEP 4 Option 5 on the main menu, Enable Camera, is only needed if you have the Raspberry Pi camera module (see page 120). We don't recommend using Option 6, Add to Rastrack, as it just adds the Pi's location to an online database. The Overclock option is of interest to those wanting to improve the Pi's performance. Open this, press Enter then choose an overclocking option. We recommend trying 'Modest' first to see if it causes any problems. Trying the faster options will make the Pi become hotter and may reduce its lifespan and cause crashes, so don't use them if you leave the Pi turned on all the time. The fastest options will give you a noticeable boost in the Pi's speed, though. The Pi needs to be restarted before the changes take effect. ▼

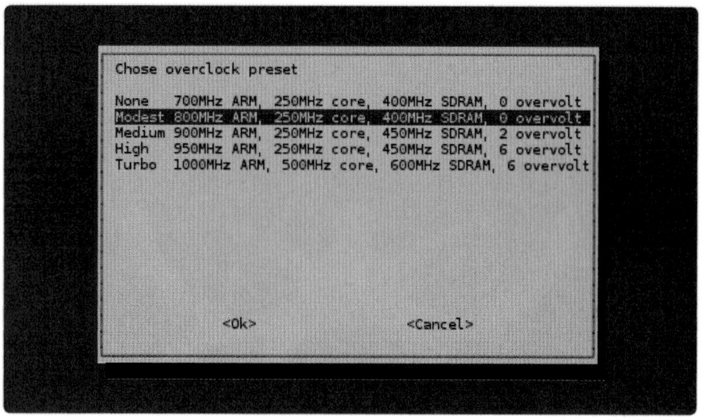

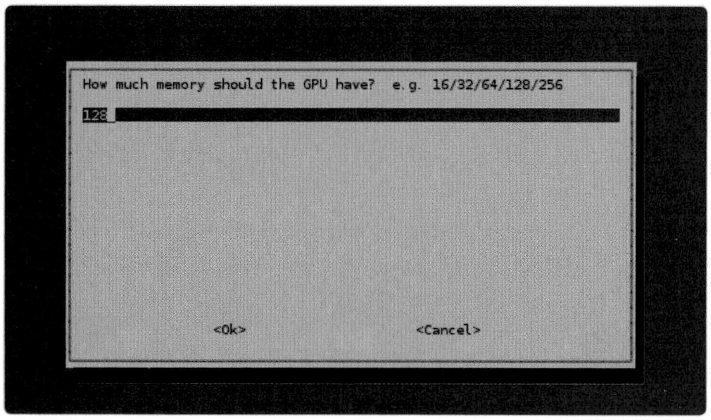

STEP 5 The Advanced Options has several useful settings. Overscan is only needed if you are connecting to a TV via the composite video connector - it removes the black bars at the edges of the screen. Hostname lets you change the Pi's network name from the default of 'raspberrypi'. Open this, press Enter, then type the new name in the box. Only standard letters and numbers can be used. Memory Split lets you change the amount of memory used for graphics. In most cases you don't need to change this, but if using it as a media player or for games you can improve performance a little by increasing this to 256MB. If you're using your Pi without a display, you could reduce the figure to 16MB. ▼

STEP 6 The next option in the Advanced Options menu is SSH. This stands for 'secure shell' and is a way of accessing the Pi's command line remotely from another computer. It is enabled by default, but can be disabled if you don't want to use it. The final option is Update, which updates the raspi-config tool to the latest version. If your version doesn't look like the one described here, it is probably out of date. Select Update and press Enter. The tool will automatically update itself and restart. An internet connection is needed for this. When you are happy with all the changes you have made, from the main raspi-config menu select Finish then press Enter. The Pi will reboot if any of the changes require it. ●

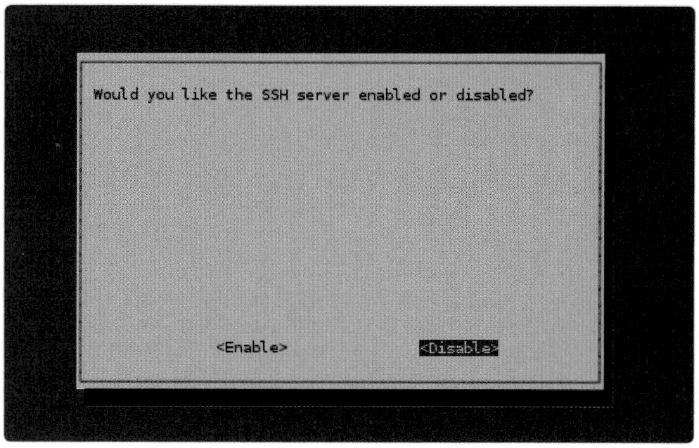

Find and install software

Discover where to get hold of the best free programs, as well as how to add them to your system

One of the major benefits of any **Linux**-based system is a huge library of free programs that are available. Finding and installing software for the Raspberry Pi is, however, very different to its Windows equivalent. Indeed, while the Raspberry Pi desktop looks superficially similar to Windows, underneath the surface there are many differences.

Rather than running a setup program, for example, with Linux you use a 'package manager' and in many cases this is done by typing in commands. Don't panic, though – it's easier than it sounds. And in this workshop we'll show you how to use a package manager as well as how to install programs via the terminal, because most online examples use this approach. ca

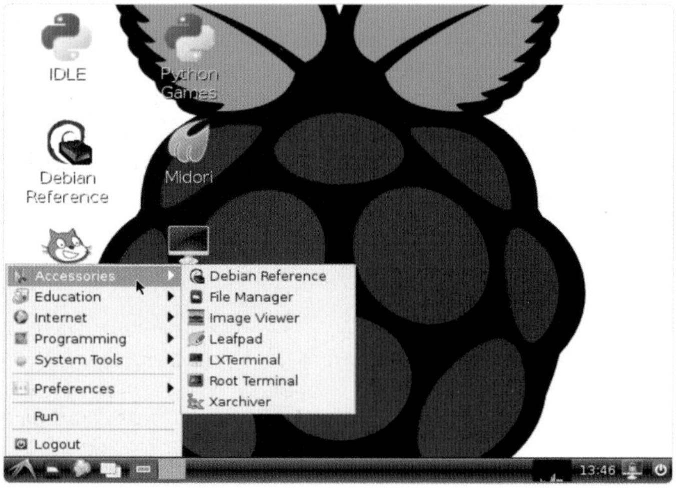

STEP 1 The Raspberry Pi comes with a basic range of software built-in. Similarly to Windows, there's a button in the bottom, left-hand corner of the screen that you can click in order to see a launch menu of programs and tools that are installed. In addition, each distribution of Linux comes with a library of optional software, called Package Repositories. You can think of the initial setup as a starting point, to which you can then add software from the repositories to suit your purpose. For a general-purpose computer, you'd probably want to install an office suite such as LibreOffice (a version of OpenOffice), and the Chromium browser (the open-source version of Google Chrome). In this case, we're going to install Chromium and then focus mainly on installing a programming editor. At various points throughout the book, we'll add extra packages. ▼

STEP 2 Let's begin by installing Chromium. Double-click LXTerminal and type: **sudo apt-get update**.followed by the Enter key. This probably looks incomprehensible, so let's take it step by step. The first command, **sudo**, tells Linux that you want to run the rest of the commands as a 'super-user'. This is similar to the Administrator user in Windows – it gives permission to change the system. This can be dangerous if not used properly, so we have to explicitly type **sudo** to confirm we want to do so. Next, **apt** is short for 'Advanced Packaging Tool' and this is the program that installs our software; **get** is the utility within apt that does this – it gets packages. Finally **update** tells apt-get to download the latest list of packages: you should always update apt-get before trying to install software. ▼

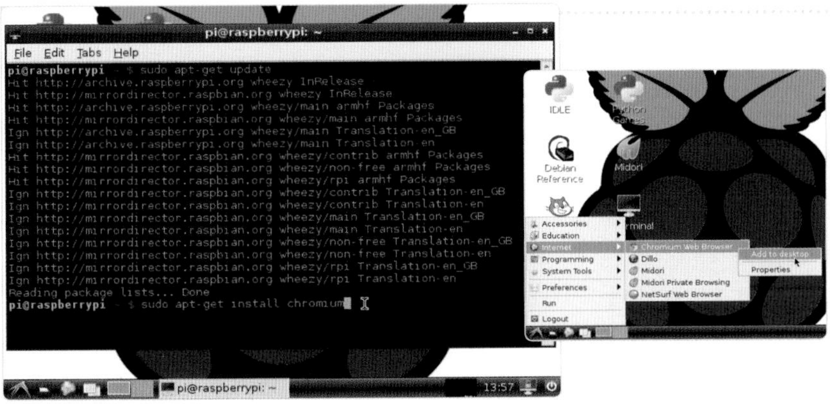

STEP 3 Wait for the update to complete; the 'pi@raspberrypi' prompt will appear once it's done. Now, to install Chromium we can type: **sudo apt-get install chromium** and Enter. This time we tell apt-get to 'install' a named package. Your terminal window will now fill with lines of text explaining what it's doing as the software installs. You may be told how much disk space the program will use up and be prompted to confirm the installation. Type **Y** and then Enter to do so. When it's done, close the LXTerminal window. Chromium will be available from the Internet submenu of the Start button. To place an icon on the desktop, right-click it in the submenu and select 'Add to desktop' ▼

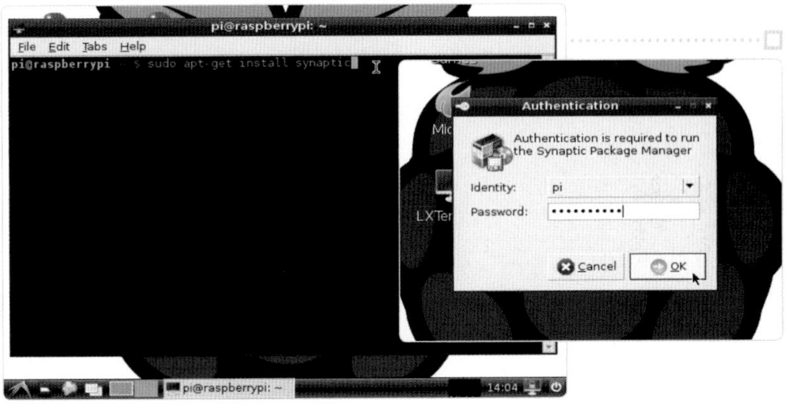

STEP 4 This is all very well, but how do you know what to install and what the package name is? One way is to Google 'office software for Raspberry Pi', but another is to install a graphical package manager. In an LXTerminal window, type: **sudo apt-get install synaptic** This will download and install the Synaptic Package Manager. Once this is done, you will find it by clicking the Start button and choosing the Other submenu. Click Synaptic and you'll be asked to type your password (which, unless you've changed it, will be 'raspberry'). You'll now see a window containing all the packages available to the Raspberry Pi, organised by type. ▼

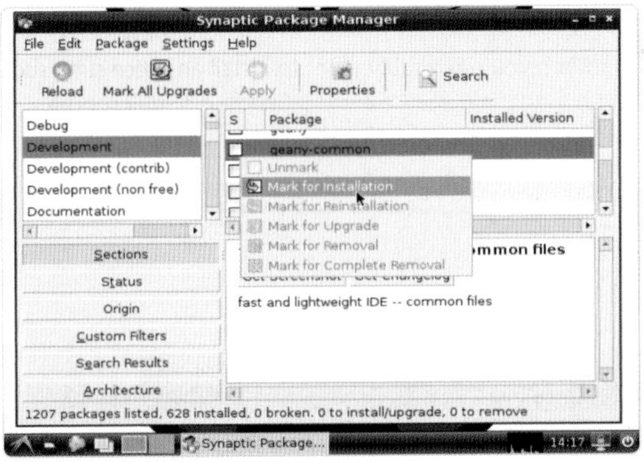

STEP 5 We're going to use Synaptic to install a code editor called Geany. On the left side of the Synaptic window, scroll down to the Development category. Now scroll through the right-hand window until you find Geany. In fact, you need to click the package geany-common first, then select Mark for Installation, before doing the same with the geany package. Once you've done this, click the Apply button to install it. This is straightforward, but remember the equivalent command in the terminal would be **sudo apt-get install geany**, which is clearly much quicker. So, if you know the package name, you should use the command line approach; if you want to browse, choose Synaptic. Why not give it a go and install LibreOffice? ●

THE FLIP SIDE

Comparatively speaking, the Raspberry Pi is a little slow. If you're used to the snappiness of a modern computer, using heavyweight software such as LibreOffice on your Pi will feel like wading through treacle. You'll notice a delay of a couple of seconds after you double-click an icon before the program launches, for example. This is partly because an **SD card** isn't as fast as a modern hard disk when it comes to reading files, as well as reflecting the speed of the processor. Once your word processor has fully loaded, you should find the performance perfectly acceptable. Some games will work well on the Pi too – 3D shoot-em-up Quake 3 was famously ported across very early on. However, the Pi is not designed for playing the latest high-end games, so don't imagine it will replace an Xbox for that purpose.

Set up Wi-Fi and print from your Pi

Find out how to configure your Raspberry Pi for wireless networking and hook up to a printer

Although the Model B Raspberry Pi can connect to a network using a standard **Ethernet** cable, upgrading to Wi-Fi makes it much easier to position your Pi wherever you like. And if you own a Model A, Wi-Fi is your only choice, as there's no network socket. Fortunately, the Pi supports a good selection of **USB** Wi-Fi adaptors (sometimes called 'dongles') out of the box (the Edimax EW-7811UN is a good choice) and you can find a complete list at ***www.snipca.com/9740***. In this guide we'll be explaining not only how to set up Wi-Fi, but also how to connect your Pi to a printer. We're connecting our printer via USB (you may need a USB hub for this) but these instructions will also work for printers on a home network.

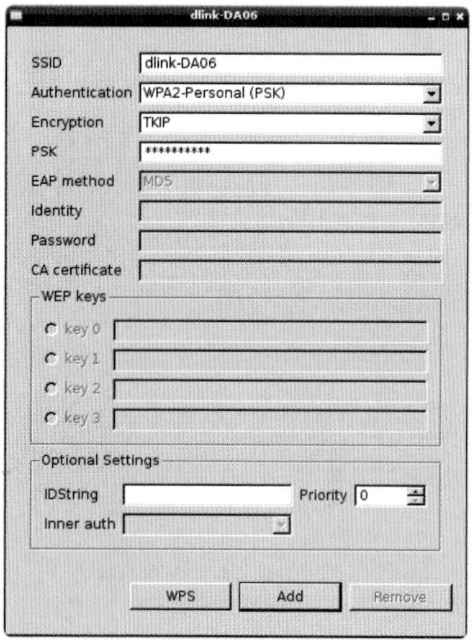

STEP 1 To get started, turn off your Raspberry Pi and plug your Wi-Fi dongle into a spare USB socket – for the Model B this can be either one of the two built-in ports. The Model A has only one USB socket so you'll need to connect the dongle to a hub. Connect your **HDMI** cable, keyboard and mouse, insert your Raspbian **SD card** and boot up. Once the desktop has loaded, double click the Wi-Fi Config icon and choose Manage Networks. Click Scan to see a list of wireless networks. Double-click your network name to select it, then add your Wi-Fi password in the field called PSK and click Add to complete the setup. Your Raspberry Pi will now automatically use that network each time you boot up. ▼

STEP 2 In order to print from your Pi you'll need to install CUPS (Common Unix Printing System). CUPS is software that allows a computer running a version of Linux, such as Raspbian, to support printers and also act as a print **server** for other computers. Before you install CUPS, however, check that your printer is supported by going to ***www.openprinting.org/printers*** and selecting your printer make and model, then clicking the 'show this printer' button. Assuming your model is on the list, this page will provide some information that might be useful later so keep it on screen. Connect your printer to your Raspberry Pi and switch them both on. Double-click LXTerminal on the desktop. LXTerminal is similar to the command prompt in Windows. Type **sudo apt-get update**, press enter, then type **sudo apt-get install cups**. The installation may take up to 30 minutes. ▼

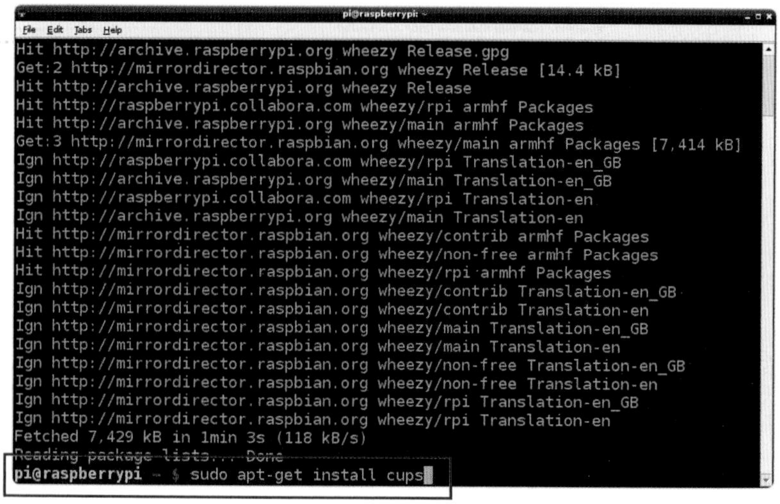

pi@raspberrypi: ~
File Edit Tabs Help
Hit http://archive.raspberrypi.org wheezy Release.gpg
Get:2 http://mirrordirector.raspbian.org wheezy Release [14.4 kB]
Hit http://archive.raspberrypi.org wheezy Release
Hit http://raspberrypi.collabora.com wheezy/rpi armhf Packages
Hit http://archive.raspberrypi.org wheezy/main armhf Packages
Get:3 http://mirrordirector.raspbian.org wheezy/main armhf Packages [7,414 kB]
Ign http://raspberrypi.collabora.com wheezy/rpi Translation-en_GB
Ign http://archive.raspberrypi.org wheezy/main Translation-en_GB
Ign http://raspberrypi.collabora.com wheezy/rpi Translation-en
Ign http://archive.raspberrypi.org wheezy/main Translation-en
Hit http://mirrordirector.raspbian.org wheezy/contrib armhf Packages
Hit http://mirrordirector.raspbian.org wheezy/non-free armhf Packages
Hit http://mirrordirector.raspbian.org wheezy/rpi armhf Packages
Ign http://mirrordirector.raspbian.org wheezy/contrib Translation-en_GB
Ign http://mirrordirector.raspbian.org wheezy/contrib Translation-en
Ign http://mirrordirector.raspbian.org wheezy/main Translation-en_GB
Ign http://mirrordirector.raspbian.org wheezy/main Translation-en
Ign http://mirrordirector.raspbian.org wheezy/non-free Translation-en_GB
Ign http://mirrordirector.raspbian.org wheezy/non-free Translation-en
Ign http://mirrordirector.raspbian.org wheezy/rpi Translation-en_GB
Ign http://mirrordirector.raspbian.org wheezy/rpi Translation-en
Fetched 7,429 kB in 1min 3s (118 kB/s)
Reading package lists... Done
pi@raspberrypi ~ $ sudo apt-get install cups

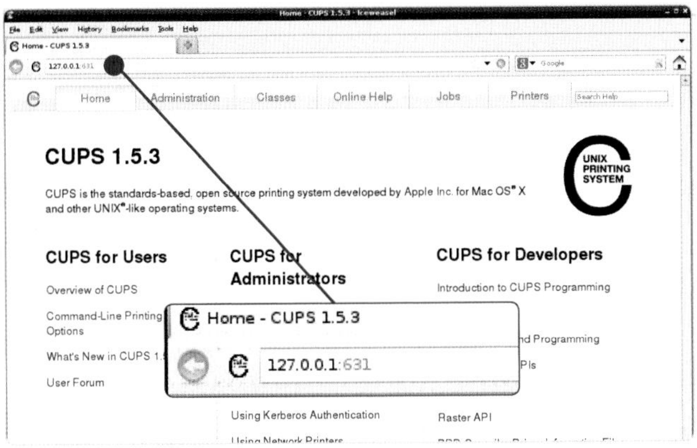

STEP 3 Once CUPS is installed, add the user pi (that's you) to the group allowed to access the printer. To do this, type **sudo usermod -a -G lpadmin pi** and press Enter. With CUPS all printer management is done via web pages, but none of the built-in browsers works well with CUPS, so we're going to install Iceweasel, the Raspbian version of Firefox. Do this by typing **sudo apt-get install iceweasel** into LXTerminal and pressing Enter. After installation, start Iceweasel by clicking the start button at the bottom left and selecting Internet. Bring up the CUPS pages by typing **127.0.0.1:631** into the address bar – that address is pointing at your Raspberry Pi. Now, click the 'Adding Printers and Classes' link, type the username 'pi' and password 'raspberry' into the pop-up box and click the Login button. On the next screen, click Add Printer. ▼

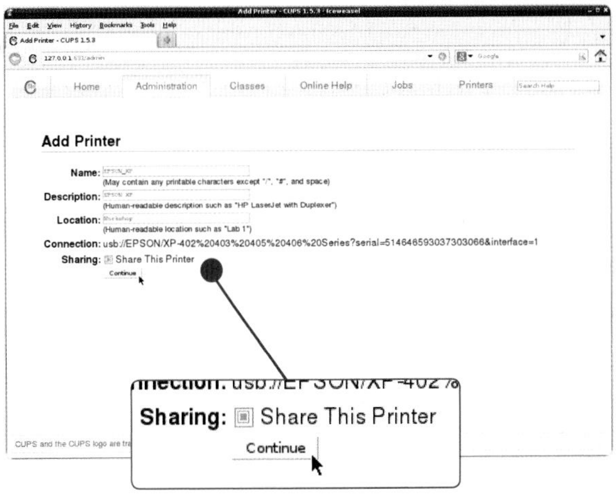

STEP 4 Assuming your printer is connected via USB, you should see your printer listed on the Add Printer page; you should also see any other printers CUPS has discovered on your home network. You might find that the name CUPS suggests for your printer isn't exactly the same as its model name; just check that it matches with the model name you came up with in step 2. Click the Continue button and, on the next page, you can add a location (for example 'spare bedroom'). If you want other people on your home network to be able to access the printer, click the Share This Printer checkbox and click Continue. ▼

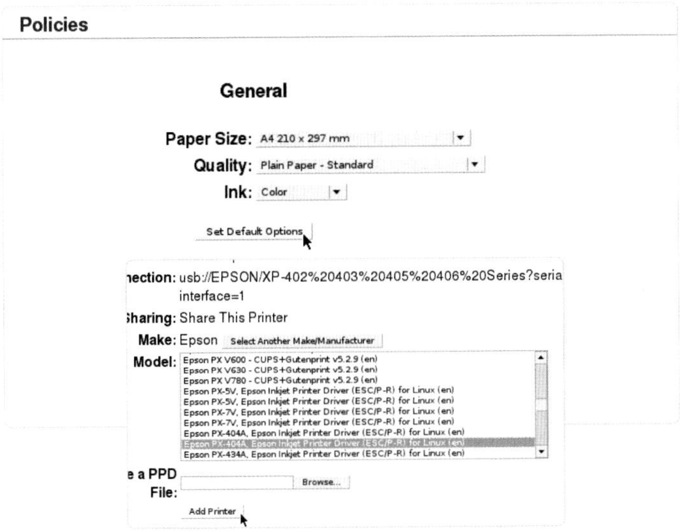

STEP 5 With any luck, the correct model name will now show next to 'model' on the Add Printer page. If it isn't, as in our case, then you may have to do a little searching on Google to find the nearest equivalent – the older your printer, the more likely it is to be on this list already. Click Add Printer and, on the next page, click Set Default Options and Continue. After a brief message confirming that the default options have been set, the printer summary screen will appear, confirming that the printer is ready. ▼

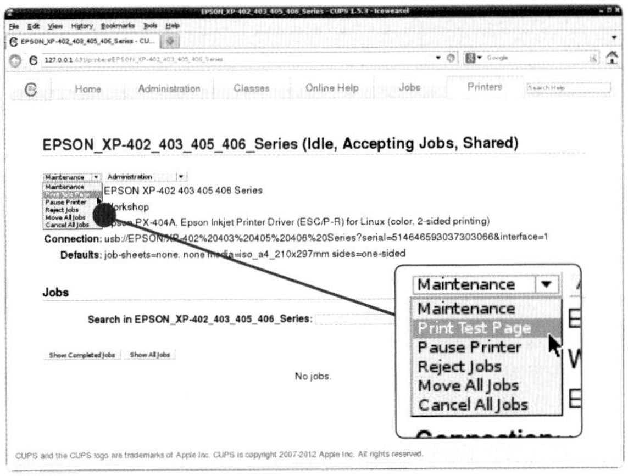

STEP 6 To check whether your printer is fully working, select the Maintenance dropdown on the left and choose Print Test Page. A message will appear to confirm that the page has been sent to the printer and you'll then see the list of print jobs with the current status. All being well, you'll also hear your printer fire up – be patient however as it can take 30 seconds for the test page to start printing. Don't despair if you get an error message – sometimes this is an issue with the browser rather than the printer itself. Check this by selecting File/Print from another application such as LeafPad. If this doesn't work, your best bet is to try another printer driver. To do this, select the Administration dropdown and choose Modify Printer – you can then walk through the steps you took to set the printer up, looking for an alternative driver. If in doubt, pick one that mentions CUPS in its driver name. ●

Add USB Storage to your Raspberry Pi

Expand your Pi's storage space beyond its SD card and make backups of valuable files

Although the Raspberry Pi boots from an **SD** memory card, it's not a good idea to store documents, photos, videos and music on it, as it's relatively slow and only has limited space. Fortunately, it's easy to add **USB** storage and whether that's by using a flash **memory stick** or an external USB **hard disk** the process is exactly the same. However, whilst you can power **flash drives** from the Raspberry Pi, if you want to add an external hard disk, you'll need to use a powered hub, or a hard drive with a separate power supply. You can also attach USB DVD drives to your Pi, though this is a slightly different process and we will be covering it in more detail later on in this guide (see page 124) ca

STEP 1 We're using a USB flash drive like the one shown but the principals are the same for adding an external USB hard disk too. Most USB flash drives come preformatted using the Windows **FAT32** file system. This will work with the Raspberry Pi but it's inefficient and easily corrupted, so the first step is to reformat the drive using the Pi's native EXT4 system. Begin by turning on your Raspberry Pi, then wait for the Raspbian desktop to load and plug in the USB drive. On a PC, Windows assigns the drive a letter such as E: or F: but a Linux system, such as the Raspberry Pi, uses 'mount points'. These are full paths such as '/dev/sda1' rather than letters to indicate where a file is stored. ▼

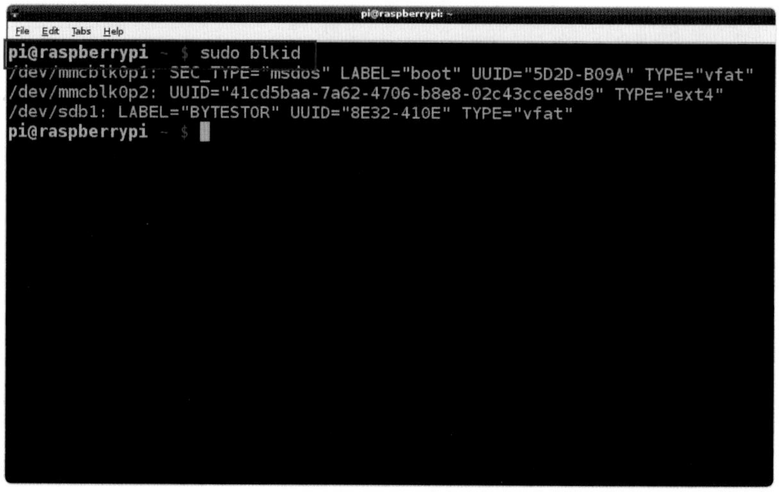
pi@raspberrypi: ~
File Edit Tabs Help
pi@raspberrypi ~ $ sudo blkid
/dev/mmcblk0p1: SEC_TYPE="msdos" LABEL="boot" UUID="5D2D-B09A" TYPE="vfat"
/dev/mmcblk0p2: UUID="41cd5baa-7a62-4706-b8e8-02c43ccee8d9" TYPE="ext4"
/dev/sdb1: LABEL="BYTESTOR" UUID="8E32-410E" TYPE="vfat"
pi@raspberrypi ~ $

STEP 2 Double-click LXTerminal, type **sudo blkid** and press Enter. You should now see a list of all attached drives. The path name for your drive will start with /dev/sd so look for a line that begins with those letters – you'll also get a clue from the label and the type – usually this will be 'vfat'. Note the path name for your drive – in the screenshot the path is /dev/sdb1. Before you can format the USB drive you need to unmount it so that the system can't access it during formatting. Type **sudo umount** followed by the path you noted earlier. In our case, we'll use **sudo umount /dev/sdb1**. ▼

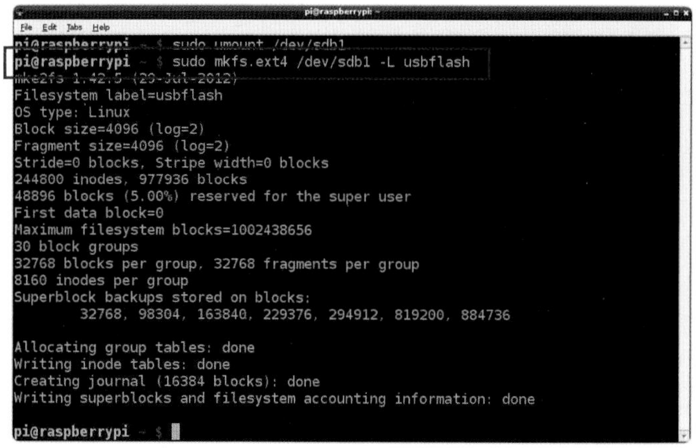

pi@raspberrypi: ~
File Edit Tabs Help
pi@raspberrypi ~ $ sudo umount /dev/sdb1
pi@raspberrypi ~ $ sudo mkfs.ext4 /dev/sdb1 -L usbflash
mke2fs 1.42.5 (29-Jul-2012)
Filesystem label=usbflash
OS type: Linux
Block size=4096 (log=2)
Fragment size=4096 (log=2)
Stride=0 blocks, Stripe width=0 blocks
244800 inodes, 977936 blocks
48896 blocks (5.00%) reserved for the super user
First data block=0
Maximum filesystem blocks=1002438656
30 block groups
32768 blocks per group, 32768 fragments per group
8160 inodes per group
Superblock backups stored on blocks:
32768, 98304, 163840, 229376, 294912, 819200, 884736
Allocating group tables: done
Writing inode tables: done
Creating journal (16384 blocks): done
Writing superblocks and filesystem accounting information: done
pi@raspberrypi ~ $

STEP 3 We're now ready to format the card. To do this, type **sudo mkfs.ext4 /dev/sdb1 –L usbflash** (substituting the path if yours is different). This creates a new file system which will appear as 'usbflash' in the file explorer. We now need to create a folder to link with the flash drive – it's a good idea to use the same name as the label you've given the drive. Create a location for it by typing: **sudo mkdir /media/usbflash**. Press Enter and then type **sudo mount /dev/sdb1 /media/usbflash** to mount the drive – again substituting the path to your flash drive. ▼

STEP 4 Now, to give permission to all users to save to the disk, type **sudo chmod 777 /media/usbflash** followed by Enter. Open File Manager and select Places from the dropdown box in the left pane of File Manager. You should see your flash drive appear beneath Applications. From now on, it will always be visible whenever it's plugged into your Pi. You can now create new folders on the USB drive – do this in File Manager by selecting it from the list of places. You'll probably see a 'lost+found' folder there; this is a system folder so don't interfere with it. Move your mouse over the white area and right-click to launch the contextual menu. Hover over Create New item, select Folder and giveit a name before clicking OK. ▼

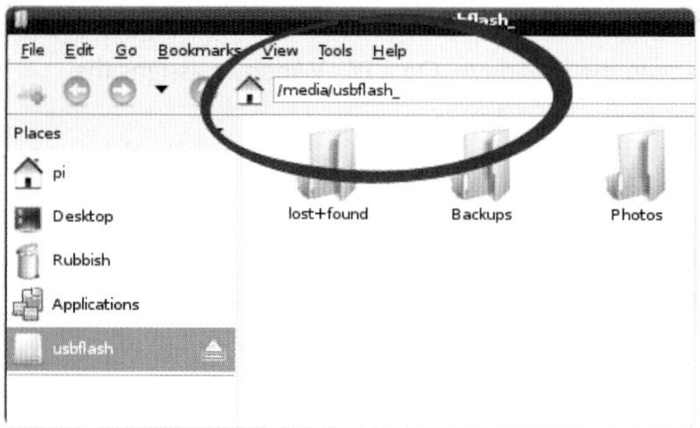

STEP 5 Now that we have a working external disk, we can use it to backup files from the Pi's SD Card. This might be something you want to do so that you can restore the files on your Pi in case something goes wrong, or you might only backup when you're about to change files or install new software. Either way, we're going to use the simple command-line program called rsync which is built into Raspbian, so you don't need to install any new software. For a simple directory backup, we use the form sudo rsync –av [source folder] [destination folder]. Begin by checking the exact name of the USB disk you're backing up to – do this by looking again in the file manager under Places. Click your flash drive and you'll see the path appear at the top – this is the path you must use. Note that in the screenshot, the Raspberry Pi has added an underscore to the end of the path, which must be included. ▼

STEP 6 In our example, we're copying a folder called 'python_games' to a directory called 'Backups' on the flash drive. To do this, we type **sudo rsync –av python_games /media/usbflash_/Backups**. The '**a**' (archive) parameter tells rsync to preserve all the file information (such as which user it belongs to) and the '**v**' (verbose) parameter causes rsync to tell us exactly what's going on – you can leave this one out once you've got used to the process. Once you've pressed Enter, rsync will copy the files over. What's really clever is that rsync supports 'differential' copying – it only copies files that have changed. So, if you ran the exact same command again, it would check to see if any new files have been added to the source folder and only copy if it detects changes. So, if you use your Raspberry Pi for writing documents or editing photos, you can run rsync periodically to back up new files as you add them. ●

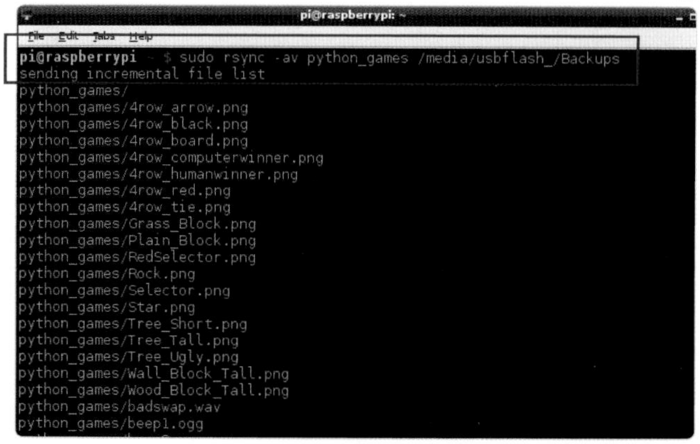

pi@raspberrypi: ~
pi@raspberrypi ~ $ sudo rsync -av python_games /media/usbflash_/Backups
sending incremental file list
python_games/
python_games/4row_arrow.png
python_games/4row_black.png
python_games/4row_board.png
python_games/4row_computerwinner.png
python_games/4row_humanwinner.png
python_games/4row_red.png
python_games/4row_tie.png
python_games/Grass_Block.png
python_games/Plain_Block.png
python_games/RedSelector.png
python_games/Rock.png
python_games/Selector.png
python_games/Star.png
python_games/Tree_Short.png
python_games/Tree_Tall.png
python_games/Tree_Ugly.png
python_games/Wall_Block_Tall.png
python_games/Wood_Block_Tall.png
python_games/badswap.wav
python_games/beep1.ogg

SECTION 2

Fun family projects

Parents and children can familiarise themselves with the Pi by working through these simple, fun projects together

Now you know the basics, it's time to get a taste of what your Raspberry Pi can really do. In this part of our guide, we've put together a selection of great Pi projects that are designed to ease you gently into the way the computer works and give you an idea of what the Pi can be used for. And the best bit is that you'll be having plenty of fun while you're doing them, too. From watching BBC iPlayer shows to programming your very first game, these initial projects are an ideal way for children and parents (or grandparents) to learn about the Raspberry Pi together.

IN THIS SECTION

Turn your Pi into a media centre and watch BBC iPlayer

We explain how your Raspberry Pi can be used as the ultimate entertainment centre

One of the Rasperry Pi's best features is the fact that the hardware is capable of playing high-quality music and videos. But, since Raspbian does not have all the necessary software, a special media centre application like XBMC is needed. You can install this manually, but NOOBS makes it much easier, as it comes complete with a great pre-configured version of XBMC called OpenELEC. This lets you play your media files in a TV-friendly interface, and you can even add the BBC iPlayer app to **stream** your favourite shows. This workshop explains the basics of getting up and running with XBMC, how to connect to a network, install iPlayer and play files from a **USB** key or via a Windows network.

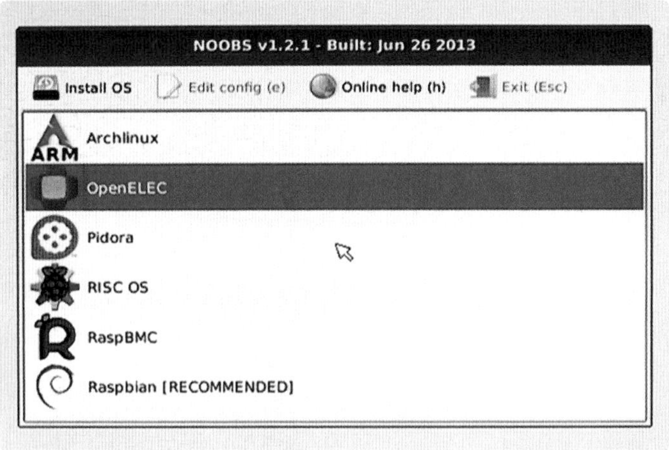

STEP 1 To install XBMC, you need an **SD Card** containing the latest NOOBS installation package (see page 18). If Raspbian is already installed on a card, you can either reinstall over the top of this (all your files on the SD Card will be deleted), or use a separate SD Card with a fresh copy of NOOBS. In the latter case, just insert the card and power on the Pi. To use an existing installation, power on the Pi while pressing the Shift key. This launches the same menu you see when first installing, where you can choose which operating system to install. Select OpenELEC, press Enter and wait for the install to complete. When done, press Enter to restart the Pi. ▼

STEP 2 The OpenELEC interface works well with keyboard and mouse, but sometimes the edges of the screen may be cut off. To fix this, use the right and left arrow keys (or push the mouse pointer to the right or left edge of the screen) until the System category is highlighted, then press Enter. Click System, click Video Output, then click Video Calibration. Move the mouse into the top left corner of the screen, click and drag the corner inwards until the two blue lines fit perfectly in the corner. Repeat for the bottom right corner. Put the mouse in the centre of the screen, and if the blue square looks rectangular, click and drag it until it is square (use a ruler to check). Press Esc three times to return to the main desktop. ▼

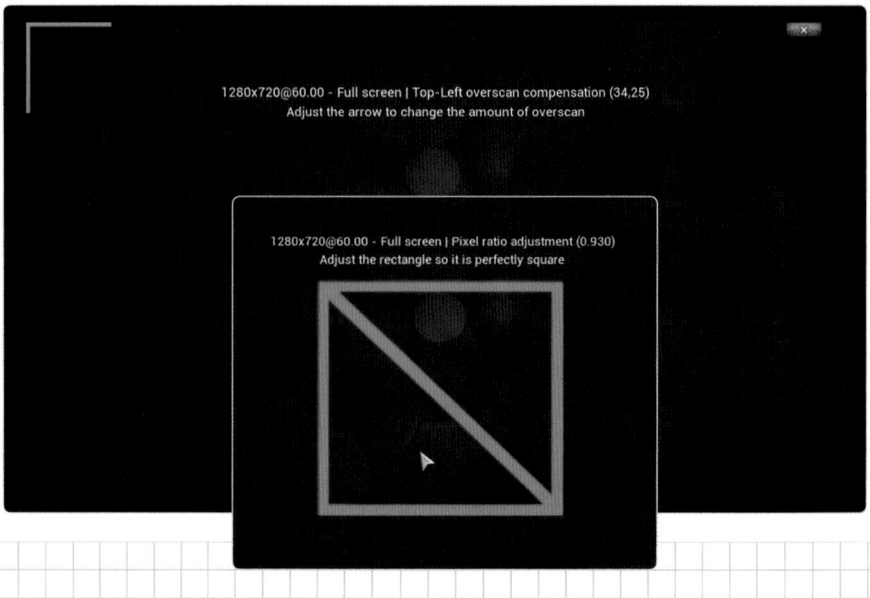

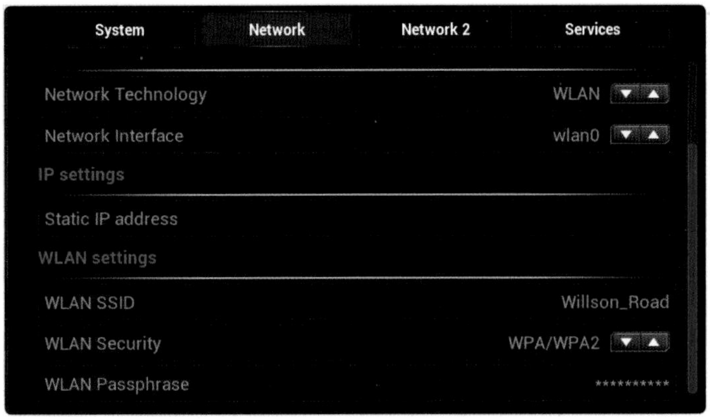

STEP 3 To use the internet, the Pi needs connecting to a **router**. If using a wired (**Ethernet**) connection no configuration is normally needed, and OpenELEC should connect automatically. Wireless dongles need setting up, though. Hover the mouse over the System category on the menu bar (see step 2), then click OpenElec. Click Network, then in the section 'Network Technology', click the small up or down arrows to choose 'WLAN'. In the Network Interface section, choose 'wlan0'. Next click WLAN SSID, then type in the wireless network name. Click Done. In WLAN Security, choose the correct security type (usually WPA/WPA2), then click WLAN Passphrase to enter the wireless password. Click Done then click OK. After a few moments the connection should be made and a small Wi-Fi icon will appear at the right end of the taskbar. ▼

STEP 4 Now OpenELEC looks good and is connected to a network, it's time to install iPlayer. Download the Zip file from *www.snipca.com/9733* and copy it onto a **USB memory key** (but don't unzip it). Plug the USB key into the Pi. Click Programs on the OpenELEC menu bar. Click Get More, then click the two dots (..) at the top of the left panel, then click them again when the second list appears. Click 'Install from zip file', then look for the USB key in the folder list in the right panel (ours is called USB_KEY). Click on this, then navigate to the zip file and click on it to automatically install it - it only takes a few seconds. ▼

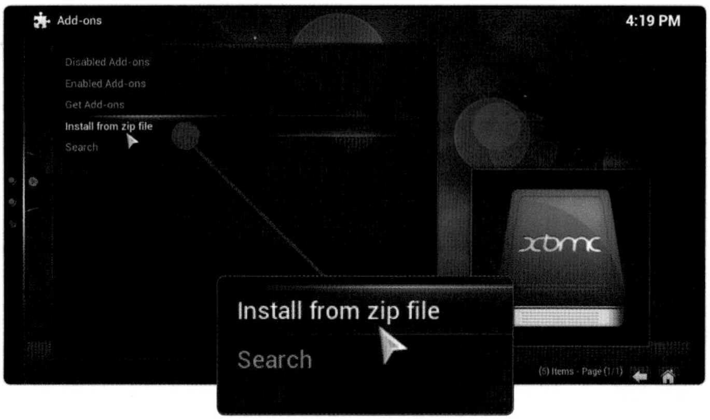

STEP 5 To use iPlayer, click Videos on the main desktop menu, then click Video Add-Ons. Click iPlayer then choose the content to watch from the list. Watching live TV is supported, via the Watch Live link, but remember that you need a valid TV licence to watch this. A good reliable internet connection is needed for an enjoyable experience, and if you have problems when using a Wi-Fi connection, switching to a wired connection should fix them. Moving the mouse while a video is playing will bring up a menu at the bottom of the screen with programme information and all the standard playback controls. To listen to live or catchup radio programs, from the desktop click Music, then Music Add-Ons, then iPlayer. Not all radio channels support the live streaming feature. ▼

STEP 6 Media files can be stored on the Pi's SD Card, on a USB key or disk, or on shared network folders. Head to page 28 for more about adding USB storage and DVD drives. Most popular audio and video formats are supported, apart from WMV and **MPEG2** videos. When playing music, the current track is shown as a thumbnail above the menu bar with play controls at the right of the screen. To play files from a USB disk or network location, click the relevant category, choose Files. USB disks should automatically appear in this list. For networks, click Add Source. Click Browse then choose Windows Network (SMB) to browse PCs on the network. To connect to a PC via **UPnP** streaming, choose UPnP Devices in the Browse window, select the PC then click OK. To learn about playing DVDs, turn to page 124. ●

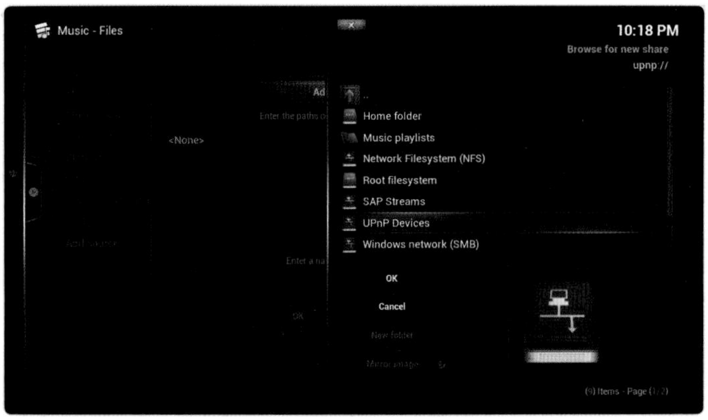

Play Minecraft on the Raspberry Pi

Play one of the most popular games around – and learn about computer programming while you're doing it

Minecraft is more than just another 'indie' game – it has become something of a phenomenon worldwide, thanks to its winning combination of attractive graphics and open-ended, creative-led gameplay. At the beginning of this year the company behind Minecraft, Mojang, announced that it was making Minecraft available for the Raspberry Pi. The Pi version is free and does not include all of the gameplay of the online and desktop versions but has something unique and very special; you can control what happens in the game using the Python programming language (see page 64 for more about Python). If you want a great way to get youngsters interested in programming, this will be the key.

STEP 1 Start LXTerminal by clicking the bottom left button, Accessories, then LXTerminal. Type **cd ~**, press Enter, then type **wget https://s3.amazonaws.com/assets.minecraft.net/pi/minecraft-pi-0.1.1.tar.gz**, press Enter, then type **tar -zxvf minecraft-pi-0.1.1.tar.gz** and Enter. This creates a folder called mcpi containing Minecraft. To start it type **cd mcpi**, press Enter, then **minecraft-pi** and Enter. Now select 'Create new'. You'll find yourself in a new Minecraft world. Press E to see a full list of items in your inventory; click one to select it. Press the right mouse button to place an item and left-click to destroy a block. Press Space once to jump or twice quickly to enter the flying mode. ▼

STEP 2 You can do more than simply build structures in Minecraft by interacting with it using the Python programming language and what's called the Minecraft API. An API is a set of programming tools; in this case these tools let you find out what's happening in Minecraft and change it while the game is running. Press Esc in Minecraft so that the normal mouse cursor appears and move the Minecraft window off to the right. Now rearrange the LXTerminal window so that it fills the left hand space left by Minecraft. It'll be narrow window but everything we're going to do can either wrap text or scroll backwards and forwards. ▼

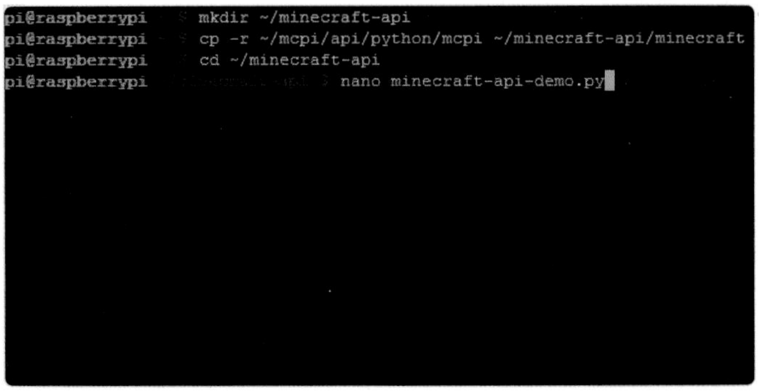

STEP 3 Create a folder to store your Minecraft programs and copy the special API files from Minecraft. Return to the LXTerminal window, type **mkdir ~/minecraft-api** and press Enter. Type **cp –r ~/mcpi/api/python/mcpi ~/minecraft-api/minecraft**, press Enter, then **cd ~/minecraft-api** and press Enter. Type **nano minecraft-api-demo.py** and press Enter to start the nano text editor and create a new file. The first part of the program is used to import the Minecraft commands and the ones used by Python to understand time, so we can use delays in between commands. Type **import minecraft.minecraft as minecraft**, press Enter, type **import minecraft.block as block**, press Enter, type **import time** and press Enter twice more. ▼

STEP 4 The next section of the program is where it actually starts. Type **if __name__ == "__main__":** and press Enter twice. Note that there are two underscores in each part of the command. Python uses tabs to understand how a program is divided, so every line following this must be preceded by at least one tab. The next command connects our program to Minecraft. Press Tab once, then type **mc = minecraft.Minecraft.create()** and Enter. Save your program by pressing Ctrl and O and then Enter. Create a message that will appear in Minecraft by typing a tab then the command **mc.postToChat("Hello World")**. Press Ctrl and O, Enter, then Ctrl and X to quit the text editor. Type **python minecraft-api-demo.py** and press Enter. The message will appear in the Minecraft window above the quick inventory list and then disappear after around ten seconds. ▼

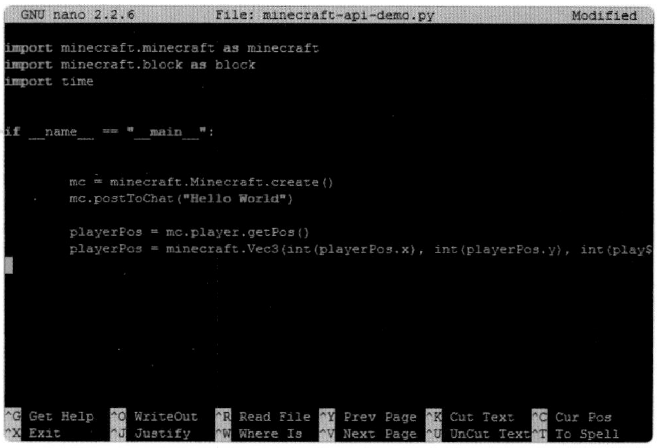

STEP 5 Return to the LXTerminal window and type **nano minecraft-api-demo.py** to load the program in nano. Use the cursor keys to move down to the bottom of the file. In order to build a tower of blocks near the player, we need to find out where they are. Enter this command below and in line with the messages, **playerPos = mc.player.getPos()** and press Enter. Press Tab again and then enter **playerPos = minecraft.Vec3(int(playerPos.x), int(playerPos.y), int(playerPos.z))** and press enter. The second command converts the players position into the correct type of data that python can use. ▼

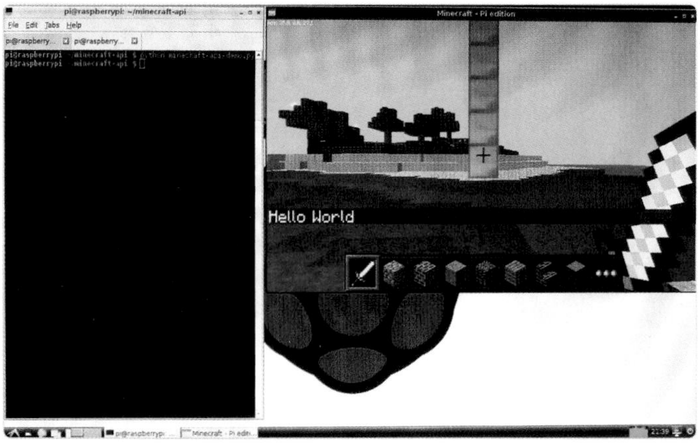

STEP 6 To create the tower as simply as possible, create a loop so you will only need to enter the setBlock command once. All the commands inside the loop must be preceded with two tabs for Python to interpret it correctly. Press Tab once, then type **for towerBlocks in [1, 2, 3, 4, 5]:** and press Enter. Press Tab twice and then type **mc.setBlock(playerPos.x, playerPos.y + towerBlocks, playerPos.z +5, block.DIAMOND_BLOCK)**. Press Ctrl and O and then Enter to save the program. Press Ctrl and X to quit. Type **python minecraft-api-demo.py** and press Enter to run the program. The program doesn't know which direction you're facing so you might need to turn around to see the tower after the Hello World message appears. ●

MORE PROGRAMMING WITH MINECRAFT

You can download some more advanced Minecraft API projects from *www.stuffaboutcode.com*. A good example is the Minecraft Clock that creates a large working clock out of blocks. The projects are hosted on a service called github. In LXTerminal, type **sudo apt-get install git-core** and press Enter. Type cd ~, press Enter, then type **git clone https://github.com/martinohanlon/minecraft-clock.git** and press Enter to download the clock. To start the clock type **cd minecraft-clock**, press Enter, then type **python minecraft-clock.py** and press Enter. Return to Minecraft and use the position values to find the clock. It is created at the co-ordinates 0, 30, 0.

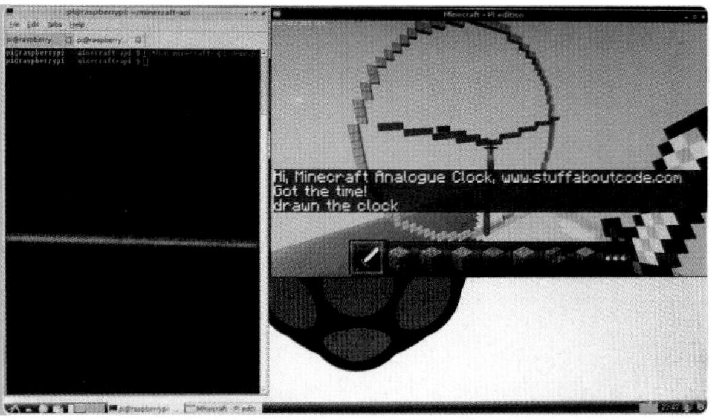

Turn your Pi into a network storage drive

Convert your Pi into a useful Nas drive for sharing photos, music and more with other PCs

Once you've attached a **USB** stick or USB **hard disk** to your Pi (see page 28) you can use it as a Nas (network-attached storage) drive. The Raspberry Pi can then be used to store digital photo albums, videos and music that everyone on the network can share, whether they're using a Windows computer, Mac, tablet, phone or another Raspberry Pi. It's a great way to keep important things easily accessible.

If possible, connect your Raspberry Pi and its USB storage to the network using an **Ethernet** lead rather than Wi-Fi – this makes transferring files faster and more reliable. It's also worth housing the Pi in a case or finding a case for both it and its disk – just bear in mind that a hard disk needs good ventilation. Site your new Nas as near to the **router** as possible and set it up so that it won't need to be turned off once it's up and running. ca

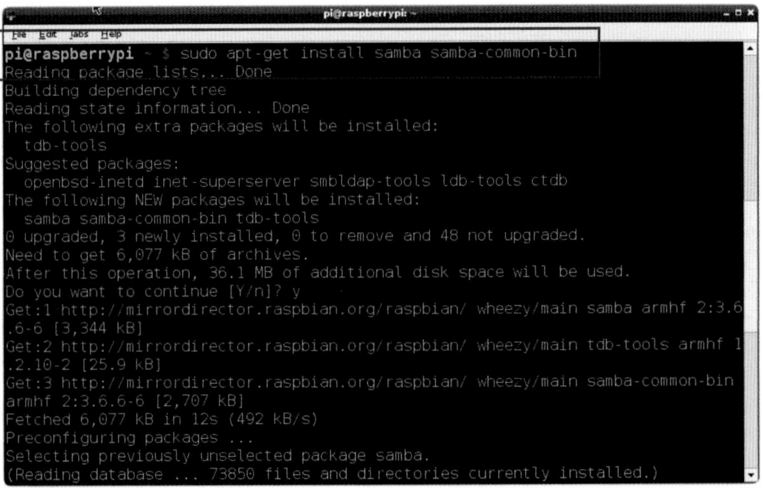

STEP 1 Samba is the software used to allow Windows machines to communicate with **Linux** computers (including the Raspberry Pi), which use different file formats – including EXT4 which we used for our USB drive on page 28. To install Samba, make sure your Raspberry Pi is connected to the internet and open up LXTerminal. Type **sudo apt-get update** to make your your system is up to date followed by **sudo apt-get install samba samba-common-bin**. This process will take up to 30 minutes, depending on the speed of your broadband connection. ▼

STEP 2 We now need to set up Samba by editing its configuration files. In common with many Linux programs, there's no graphical user interface but you only have to set it up once. We're going to use nano - one of the Raspberry Pi's built-in text editors.

In LXTerminal, open the configuration file in nano by typing **sudo nano /etc/samba/smb.conf**. You use the keyboard rather than your mouse to edit files in nano but it's straightforward. Navigate through the file using the arrow keys until you reach a section called Authentication. We want to add some security to our network so find the line # security = user and remove the hash symbol at the beginning of the line. Hash is often used to tell computers not to pay attention; by removing it we're turning on user level security and preventing people who connect to your network as guests from having access. ▼

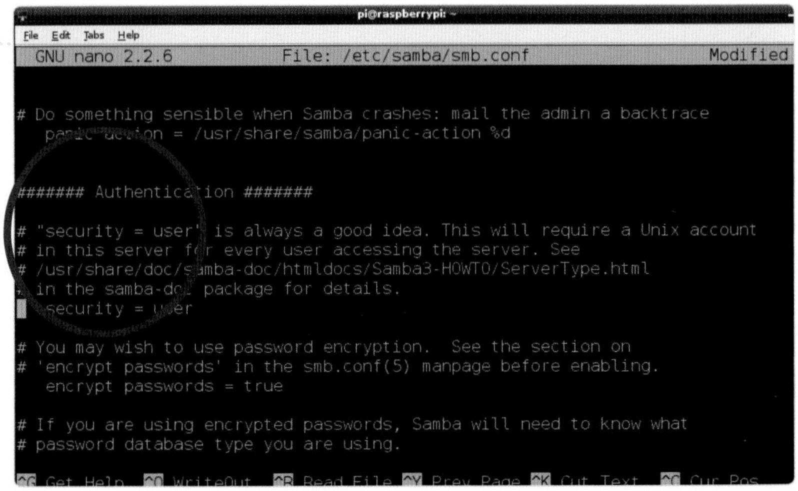

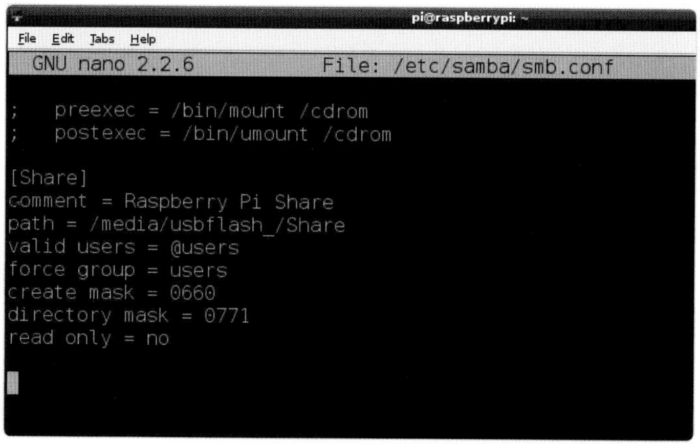
pi@raspberrypi: ~
File Edit Tabs Help
GNU nano 2.2.6 File: /etc/samba/smb.conf
; preexec = /bin/mount /cdrom
; postexec = /bin/umount /cdrom
[Share]
comment = Raspberry Pi Share
path = /media/usbflash_/Share
valid users = @users
force group = users
create mask = 0660
directory mask = 0771
read only = no

STEP 3

Use the arrow keys to move down to the very bottom of smb.conf and press the Enter key at the end to insert a new line. Add these lines to the file, pressing Enter at the end of each:

[Share]
comment = Raspberry Pi Share
path = /media/usbflash_/Share
valid users = @users
force group = users
create mask = 0660
directory mask = 0771
read only = no

Once you've done this, press the Ctrl key and O to save the file, then Enter to confirm. Press Ctrl-X to exit nano and you should return to the command prompt in LXTerminal. ▼

STEP 4

We need to restart Samba so that it reads the configuration file back in – to do this type **sudo /etc/init.d/samba restart**. We now create a Raspberry Pi user who can access the share - we're choosing the username 'networkuser' and password 'raspberry'. It'll be these details that people using other computers to connect to your USB drive will be asked for. To do this, type **sudo useradd networkuser –m –G users** and Enter followed by **sudo passwd networkuser**. After pressing Enter, the Pi will ask you to set a password. Make sure you write this down as you and all your Nas drive's other users will need it! ▼

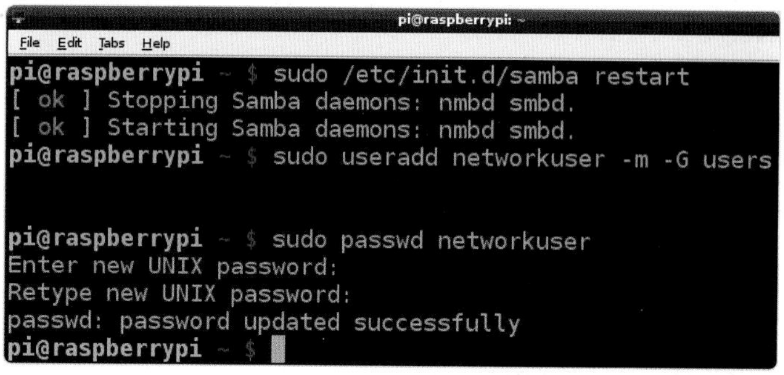
pi@raspberrypi: ~
File Edit Tabs Help
pi@raspberrypi ~ $ sudo /etc/init.d/samba restart
[ok] Stopping Samba daemons: nmbd smbd.
[ok] Starting Samba daemons: nmbd smbd.
pi@raspberrypi ~ $ sudo useradd networkuser -m -G users
pi@raspberrypi ~ $ sudo passwd networkuser
Enter new UNIX password:
Retype new UNIX password:
passwd: password updated successfully
pi@raspberrypi ~ $

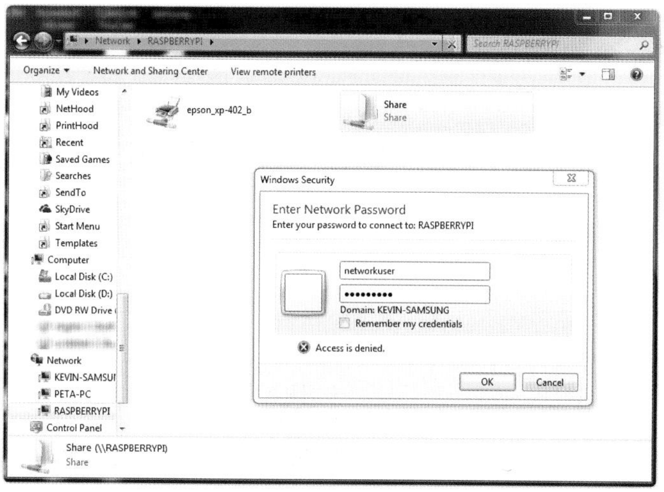

STEP 5

We need to add this new user to Samba's list of authorised people. Type **sudo smbpasswd –a networkuser** and enter the password when prompted. Finally, we're going to set the permissions on the share folder so that anyone on the network can add, edit or delete files. To do this, we use the chmod command followed by the permission and the name of the folder. Type **chmod 777 /media/usbflash_/Share** followed by Enter. Now start Windows Explorer on a PC and you should see 'Raspberry Pi' on the list of devices. Double-click it to see the Share folder. Try to open it and you should be prompted for a username and password. Once you've done that, you can **drag and drop** files. ▼

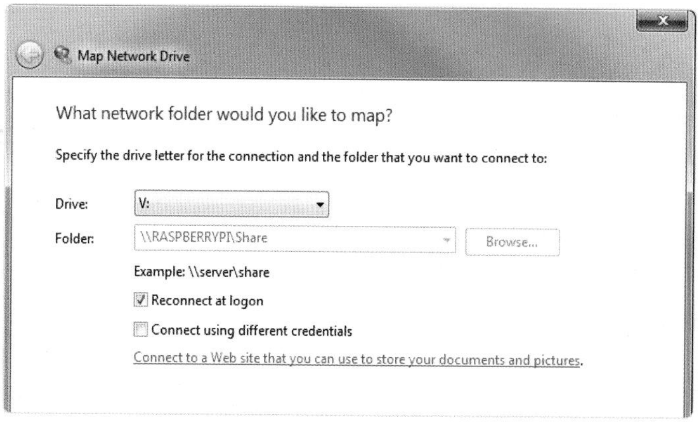

STEP 6

To make the shared folder easy to use, we can assign it a drive letter in Windows so that it appears just like a disk drive. In Windows Explorer, **right-click** the Raspberry Pi's Share folder and select Map Network Drive from the **dropdown menu**. Choose a drive letter from the dropdown menu – it's probably a good idea to pick a high letter so that it's clear which are true disk drives and which are network storage. Leave the 'Reconnect at logon' check box selected and click Finish. After a few seconds, it'll appear in its alphabetical order under Computer on your Windows PC. ●

Take time-lapse photos with your Raspberry Pi

Use your Pi to take automatic snapshots via a webcam and build the photos into a time-lapse movie

The tiny, low-power Raspberry Pi is ideal for taking time-lapse photography, where a device needs to be left alone for long periods of time and where there might not be space for a normal computer. The Pi will work with most standard webcams. Snapshots can be taken by a free program called Motion, either at timed intervals for things like a night sky, or when your webcam detects movement.

We're using a Model B Pi. Since both **USB** sockets will be taken up by the webcam and Wi-Fi adapter, we're going to set up the Pi so it can be controlled remotely using a free program called PuTTY (*www.snipca.com/9770*). PuTTY gives you command line control of your Pi from a Windows PC.

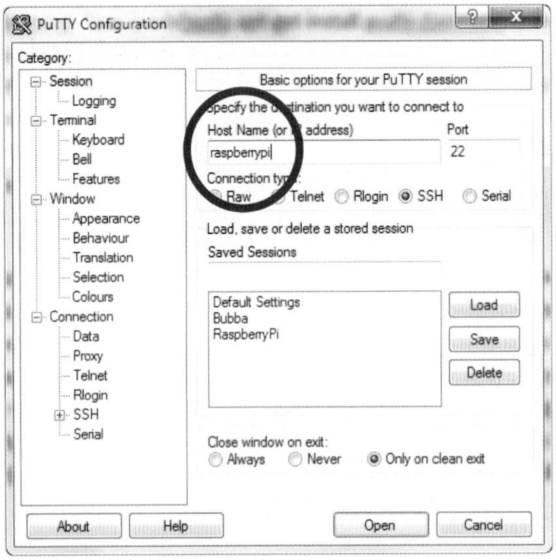

STEP 1 To make it easier to locate and control your Pi remotely over a network, we'll be using a program called Avahi. Start your Raspberry Pi as normal and make sure it's connected to the internet. Open LXTerminal and type **sudo apt-get update**, press Enter, then type **sudo apt-get install avahi-daemon**, press Enter and then Y when asked to confirm. Now start PuTTY on your Windows PC. It should find the Pi on your network, listing it as either raspberrypi.local or raspberrypi. If not, you may need to install a free Apple utility called Bonjour (*http://support.apple.com/kb/DL999*) on your PC, or follow our instructions on page 124 to give your Pi a fixed **IP address**. ▼

STEP 2 Remotely controlling your Pi via PuTTY on your PC, type **sudo mkdir /public** at the command line and press Enter to create a public folder. To share the folder over your network type **sudo apt-get install samba** and press Enter. Next, type **sudo nano /etc/samba/smb.conf**, press Enter and then scroll to the bottom and enter the text from [public] onwards as it appears in the image to the right. Press Ctrl and X, Y and then Enter to save the changes and quit. Type **sudo chown -R root:users /public**, press enter, then **sudo chmod -R ug+rwx /public/** and press Enter. Restart the Samba **server** by typing **sudo service samba restart**. Finally, type **mkdir /public/motion** and press Enter. See page 36 for more about Samba. ▼

pi@raspberrypi: ~
GNU nano 2.2.6 File: /etc/samba/smb.conf Modified
[public]
comment = Public files
path = /public
valid users = @users
force group = users
create group = 0660
directory mask = 0771
read only = no
^G Get Help ^O WriteOut ^R Read File ^Y Prev Page ^K Cut Text ^C Cur Pos
^X Exit ^J Justify ^W Where Is ^V Next Page ^U UnCut Text ^T To Spell

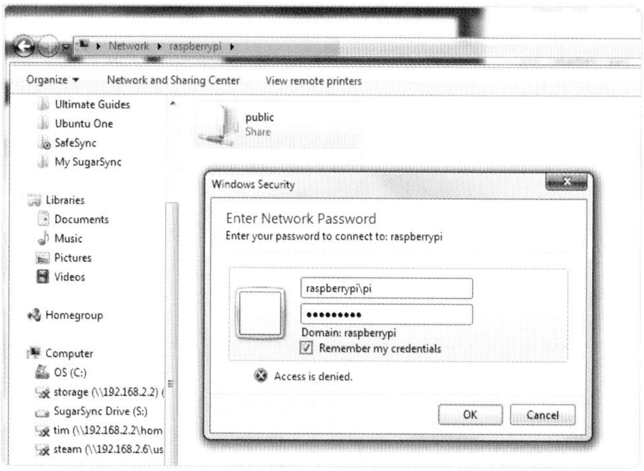

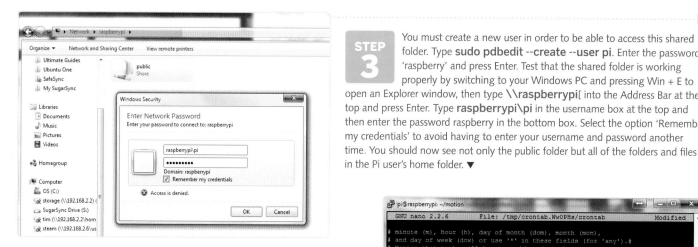

STEP 3 You must create a new user in order to be able to access this shared folder. Type **sudo pdbedit --create --user pi**. Enter the password 'raspberry' and press Enter. Test that the shared folder is working properly by switching to your Windows PC and pressing Win + E to open an Explorer window, then type **\\raspberrypi[** into the Address Bar at the top and press Enter. Type **raspberrypi\pi** in the username box at the top and then enter the password raspberry in the bottom box. Select the option 'Remember my credentials' to avoid having to enter your username and password another time. You should now see not only the public folder but all of the folders and files in the Pi user's home folder. ▼

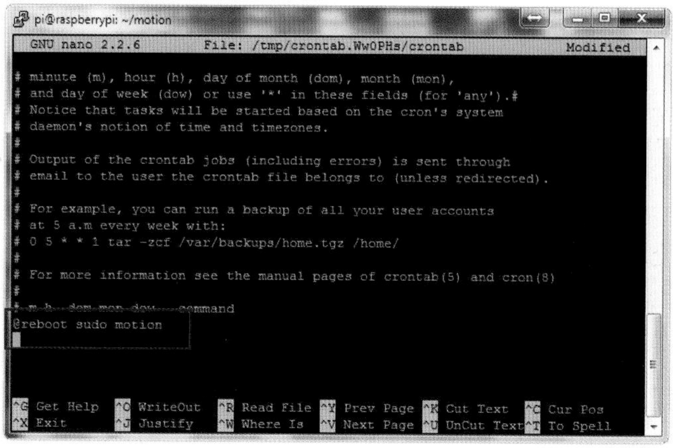

STEP 4 Return to PuTTY. Install Motion on your Raspberry Pi by typing **sudo apt-get install motion** at the command line and pressing Enter. Press Y when asked to confirm the installation. When it has finished you should set Motion to run at startup by typing **crontab -e** at the command line and pressing Enter. Move down to the bottom of this file and enter the following text **@reboot sudo motion**. Press Ctrl and X and press Y when asked whether to 'Save modified buffer', then press Enter to confirm. ▼

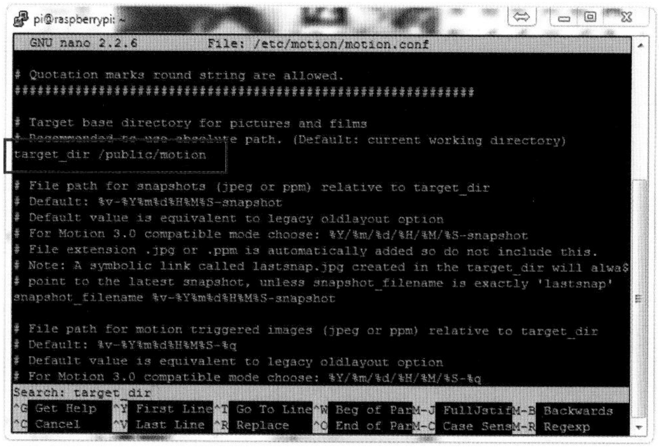

STEP 5 You can set exactly how Motion will work by editing a single text file. Type **sudo nano /etc/motion/motion.conf** and press Enter. The text document is rather long so to find the setting we want, press Ctrl and W, type **target_dir** in the Search section that appears at the bottom of the screen and press Enter. The cursor will jump to this setting. Replace the text after target_dir with **/public/motion**. Press Ctrl and W again, type **snapshot_interval** and press Enter. Delete 0 and replace with the number of seconds you want between each time-lapse shot. ▼

STEP 6 You can improve image quality by increasing the **resolution** of the captured snapshots. Press Ctrl + W, type 320 and press Enter to find these settings in the settings file. Change the image width and height settings to your webcam's upper limit. Our Microsoft LifeCam HD-5000 can manage 1280x720. Press Ctrl + X, then Y when prompted to save, and then Enter. Shutdown the Pi by typing **sudo shutdown -h now**. When all the LEDs apart from the red PWR one have gone off, it's safe to unplug the Pi, remove the keyboard and mouse from the USB ports, then plug in the webcam (and Wi-Fi adapter for wireless network access) and position it where you want it. Now power it up again to start taking the time-lapse photos. ▼

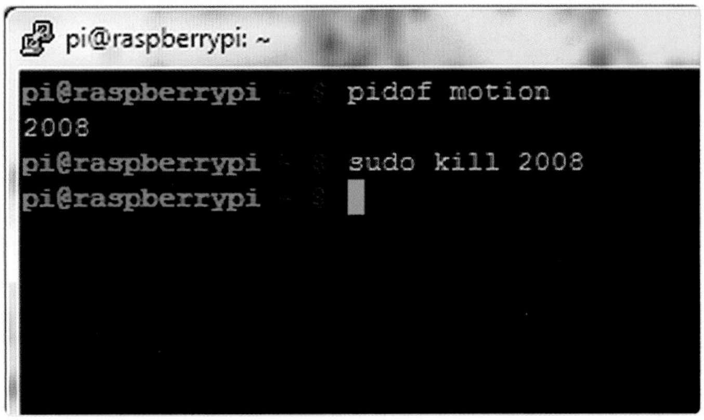

STEP 7 When you've finished capturing the time-lapse videos you need to stop the Motion app from taking any more images. To do this in PuTTY, type **pidof motion** at the command line then press Enter. Next, type **sudo kill** followed by the number that appeared after you typed the last command. Should you ever need to, you can stop Motion running whenever the Pi starts up by typing **crontab -e** and pressing Enter. Scroll down to the setting shown in Step 4 and add a **#** at the beginning of the line to make Raspbian ignore it. Press Ctrl + X, then Y and then Enter to save your changes and quit. ▼

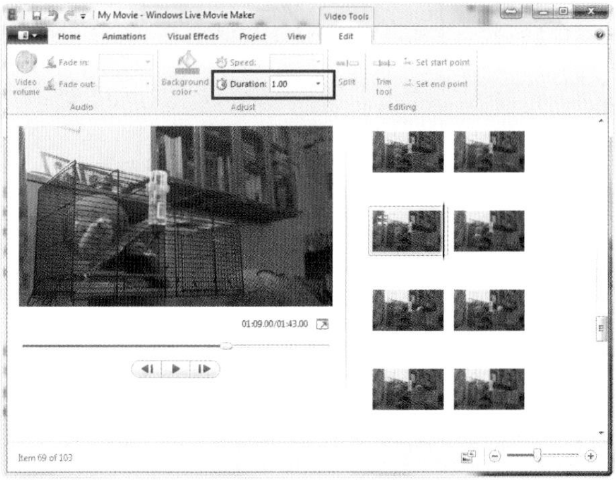

STEP 8 To make a video from your time-lapse images, return to your Windows desktop and launch Windows Movie Maker. Click the 'Add videos and photos' button in the Ribbon. Navigate to your Pi's folder, press Ctrl + A to select all the photos, then click Open. By default, Movie Maker gives each picture seven seconds on screen, which is far too long. So, press Ctrl + A to select all the pictures, then click the Edit tab in the Ribbon, then type a smaller number in the Duration text box. To see what duration works best with your captured images, click the play button underneath the video preview. ▼

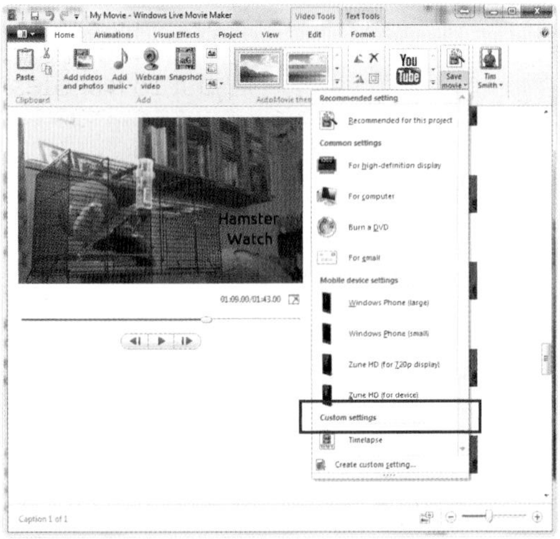

STEP 9 Add a title to the video by clicking the Home tab, then the Title button. Use captions to describe moments of interest during the video. When you're happy with the video, click the 'Save movie' button in the Home tab of the Ribbon and then create a customised time-lapse setting. Name the setting 'Webcam Time-lapse' and set the resolution to that of your webcam. Click Save twice, then Close. Click the 'Save movie' button again and select the time-lapse setting you just created. Give the video a name and then click Save. ▼

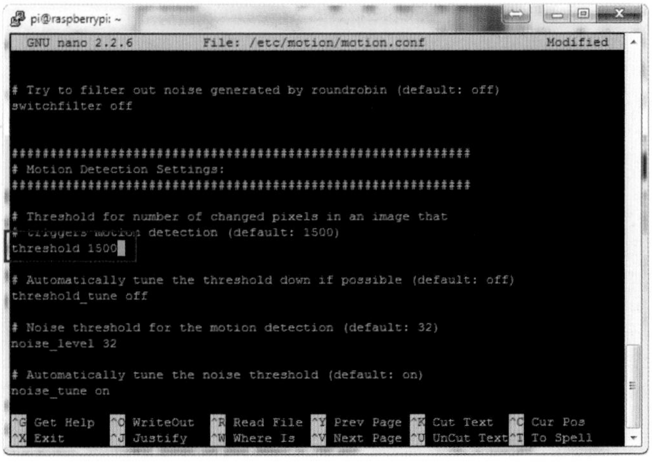

STEP 10 You can also use the motion app to capture video when movement is detected on the webcam. Open the Motion.conf file for editing (see Step 5), press Ctrl + W, type **snapshot_interval** and press Enter. Change the number to 0 to disable snapshots. Next, press Ctrl + W, type **threshold**, then press Enter. Change the number for the threshold setting to 1500. Motion capture is more complicated than time-lapse and you can find more detailed instructions at *www.snipca.com/9817*. This describes how to ignore portions of the view if cars passing by start the motion-capture and how long to keep recording after no more movement is detected. ●

Use Scratch to program a quick game

Computer programming is easier than you think. Get coding with your kids

The little Raspberry Pi computer has led to a resurgence of interest in the more technical aspects of computing, including programming. We'll explore coding in much more detail later on in this guide, demonstrating the theory behind it and helping you to learn how to create your own programs.

However, the challenge with many programming languages – even Python – is that they don't always offer the quick gratification needed to keep novices interested.

But a free tool called Scratch takes a different approach – one that offers an engaging experience from the start. Programs are created simply by dragging and dropping elements around on screen. A complete novice can create a working program quickly, and projects can be shared with other users on the Scratch website. So, to learn how to program a game in just 15 minutes, read on.

Understanding the interface

Scratch comes built into the Raspberry Pi's Raspbian operating system. You'll find a shortcut for it on your Pi's desktop. A Windows version is also available to download free of charge from ***http://scratch.mit.edu/scratch_1.4***. We'd also suggest signing up for a Scratch account. This is free, and will allow you to share your work with other people. Visit ***http://scratch.mit.edu*** and click the Signup link at the top of the web page. Fill in the registration form and the blue 'sign up' button at the bottom. Your Scratch profile page will appear; we'll return here later.

Flip back to the Scratch program window. There

▲ **Scratch is a great way to start learning about computer programming, on Raspberyy Pi or Windows**

are several panes; the window in the top-right corner, with the picture of a cat, is the 'stage' and this is where the results of the program will appear. It also controls the starting and stopping of programs, with the green flag and red dot respectively.

Objects on the stage, such as the cat, are known as 'sprites'; they are listed in the pane below the stage – the cat is named 'Sprite1'. This is where you can add new sprites and change their properties.

The tall pane to the left-hand side of the stage is known as the 'scripts area'; this is where the programming code is developed and shaped. Programming essentially involves creating a series of commands to control something – sprites on the stage, in this case. A complete series of commands is known as a 'script'.

WHAT YOU'LL LEARN

- Create a working game in just 15 minutes using a simple programming language
- Encourage children to create games and interactive stories
- Share and run your programs online at the Scratch website

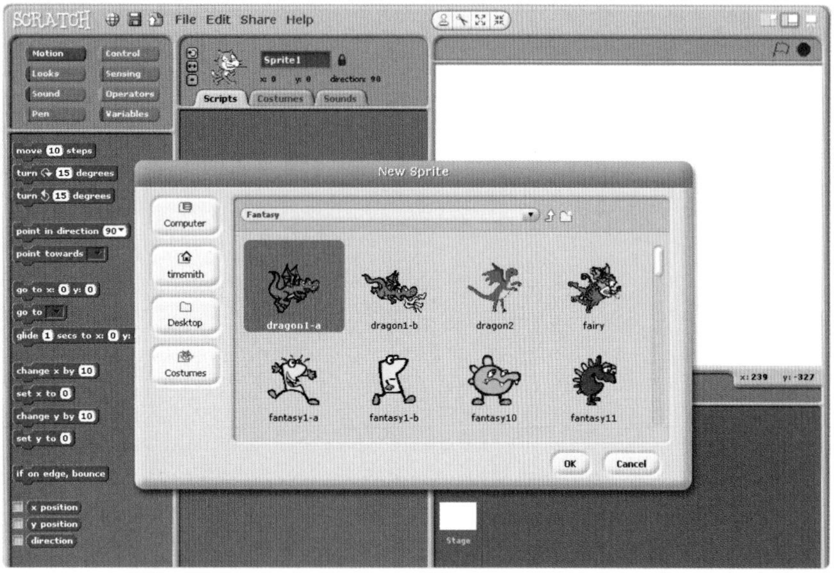

▲ **In Scratch, you can build up a program just by dragging and dropping**

Scratch's commands are arranged into eight different categories, which can be selected by clicking one of the eight labelled buttons in the top-left corner of the Scratch program window. Scripts are created by dragging items from the commands pane into the scripts area.

Programming primer

Let's do that now. Click the Control button in the top left-hand corner and the commands pane will fill with command **icons**, coloured orange. To start, drag and drop the 'when [green flag icon] clicked' command into the scripts pane. Place it near the top-left corner but don't worry too much about its precise position.

Now click the Looks category button and find the 'say Hello! For 2 secs' command – drag the first (orange) command in the scripts pane. As you do, notice how a white line appears below the orange command; this indicates that the command being dragged can naturally follow the existing command. Now drop the new command below the existing one and the two will 'snap' together. Indeed, examine the command icons and you'll see they are shaped a bit like puzzle pieces – commands that fit together can work together.

Remarkably, you have already created some working computer code. To try it, click the green flag icon above the stage to start the program. A 'Hello!' speech bubble will appear above the cat for a couple of seconds, and then disappear. Now examine the fledging script to consider what is going on. The two commands read 'when [green flag icon] clicked' and 'say Hello! For 2 secs' – and that's precisely what has just happened.

Creating a game

Let's make a game of chase in Scratch. The player will control the cat sprite in an effort to try to reach a snowman, while avoiding a ball that moves across the stage. We'll create the program so that the two characters appear in opposing corners at the beginning of the game, and apply random movement to the ball.

Create a new script by selecting New from the File menu and click No when asked if you want to save your work. **Drag and drop** the 'when [green flag icon] clicked' command into the scripts pane. Now select the Motion category and drag the 'go to x:[X] y:[X]' and the 'point in direction [X]' icons to join them to the first command. Click in the 'x:' box and type -182 as the new value, and set 'y:' to '-112'

To make the cat react to the cursor (arrow) keys, return to the Control category and drag 'when [X] key pressed' to the scripts pane – this will not join up with the previous three commands. Click this command's down-pointing arrow and choose 'up arrow' for the [X] value. Return to the Motion category. Drag both the 'point in direction [X]' and the 'move [X] steps' commands to join up with the second orange command. Click the down-pointing arrow to ensure that the 'point in direction' [X] value is set to '0 (up)'. For 'move [X] steps', the [X] value should be '10'.

Click Control and drag another 'when [X] key pressed' command to the scripts pane, choosing 'down arrow' for [X]. Add 'point in direction [X]' and the 'move [X] steps' commands as before, changing the first [X] value to 180. Repeat twice more, for the left and right arrows, using '-90' for the left arrow [X] value and '90' for the right arrow.

Click the green flag icon to check your work – tapping the arrow keys should control the cat.

Adding the snowman

To add a new sprite, click the middle star-shaped icon under the stage. In the New Sprite dialogue box, click the Costumes button on the left and then

BEYOND SCRATCH

Scratch has the potential for creating some fairly sophisticated programs. For example, it makes it easy to perform several tasks at simultaneously, which can be quite tricky with traditional coding methods. However, if you want to develop your skills then at some point it will become necessary to move to a more traditional programming language. Small Basic (***http://smallbasic.com***) would be a good one to try. The next step up is Visual Studio. Microsoft produces a free version called Visual Studio Express (***www.snipca.com/9818***). Although some handwritten code is required, it is also possible to design programs by dragging and dropping commands in similar way to Scratch. Another good choice is Game Maker Studio (***www.yoyogames.com/gamemaker/studio***). The best way, however, would be to turn to our section on Python (from page 50) where you'll find everything you need to learn this simple, free programming language using your Raspberry Pi.

double-click the Fantasy folder. Scroll down to find and double-click 'snowman2' – he will appear in the stage. Double-click the snowman to make him the subject of scripts pane. As before, add a 'when [green flag icon] clicked' command. Then join a 'forever' command beneath it, followed by an 'if' command inside that. The 'forever' command grows to allow 'if' to fit inside.

We have created a 'loop'. Loops are used to repeat actions either endlessly, or based on a particular condition that will be checked by the 'if' command.

We need the 'if' command to check whether or not the cat has touched the snowman. Click to select the Sensing category and drag the diamond-shaped 'touching [X] ?' command into the diamond-shaped depression inside the 'if' command. Click the down-pointing arrow to change the 'touching [X] ?' command's [X] value to 'Sprite1' – this is the cat's sprite.

Select the Looks category and drag and drop the 'say Hello!' command inside the 'if' loop. Double-click on the 'Hello!' text, delete it and replace by typing 'You Win!'. Return to the Control category and drag and drop a 'stop all [red circle icon]' command (you may need to scroll down the commands list to find it) below the 'say' command. This will end the game when the cat sprite touches the snowman.

Adding the ball

Click the middle star-shaped icon under the stage. Click Costumes then double-click Things followed by 'beachball1'. Double-click the ball in the stage to make it the focus of the script area. Drag a 'when [green flag icon] clicked' Control command into the scripts area, followed by a 'go to x:[X] y:[X]' Motion command. Change 'x:' to '178' and 'y:' to '106'.

To make the snowman move, add a 'forever' loop and then a 'repeat' loop within that. From the Operators category, drag a 'pick random [X] to [X]' command into the number field in the 'repeat' command, and change the [X] values to '1' and '5' respectively. Below this, attach a 'move [X] steps]' command (from the Motion category) and another 'pick random [X] to [X]' command in to the move command, setting the [X] values to '5' and '15'.

Drag a 'point towards [X]' Motion command so that it appears underneath the 'repeat' loop but still inside the 'forever' loop. Click on the down-pointing arrow and choose 'Sprite1'. Now insert a 'turn [X] degrees' command underneath this. Drag a 'pick random [X] to [X]' Operator command into 'turn [X] degree' command's number field and set the values to '-90' and '90'. This is to make the ball travel in the general direction of the cat but with some randomness, so the game isn't impossible.

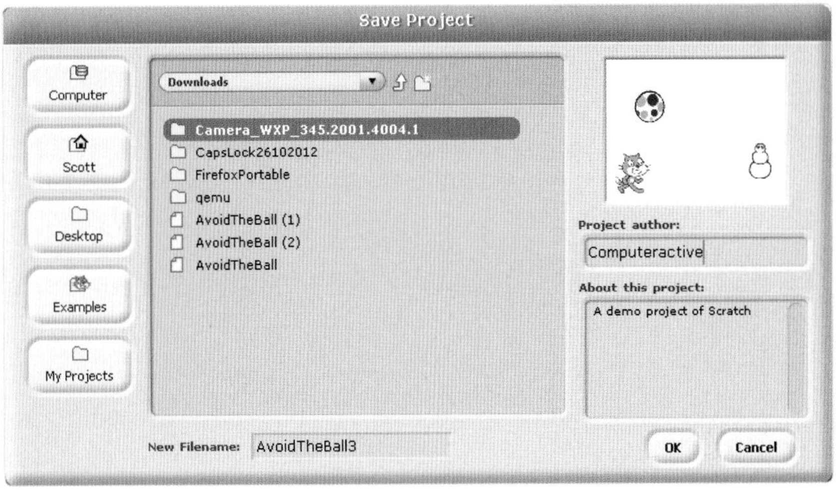

▲ It won't take long before you've created a simple script using Scratch

Finally the ball needs to know whether or not it has touched the cat. Insert an 'if' command after the 'turn [X] degrees' command, but still within the forever loop. From the Sensing category, drag a 'touching [X] ?' command into 'if' command's gap, choosing 'Sprite1' as the [X] value. Add a 'say' command from the Looks category and change the text to read 'Got You!'. Add a 'stop all [red circle icon]' after this 'say' command to end the game.

If you ran the program now (by clicking the green flag icon) you'd discover the ball moves too fast. This can be fixed by adding a 'wait' command (from the Control category) to the very end, but still within the 'forever' loop. Set it to 0.2 seconds.

Now run the program. The ball will move and the cat will respond to direction commands from the cursor (arrow) keys. Try to get to the snowman without being touched by the ball.

If something's wrong, check the code carefully or download the completed program from ***www.snipca.com/7950*** – click the AvoidTheBall link.

Save and share

Save your work often. Type a name at the bottom of the window. If planning to share, add your name in the Project author box and a description in the 'About this project' box. Click OK.

To share the program with other people using your Scratch account, click the orange icon. Enter your Scratch login details and some information about the program, then click OK. ca

“ Even if you've never programmed before, Scratch makes it very simple. ”

Build your own games controller

Learn simple electronics skills to create a homemade gamepad for your Pi

WHAT YOU'LL LEARN

- How to build a gamepad from scratch
- Create a device without previous electronics experience
- Modify your existing programs to add controller support

Building custom hardware is not as difficult as it may sound, but it does require some equipment and supplies not usually found in the average household. These do not have to cost a fortune and are easily available.

The equipment needed includes a basic soldering kit (around £10, *www.snipca.com/7225*), a wire-cutter tool (£5, *www.snipca.com/7226*), a wire stripper (£5, *www.snipca.com/7227*), some lengths of wire (£3, *www.snipca.com/7228*), some button-type switches with matching resistors (£3, *www.snipca.com/7229*) and some female-to-female jumper wires (£4, *www.snipca.com/7266*) to connect the finished device to the Raspberry Pi.

The only additional piece of equipment required is a length of stripboard – a type of circuit board suitable for creating prototype devices by soldering components through a grid of holes. A good source is maplin, where it is available to order using code FL17T (£6, *www.snipca.com/7230*.) You will also need to download the code for a basic game of Snake to play with your new controller from *www.snipca.com/7157*. We will be showing you how to modify this code for use with the gamepad.

Start with the stripboard

This controller will connect to the Pi's GPIO (general-purpose input/output) port at the top-left of the Pi. This might sound complicated but it is very easy to build and an excellent way to practise soldering.

First, get a piece of stripboard and snap it to length by counting at least 15 holes from one end

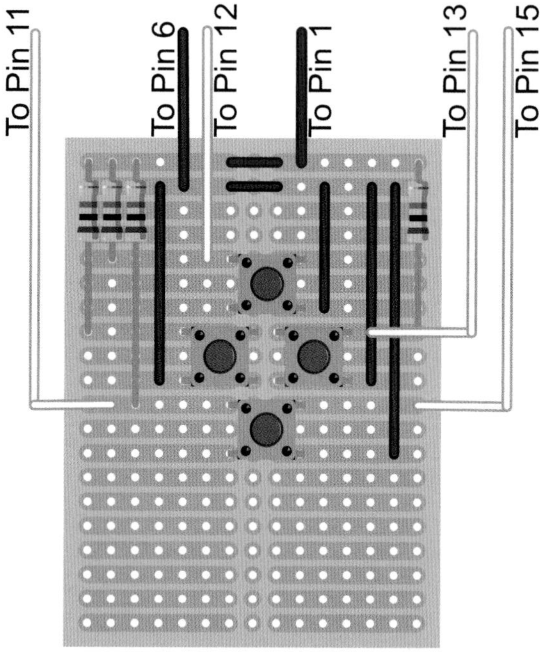

▲ Wire up your gamepad following our diagram and you'll have a cool accessory for your Raspberry Pi

along the length, not the width. Place some pliers or side-cutters alongside the required break line and twist, but be careful – the snapped edges of the stripboard can be sharp. Trim them with side-cutters or file them down.

Look at the stripboard's underside: copper strips run across the board with a break in the middle. These strips connect the holes in each row together electrically so be sure to position components carefully in the correct holes before soldering. Choose an end of the stripboard to be the 'top', ensuring the strips run side-to-side, not up-and-down.

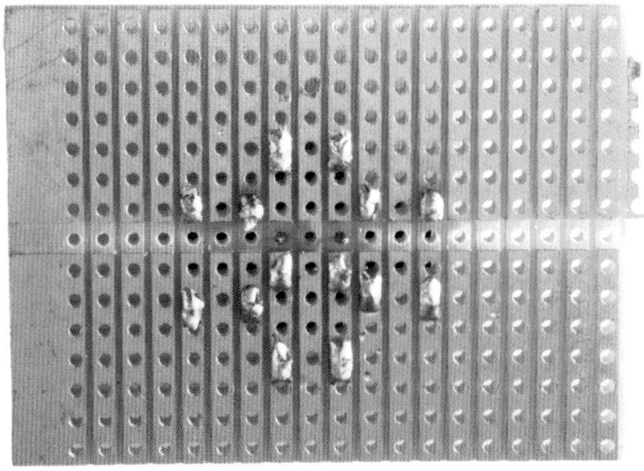

▲ Make sure all the components are in the correct positions on the board before starting to solder

> "Building a simple gamepad shows just how easy it is to make your Raspberry Pi talk to the real world."

Adding the switches

Four switches will be used to represent the snake's four directions. Each switch has four legs, set in pairs. When inserting the switches into the stripboard, they should be turned so that the legs are sticking out from the sides, not the top. Check the photograph at the bottom right if you're not entirely sure what things should look like.

Count five holes down from the top of the stripboard and six holes in from the right-hand side, and place the top-right leg of one of the switches into the hole. The top-left leg should be on the same row seven holes in from the left, and the bottom two legs in the same column two holes down from the top legs. If necessary, bend the legs slightly to fit.

The next two switches should go immediately beneath the first switch, with the top-right leg of the right-hand switch sitting four holes in from the right and the top-left leg of the left switch five holes from the left. There should be no holes showing between the tops of these switches and the bottom of the first switch.

The final switch goes directly beneath the last two switches, lining up with the first switch. The top-right leg should be six holes from the right-hand side of the board, and 11 holes from the top of the board. Check your work against the diagram on page 44.

Now turn the board over and solder the legs of the switches into place. Do this by pushing the hot tip of the soldering iron against both a leg of a switch and the copper track, then wait for a few seconds and push a length of solder against both. When the solder melts to cover the hole, retract the solder, then the iron.

Repeat the process for each of the legs, except the two legs which are poking through holes in the middle of the board, where there is no copper track; these legs should be left unsoldered.

Connecting the resistors

For the Pi to detect the switches, the controller needs some resistors on each switch. These will connect to the Pi in such a way as to provide power to pins on the GPIO port until the switch is pressed. Insert the resistors into the stripboard so that one end of each is pushed through holes at the very top of the board. Three resistors should be pushed into the top-left-most holes, and one into the top-right-most hole (again, check our diagram).

The opposing end of the far-left resistor should poke through a hole eight down from the top of the board, in-line with the top-left pin of the left-most switch. The next resistor on the right should have its end pushed through the hole five down from the top, and the next resistor 11 down from the top. The right-hand resistor should be pushed through the hole eight down from the top.

To recap, each resistor should be connected to the top row of holes and to one of the two top legs of a switch. Now turn the board over and solder the components into place as before. The resistors have long legs, so there will be some excess left over when the soldering is finished; snip this off with the side-cutters.

Wiring up

Jumper wires are needed to connect copper rows on the stripboard to other rows, forming an

▼ Our gamepad is simple to wire up, and you don't need experience with electronics

BEYOND PI

The Raspberry Pi's GPIO port gives it impressive capabilities for controlling external hardware, but there are more flexible devices on the market. The £20 Arduino, for example, uses a special processor known as a microcontroller. This isn't powerful enough to run an **operating system** like Raspbian but it is specifically optimised for controlling external hardware. As a result, it's possible to create projects requiring more pins than offered on the Pi or analogue-to-digital conversion facilities – for example, to read a temperature sensor. The Arduino can even connect to a Raspberry Pi, either through GPIO or via a USB port, offering users the best of both worlds in a remarkably compact package. To find out more, visit ***http://arduino.cc***.

▲ **The gamepad connects to the Raspberry Pi's GPIO connector**

electrical circuit. These are just normal wires cut to length with the ends stripped of insulation.

Measure each jumper wire against its position on the stripboard, and add on a couple of centimetres for pushing through the holes. Use wire strippers to remove a centimetre of insulation from the end and bend the exposed wire at a 90-degree angle, to push into the stripboard.

The first jumper wire should connect the fourth hole from the left on the second row from the top to the same hole on the tenth row from the top, inline with the bottom-left leg of one of the switches. The next should connect the fifth hole from the right on the second row from the top to the same hole on the seventh row.

Next, a wire should connect the third hole from the right on the second row from the top to the same hole on the tenth row, and the final wire from the second hole on the right on the second row from the top to the same hole on the 13th row.

Finally, two small jumper wires are needed to bridge the gap in the middle of the top two rows. Place a wire through the holes next to the very middle hole on both rows, jumping over the empty middle hole. Turn the board over, solder each wire into place and trim off any excess from the bottom.

Finishing the job

Take six female-to-female jumper wires, cut off one of the female ends and strip the insulation back by a centimetre. The female end will be left free to connect to the Pi in the next step.

The first wire should go into the hole on the second pin in from the left on the 11th row from the top, and the second wire into the fifth hole from the left on the second row. The next wire goes through the sixth hole from the left on the fifth row, and the next through the sixth hole from the right on the first row. Place the next wire through the third hole from the right on the eighth row from the top, and the final wire through the right-most hole on the 11th row. Solder these final wires into place to complete the controller.

Check all the positions against the diagram: a mistake could damage the Raspberry Pi by causing a short-circuit. Switch off the Pi. From the left-most wire on the stripboard, connect the free ends to the Pi's GPIO port by pushing the male headers down onto the pins in the following order: pin 11, pin 12, pin 6, pin 1, pin 13, pin 15. The pins are numbered from pin 1 (marked 'p1' on the Pi) at the bottom-left and are counted in pairs: the bottom-left pin is pin 1, the top-left pin pin 2 and so on. Again, check your work against our diagram.

Updating the software

The snake game you downloaded needs some alterations to work with the controller rather than the keyboard, which includes installing an add-on piece of software known as a 'module'.

If the Pi is already switched on and with the Raspbian graphical user interface running, click the menu button at the bottom left, choose accessories and then LXTerminal to open a command line. If

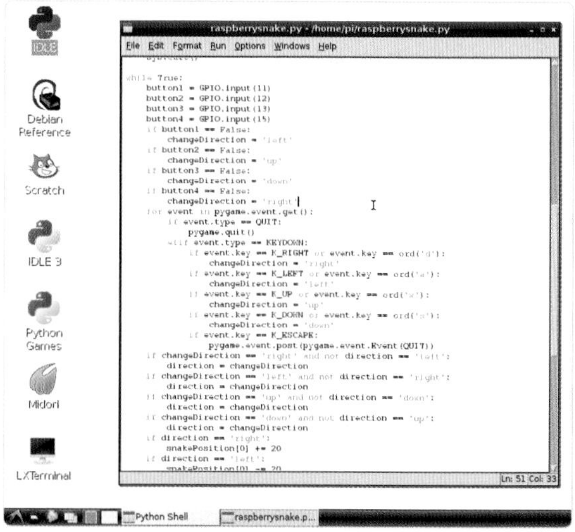

▲ **It's very easy to adapt the snake game to work with our home-made gamepad for the Raspberry Pi**

◀ Once connected up, you can use your home-made pad to play lots of games

> “ Once you've built your pad, you can use it to control many more programs on your Pi, with a few lines of code. ”

the Pi has only just been switched on, log in and type 'startx' to launch the graphical user interface first.

To install the required software, type the following instructions into the command line. Pay close attention to capitalisation, as each instruction is case-sensitive, and remember to press the Enter key after each line:

```
wget http://raspberry-gpio-python.googlecode.»
com/files/RPi.GPIO-0.2.0.tar.gz
tar xvzf RPi.GPIO-0.2.0.tar.gz
cd RPi.GPIO-0.2.0.tar.gz
sudo python setup.py install
```

Note that there are only four commands to type here, not five – the first line has been wrapped just after the '»' symbol to fit our column width. Now double-click the idle icon on the Pi desktop, then click the file menu and choose open. Find the raspberrysnake.py file and click open to view it in the idle editor. The first modification is to load and configure the GPIO module installed earlier. Click at the end of the second line and press enter to insert a new line, then type:

```
importRPi.GPIO as GPIO
GPIO.setup(11, GPIO.IN)
GPIO.setup(12, GPIO.IN)
GPIO.setup(13,GPIO.IN)
GPIO.setup(15,GPIO.IN)
```

These lines tell the program to use certain pins on the GPIO port as inputs for the switches, but the program still doesn't know what to do when each switch is pressed. Scroll down to the line 'while true:', click on the end of the line and press enter to insert a new line, then type:

```
button1=GPIO.input(11)
button2=GPIO.input(12)
button3=GPIO.input(13)
button4=GPIO.input(15)
if button1 == False:
        changeDirection = 'left'
if button2 == False:
        changeDirection = 'up'
if button3 == False:
        changeDirection = 'down'
if button4 == False:
        changeDirection = 'right'
```

Pay attention to the indentation; each line should have four spaces at the start, except the 'changedirection' lines – those require eight spaces.

Click on the file menu and click save to save these changes to the file.

Playing the game

Because the game now uses the GPIO port, it's not possible to run it the usual way through Idle's run menu.

Instead, go back to the command line by clicking on the window's entry along the bottom or by clicking the bottom-left menu button, then accessories and LXterminal. With the terminal open, type **sudo python raspberrysnake.py**. The sudo command, used earlier to install some software, tells the Raspbian operating system to run a command as the 'root user', which has unrestricted access to the system. If the code fails, check your work or download the finished program from ***www.snipca.com/7439***.

The controller can now be used to play the game, turning the snake to face left, right, up or down.

The same python code can be used for other programs and not just games. For example, it would be possible to have the Pi execute certain commands on each button press, to shut itself down or provide quick access to commonly-used programs.

For more information on interfacing hardware with the pi, try the Raspberry Pi user guide (***www.snipca.com/7233***) or browse the official forums, at ***www.snipca.com/7231***.

SECTION 3

Programming for Key Stage 3 & 4

With our beginner's course in computer programming you'll learn a valuable skill for the classroom – and have loads of fun too!

Have you ever dreamt of creating your very own video games? Fancy making your fortune designing mobile apps? If so, you'll need to learn about computer programming. The good news is that it isn't as hard as it sounds and your Raspberry Pi provides an ideal environment to acquire all the skills you need. In this section we're going to show you how to understand the thinking behind programming, explain how to master the basics and demonstrate just how easy and how much fun programming can be. You'll even learn how to write your first simple programs.

IN THIS SECTION

What is programming?

Learning about computer programming is one of the best ways to use your Pi – we explain how to get started

WHAT YOU'LL LEARN

- Discover what programming is and why it's so useful to learn
- Find out where and how programming is used in daily life
- See how creative coding can be

Mention the word 'programming' to most people and one of two images will pop into their minds – the T-shirted hacker wreaking havoc with sensitive government **servers**, or lines of incomprehensible code streaming down a screen. Not surprisingly, real programming is nothing like either.

Wikipedia defines programming as "the process of designing, writing, testing, debugging, and maintaining the source code of computer programs", which is a bit like saying that running is something you do when you run. Of course, programming means to write code – but what does that code do? What is the point of creating it?

The fact is that almost every single electronic device you might come across in your daily life is controlled by code that was written by a programmer. It's barely an exaggeration to say that programming is what makes the modern world go round. By learning how to code, then, you are equipping yourself with the knowledge and skills you need to take an active part in shaping the environment in which you and others live.

Cracking the code

Whilst that might sound a little grand or abstract, just remember that a person, or a team of people, created the code that runs the microwave you use to make cheesy beans for supper, the fuel injection system that gets your family car from A to B, and the set-top box you use to watch your time-shifted TV programmes – as well as the more obvious code you encounter on your computer, games console or smartphone.

Someone must write the instructions that make these devices carry out their useful functions and, despite what you might imagine, you don't need to be a genius to code. Above all else, programming involves two main skills: creative imagination and the ability to think in a logical, structured way. It certainly doesn't involve remembering every obscure command of every coding language (that's Google's job). Programming is a process in the same sense as planning a presentation, cooking a complex meal or coming up with next season's Fantasy Football strategy. It's like solving a puzzle and it's one of the most enjoyable and creative things you'll ever do.

Don't believe us? Just have a little patience and you'll soon discover the thrill of taking control of your computer rather than feeling a slave to it. This is at the heart of programming: having an impact in the real world whether that's on a PC screen, smartphone or a hacked-together robot trundling after the dog. This impact can be profound and, when the penny drops, you'll realise that programming frees you from being a passenger in this technological world and provides the toolkit to take hold of the wheel for yourself.

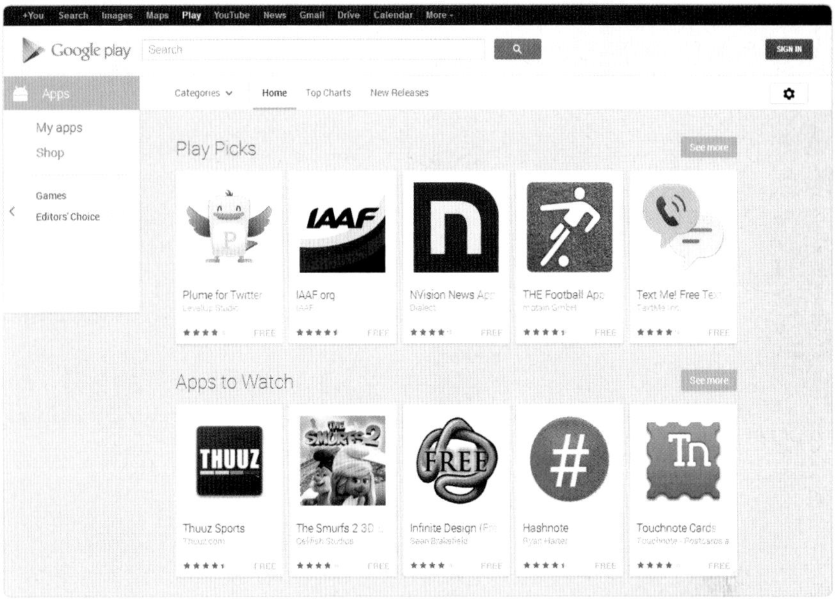

▲ It's easy to publish homemade apps for mobile platforms, thanks to their online stores

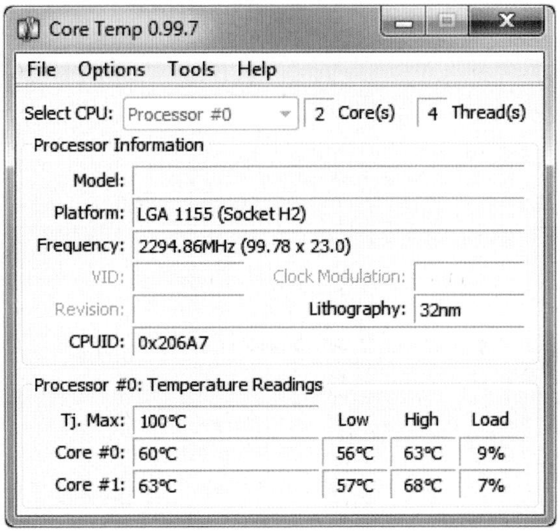

◀ Programming can be as simple as just displaying essential information about your PC

Setting your sights

With such a wealth of possibilities it's important to think about what you want to achieve with your programming skills. Having a practical goal in mind will help make sense of what you're learning,

> "From a microwave to a car's fuel system, programming is everywhere."

as well as providing an opportunity to practise and get a sense of real achievement. The best advice is to follow your interests and choose a project you'll enjoy. Whether or not you want to become a professional programmer, by focusing on something that you'll enjoy for its own sake, you'll become better quicker. The people at the top of the industry, earning the significant pay cheques by creating the software that runs the banks and major businesses, for example, almost always began this way – and many continue to code for fun in their spare time.

So what is achievable for a keen beginner willing to invest some time, effort and brain power to learn programming skills?

Making games

Most coders begin by creating games because most like playing games. Whether you realise it or not, when you play a game you're gaining an understanding of how games work. Crucially, this means you know what you're aiming for when developing your own game.

The games category covers everything from basic word-guessing puzzles through 2D platform adventures to immersive first-person extravaganzas such as the Call of Duty series. As a new programmer, you'll begin at the simple end before settling on your favourite form; many people choose arcade puzzlers or point-and-click adventures, for example, because these can be created in small teams or even by coders working alone. Whatever your ultimate ambition, games are a great way to learn programming.

▲ Thanks to devices like Arduino, it's possible to control your home with your programming skills

▼ The latest web browsers can run complex apps

Mobile apps

The market for smartphone and tablet apps has become hugely popular in the past few years, especially amongst 'indie' developers (that's you). One reason for this is that mobile devices represent the fastest growing category of internet-connected hardware. Even more importantly, each main platform (iOS, Android, BlackBerry and Windows) is served by marketplaces that make it easy for individual developers to publish their work. You don't need to sign a deal with a major distributor such as EA Games to get your masterpiece into the hands of your audience; you can create it and publish it yourself via Google or Apple's app store, at minimal cost.

That's not to say it's all plain-sailing. Despite what you might hear, mobile app development is no gravy train. But it is the leading modern platform and a good sector to learn in if you're looking for a career in programming.

Web development

By creating applications that run on a web **server**, you potentially gain all the benefits of developing apps for mobile devices as well as having your software available to the billions of users of standard PCs. Whilst there are many situations where a 'native' app is a better choice (games being one), it's often most effective to put the code on the web and have people access it via a browser.

Much of this programming goes unnoticed, but it's there lurking in the background every time you order something from Amazon or post a status update on Facebook. Anything that happens on the web beyond serving up static web pages is programming. To see an example of just

PYTHON SQUARED

There are two families of Python in common use: 2.x and 3.x. This may seem odd, as it's usually the case that when a new version of any software is released (Python 3 was released in 2008) users tend to upgrade. However, one of Python's great strengths is the huge library of add-ons created by the community and some of these are written in version 2, making them incompatible with the latest version.

The differences between versions 2 and 3 aren't huge so, in this book, we're focusing on Python 2.7 – the version that comes installed by default in Raspbian at the time of writing this book. This means we can use just about every available Python library but still move interchangeably between it and version 3 when the time comes.

how stunning this can be, take a look at ***www.movikantirevo.com***.

PC applications

There's still a big market for software that users download and run on their computers. This can include utilities, games, educational software and creative programs such as music editors and art packages. In practice, this usually means that you spot a problem that needs solving and, if you can't find a good pre-existing solution to it, you write your own program. You'd be amazed at the tiny niches some of this software serves – there are, for example, several 'explosion generator' applications that satisfy the need for arcade game developers to blow up enemy spaceships in spectacular style.

Typically, the coder hacks together a solution to their own problem and then, if they think there would be an audience for it, spends time adding an effective user interface (windows, **dialogue boxes** and buttons) before releasing it for general use. It's also common to contribute the code to the open-source community, which means that anyone can amend and update it. Done in an organised way, this can result in a much better, more widely used program – for which you receive the main credit. all of which is very good for your CV!

Controlling your home

With the Raspberry Pi and related technologies such as the Arduino (***www.arduino.cc***), it's become much simpler to program real-world objects as well as traditional computers. There's nothing quite as cool as connecting with your environment, whether that's keeping tabs on your energy bills, watching a robot you've made from an old remote control toy make its way around the living room floor, or taking pictures from a weather balloon. The range of possibilities is infinite and it's in this area that the Raspberry Pi has a big advantage over, say, a laptop – its diminutive size, modest power requirements, robustness and, above all, low cost make it ideal for real-world projects.

▲ Playing games like Call of Duty can help when it comes to creating your own

And that's only the beginning. As you develop your programming skills, you'll notice more opportunities to put them to work. So, enough talk: now it's time to tool up and get cracking.

What do you need?

If you want to be a coder, you'll need both hardware and software to get started. The good news is that the hardware is cheap – and the software is free. By using a version of **Linux** as the **operating system**, you can learn to code on a low-cost computer such as the Raspberry Pi or a repurposed laptop or desktop that's now too slow to run Windows. Popular Linux variants such as Raspbian, Debian and Ubuntu are free, as is most of the software you can run on them – including many of the most popular programming languages.

Parlez-vous Python?

The first decision you need to make is which programming language to learn. There are hundreds to choose from, but a good choice would be one that's widely used, easy to learn, applicable to lots of programming tasks, and similar enough to other languages to make it easy to spread your wings later. It should also be free to download and use. At ***www.snipca.com/9764*** you'll find a table of languages in order of their popularity, in terms of jobs and online resources. The only candidate that meets all our criteria is Python. Why? Well, for starters it's very widely used. Python appears in the top ten of the TIOBE index (at the time of writing), which means that many skilled engineers use it and there are many jobs for Python programmers. Plus, there are plenty of resources to help learn it.

Python is also easy to learn. The Raspberry Pi Foundation chose Python as its recommended programming language for this reason. One way to describe a language is to say how 'high level' it is: broadly speaking, the more English-like it looks, the more high level it's considered. Take a look at the following code. It shows how to simply make the words "Hello World!" appear on-screen, and it's written in C, a very widely used but low-level language:

```
#include <stdio.h>
int main(int argc, char *argv[])
{
```

> **"** If you've got a problem, and no one else can help, why not create your own program to solve it? **"**

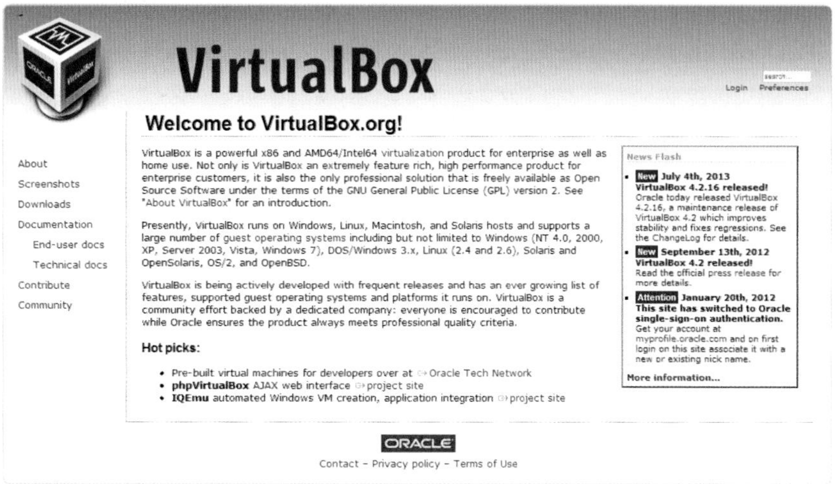

▲ You can run Linux inside Windows by using VirtualBox

```
        printf("Hello world!\n");
        return 0;
}
```

Don't worry if you didn't follow that – it's clear that there's a considerable learning curve involved in understanding C, let alone creating it for yourself. Now, for comparison, let's look at another section of code that does exactly the same thing, only this time written in Python:

```
print ("Hello World!")
```

Not only is this Python example much closer to English, and therefore easier to understand, it's also much shorter – in this case reducing six lines of low-level C into a single concise instruction. This is another characteristic feature of high-level languages.

Python's flexible. You've probably heard of BASIC, which is another well-known and easy-to-learn language. However, these days BASIC isn't as popular as it used to be. Visual Basic is the only dialect that appears in the top ten and it's restricted to Windows computers; the commercial version is also relatively expensive. Python, on the other hand, can be used on Windows, Mac and Linux computers, as well as on many other platforms. It's also able to access libraries of code created in C and C++.

Python's a good first language. The concepts that underpin Python are similar to those found in other popular languages. So once you've learned to code in Python, you'll find it much easier to get to grips with almost any other mainstream language. And if you need any other reason... it's named after Monty Python!

Tools of the trade

Even though you already own a Raspberry Pi, it's often more convenient to develop on another, more

▲ Games are a great way to learn programming - and they donn't have to be fast-paced first-person shooters

powerful computer and then move the code across to the Pi. Even if you've set up the Pi in your living room, hidden it in a shed or built it into a toy robot, this can be a convenient way to work, since it's very easy to connect to the Pi across a network.

The good news is that an old laptop – or a modern PC or Mac – will do fine for Pi development. However, whilst Python is available for all the main operating systems, its natural home is Linux. If you're using Windows or OS X, it's a good idea to install a Linux distribution alongside your existing operating system – or, even better, set up a dedicated computer.

Ubuntu

If you're using a Raspberry Pi, you should already be set up with Raspbian. What if you want to stick with your existing PC? You can install Python for Windows (see left), but we recommend using Linux as the basis of your programming environment,

PYTHON ON WINDOWS

Windows is the only major operating system that doesn't come with Python built in. If you have to work in Windows, you should download the Windows installer at ***www.python.org/getit***. Choose the latest version of Python 2.7. Don't choose a 64-bit version (you'll see the number '64' in the description) since this would make it incompatible with many important libraries.

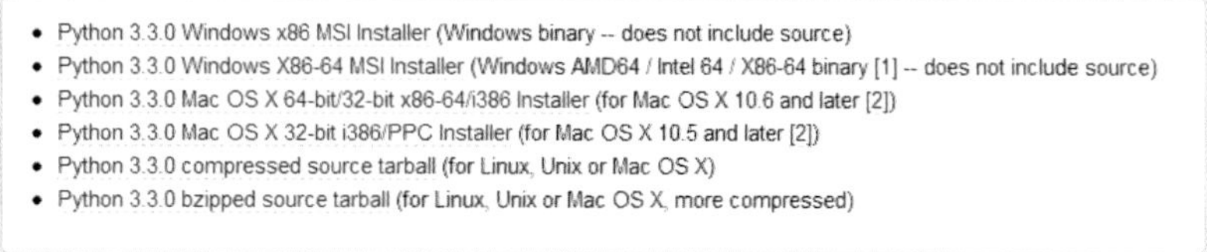

- Python 3.3.0 Windows x86 MSI Installer (Windows binary -- does not include source)
- Python 3.3.0 Windows X86-64 MSI Installer (Windows AMD64 / Intel 64 / X86-64 binary [1] -- does not include source)
- Python 3.3.0 Mac OS X 64-bit/32-bit x86-64/i386 Installer (for Mac OS X 10.6 and later [2])
- Python 3.3.0 Mac OS X 32-bit i386/PPC Installer (for Mac OS X 10.5 and later [2])
- Python 3.3.0 compressed source tarball (for Linux, Unix or Mac OS X)
- Python 3.3.0 bzipped source tarball (for Linux, Unix or Mac OS X, more compressed)

Home Ubuntu Business Devices Cloud Download Support Project Community Partners Shop
ubuntu®
Desktop Server Cloud
Type to search
Download the Windows installer for Ubuntu Desktop
Windows installer for Ubuntu Desktop
With our officially supported Windows installer, you can install and uninstall Ubuntu easily and safely. Choose either the 12.10 release for all the latest software or 12.04.1 LTS for long-term support.
Read the installation instructions ›
Choose your release
12.10
Get the installer

▲ Ubuntu can be easily installed on a system that's already running Windows

▼ An old laptop is an ideal choice for installing Linux to learn programming

since it's Python's natural environment and if you intend to do any serious coding you'll almost certainly encounter Linux at some point, especially if you develop for the internet.

On top of this, Linux is made for tinkering; it's a much more open OS than either Windows or OS X, and has an active community providing all the bits and pieces you need to create great programs. You can also find plenty of generous and enthusiastic advice.

For most people, Ubuntu is the best Linux distribution to choose. It's based on Debian (like Raspbian) but is more user friendly. It's the most widely used and most actively developed version of Linux. You can also install it in several ways, depending on your situation.

1. Wipe and replace

If you want to repurpose an old laptop that no-one's using anymore, then your best bet is probably to wipe whatever version of Windows is already on it and replace it with Ubuntu (having backed up any documents you want to keep). To do this, go to ***www.ubuntu.com/download/desktop*** and download the newest 32-bit version. The download is in the form of an **ISO** file, which you can either **burn** to DVD (double-click it and follow the prompts) or transfer to a **USB flash drive**. When you're ready to install it on the target computer, insert the DVD or flash drive and follow the prompts. Full instructions are on the Ubuntu downloads page.

2. Side by side

Another option is to install Ubuntu alongside Windows so you can use both. To do this, download the WUBI Windows installer from ***www.ubuntu.com/download/desktop/windows-installer***. This is a standard Windows program that downloads and runs the Ubuntu setup. As part of the process, your hard disk is divided up into sections so that Ubuntu and Windows can co-exist; make sure you have backed up your PC before starting. Once Ubuntu is successfully installed, you'll choose which OS to use when you boot up your computer. It's also easy to uninstall Ubuntu from within Windows.

3. Virtual Ubuntu

Perhaps the most flexible option is to set up Ubuntu as a 'virtual machine' (VM) running in Windows. A VM is a software program that pretends it's a hardware computer running your chosen operating system (in this case, Ubuntu). The great benefit of this approach is that if something were to go wrong, you could very quickly wipe it and start again. To create a VM, you need software such as Oracle's VirtualBox (***www.virtualbox.org/wiki/Downloads***). Once your virtualisation software is installed, you can set up a VM and then load the Ubuntu ISO file into it. In fact, you can create as many VMs for which you have space, allowing you to try out any number of different versions of Linux.

Of the three approaches, using WUBI to install alongside Windows is the simplest, whereas the VM option is the most flexible but requires more technical confidence. ca

“ If you install Ubuntu, you can test your programs quickly and easily. ”

The programmer's toolkit

There are a few tools you'll need before you start programming – luckily they're all available free of charge

WHAT YOU'LL LEARN

- Find out what you need to start programming
- Discover where to get your tools for free
- See how the Geany text editor works

So now you know what programming actually is, it's time to put together a suite of tools to help you get started. There are three things you'll need for most coding tasks: a programming language, an editor, and – if your project is going to make use of graphics and sound – a set of software tools for creating and editing these resources. And you'll be pleased to learn that you won't have to pay a single penny for any of these things. In this feature we will show you the best tools to use and where to find them.

Programming language

The Raspberry Pi comes with Python 2.7 built in. This is the final version of the Python 2 family and the code examples in this book are aimed at version 2.7. When the educational version of the Raspberry Pi is released, it's possible that it will default to Python 3, but it will almost certainly also include version 2.7 – and this is the one we recommend you use. We'll cover how to make sure you're targeting the right version below.

Editor

Computer programs are usually text files, which means you can edit them using any word processor or text editor. However, by using an IDE (Integrated Development Environment) rather than, for example, Leafpad (the Raspberry Pi's equivalent of Windows Notepad), you get access to all sorts of tools that help with your programming.

Raspbian includes two versions of an editor

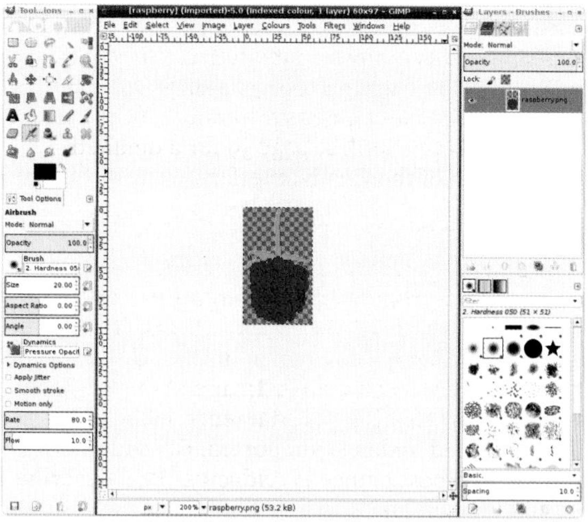

▲ The free GIMP program is great for creating and editing the images you'll need in your programs

called IDLE – one for Python 2.7 and one for Python 3 – but it's rather too basic for convenient programming. For that reason, we've created the examples in this book using a more advanced editor called Geany. You may have already installed Geany. If not, simply open up LXTerminal and type:

```
sudo apt-get update
sudo apt-get install geany
```

...and press Enter. The first line ensures the list of packages on your Raspberry Pi is up to date, the

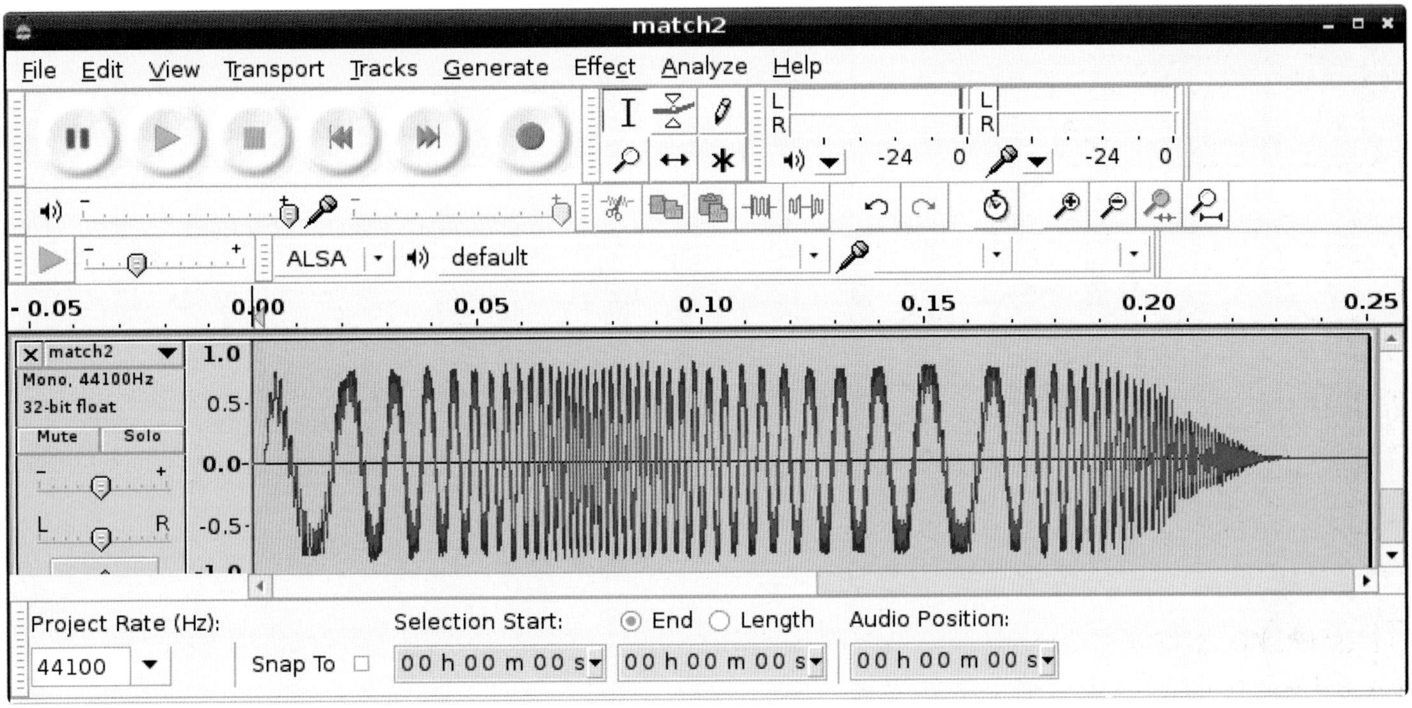

▲ Use Audacity to edit the sounds for your own programs

second line performs the actual install. Geany is available for Windows computers too. If you're using Windows, go to ***www.geany.org/Download/Releases*** and select the latest version of the Full Installer. Have a look at page 59 for a detailed explanation of the Geany interface.

Media

Many projects require custom graphics, and for games you'll probably need to create or edit your own sound effects. As with text editors, there are many choices available to Linux users but the gloriously named 'GNU Image Manipulation Program', or GIMP to its adherents, is the most fully featured and best supported. For sound editing, the best choice is Audacity. We'll describe how to find and install them both.

GIMP

To install GIMP on your Raspberry Pi, start up Synaptic Package Manager and find 'gimp' in the Graphics category. Select this and also 'gimp-data' then click Apply. Alternatively, from LXTerminal, enter the following lines:

```
sudo apt-get update
sudo apt-get install gimp
```

Once installed, you'll find an icon to run GIMP in the Graphics folder of your Start menu. Since GIMP is a processor-intensive application, it will run fairly slowly on your Raspberry Pi, but it's perfectly usable. To get the best performance, shut down any other applications before running it. Windows users can download the installer from ***http://gimp-win.sourceforge.net/stable.html***.

Whichever OS you're using, you'll find GIMP reasonably familiar if you've used any other photo-editing package, whether that's Windows Paint or Photoshop. You can find out more about GIMP at ***www.gimp.org***.

Audacity

Most games include sound effects and, even if you use pre-existing resources, the chances are you'll need to edit them to fit your project sooner or later. Audacity is a basic sound-editing package that includes all the features most people require, and it's free. In Synaptic, you'll find Audacity in the Multimedia category; again, you need to make sure that both 'audacity' and 'audacity-data' are selected before you click Apply. To install via LXTerminal:

```
sudo apt-get update
```

> “Graphics and sound bring your programs to life - and there are great free tools to help you with both.”

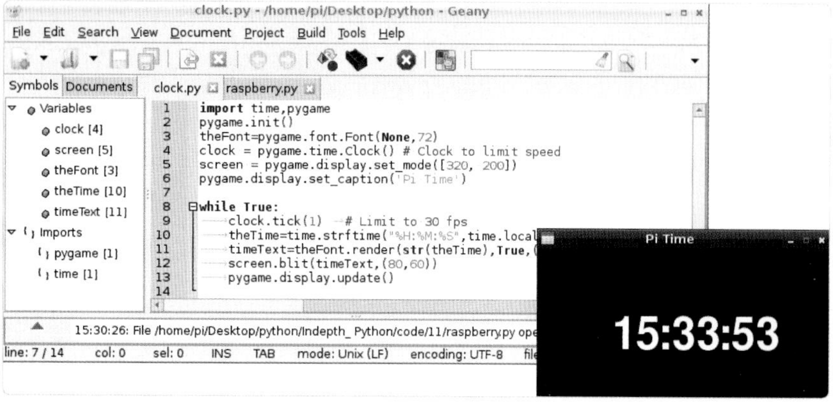

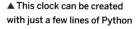

▲ This clock can be created with just a few lines of Python

```
sudo apt-get install audacity
```

Bear in mind that if you've only just installed GIMP, you don't need to run the update command again, as apt-get will have the most up to date information.

Once installed, you'll find Audacity in the Sound & Video section of your Start menu. You can find more information and download links for Windows and Mac versions at ***http://audacity.sourceforge.net***.

Let's get cracking

The final step before we get into coding is to check that your Python environment is working as expected. Rather than bashing out the bog-standard "hello world" program, we're going to create a real-time clock for your desktop. This is not only more interesting and useful, it will also test whether you have two of the most important Python libraries installed and working, as well as Python itself.

Connect your Pi and load up the desktop. Open Geany by going to the Programming folder of the Start menu.

Click File, New and then immediately save it as 'clock.py'. The 'py' extension tells Geany you're creating a Python file and switches on its built-in help and syntax colouring. Now, go to the Edit menu in Geany and click Preferences. Pick the Editor tab on the left followed by the Display tab along the top, then click next to 'Show white space' to fill in the checkbox. This means that all spaces and tabs are marked in the editor window, which is helpful when typing and editing Python code.

Type the code from the listing below into Geany:

```
import time,pygame
pygame.init()
theFont=pygame.font.Font(None,72)
clock = pygame.time.Clock()
screen = pygame.display.set_mode([320, 200])
pygame.display.set_caption('Pi Time')
while True:
	clock.tick(1)
	theTime=time.»
strftime("%H:%M:%S",time.localtime())
	timeText=theFont.render(str(theTime),»
True,(255,255,255),(0,0,0))
	screen.blit(timeText,(80,60))
	pygame.display.update()
```

Be careful to type the code exactly, including punctuation, and make sure you put line breaks in the correct places. The » symbol means a line continues, so just carry on typing. Use the tab key at the start of lines to indent your code exactly as it's shown in the listing. If you prefer, you can download the file from ***www.snipca.com/9785***.

Although what you've just typed in probably looks mystifying at the moment, you can see how little code is needed to create an application. For now, we're just testing that your setup is working so, once you've typed in the code and checked it for errors, click the Cog icon on the Geany toolbar to run it. All being well, after a brief pause, your clock will start ticking away. If so, congratulations.

If the clock doesn't appear, don't despair – it's common for programs not to work first time. Take a look at the LXTerminal window, which will show a message that can help you fix the problem. More often than not, the cause will be a mistake in typing the code, but another possible problem could be Python complaining that it's missing the Pygame module. If it is, and you're using a Raspberry Pi, the chances are that your machine has been set to run Python 3 by default. This is an easy problem to fix: go to the Build menu in Geany and select 'Set build commands'. In the field next to Execute, remove the number 3 to set it to run the older version.

Once the clock is working, you know Python is correctly installed and working on your Raspberry Pi. Congratulations! You now have everything you need to begin your career as a programmer.

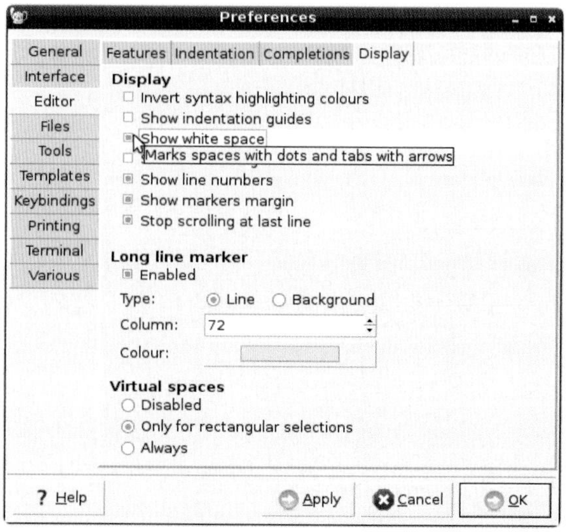

▶ Geany can use colour to help make your code easier to follow

GEANY'S INTERFACE EXPLAINED

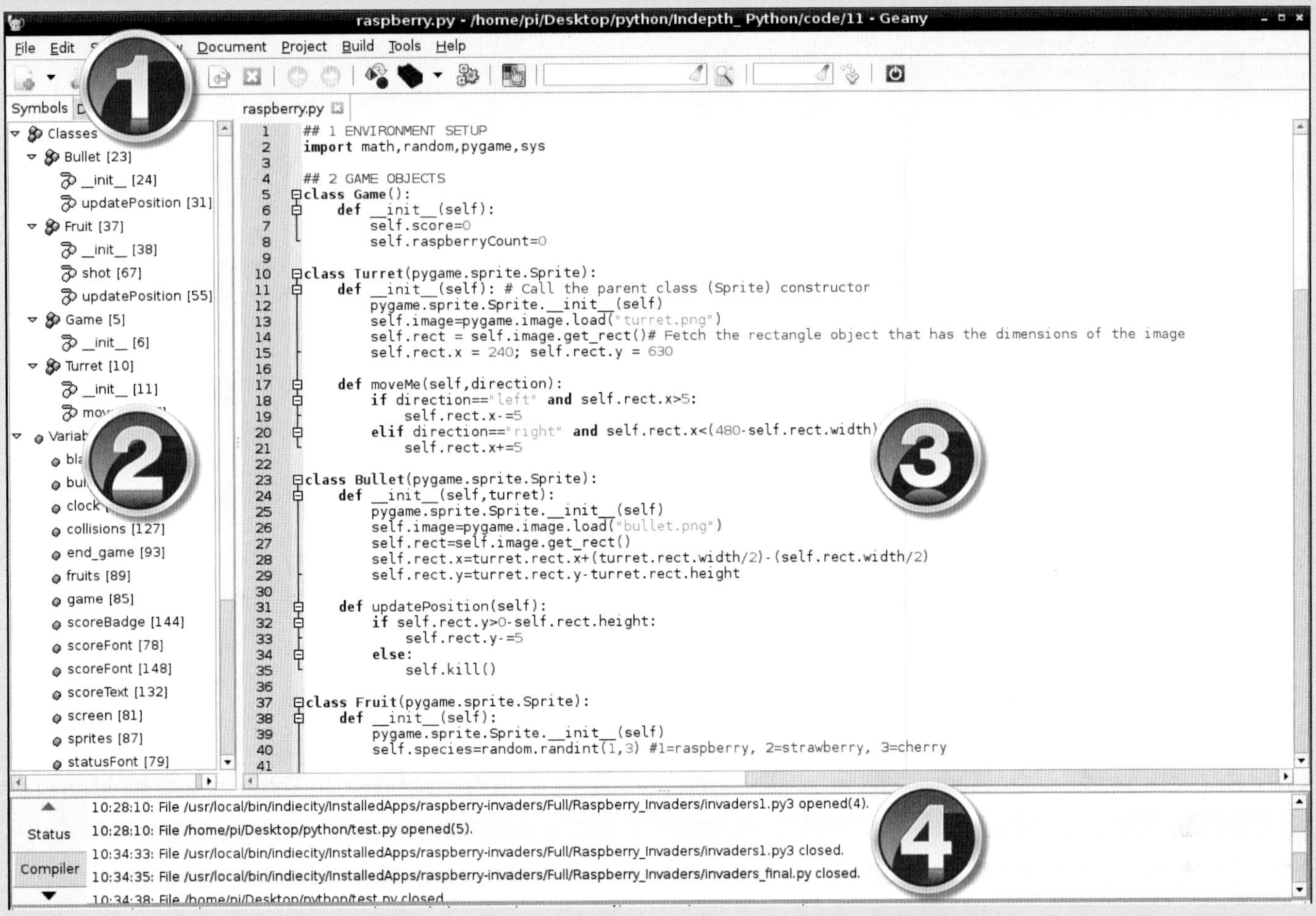

raspberry.py - /home/pi/Desktop/python/Indepth_ Python/code/11 - Geany
File Edit Document Project Build Tools Help
1
2
3
4
Symbols
Classes
Bullet [23]
__init__ [24]
updatePosition [31]
Fruit [37]
__init__ [38]
shot [67]
updatePosition [55]
Game [5]
__init__ [6]
Turret [10]
__init__ [11]
collisions [127]
end_game [93]
fruits [89]
game [85]
scoreBadge [144]
scoreFont [78]
scoreFont [148]
scoreText [132]
screen [81]
sprites [87]
statusFont [79]
raspberry.py
1 ENVIRONMENT SETUP
import math,random,pygame,sys
2 GAME OBJECTS
class Game():
def __init__(self):
self.score=0
self.raspberryCount=0
class Turret(pygame.sprite.Sprite):
def __init__(self): # Call the parent class (Sprite) constructor
pygame.sprite.Sprite.__init__(self)
self.image=pygame.image.load("turret.png")
self.rect = self.image.get_rect()# Fetch the rectangle object that has the dimensions of the image
self.rect.x = 240; self.rect.y = 630
def moveMe(self,direction):
if direction=="left" and self.rect.x>5:
self.rect.x-=5
elif direction=="right" and self.rect.x<(480-self.rect.width):
self.rect.x+=5
class Bullet(pygame.sprite.Sprite):
def __init__(self,turret):
pygame.sprite.Sprite.__init__(self)
self.image=pygame.image.load("bullet.png")
self.rect=self.image.get_rect()
self.rect.x=turret.rect.x+(turret.rect.width/2)-(self.rect.width/2)
self.rect.y=turret.rect.y-turret.rect.height
def updatePosition(self):
if self.rect.y>0-self.rect.height:
self.rect.y-=5
else:
self.kill()
class Fruit(pygame.sprite.Sprite):
def __init__(self):
pygame.sprite.Sprite.__init__(self)
self.species=random.randint(1,3) #1=raspberry, 2=strawberry, 3=cherry
Status
Compiler
10:28:10: File /usr/local/bin/indiecity/InstalledApps/raspberry-invaders/Full/Raspberry_Invaders/invaders1.py3 opened(4).
10:28:10: File /home/pi/Desktop/python/test.py opened(5).
10:34:33: File /usr/local/bin/indiecity/InstalledApps/raspberry-invaders/Full/Raspberry_Invaders/invaders1.py3 closed.
10:34:35: File /usr/local/bin/indiecity/InstalledApps/raspberry-invaders/Full/Raspberry_Invaders/invaders_final.py closed.

1. Toolbar

The Geany toolbar contains shortcuts for moving quickly through your code, picking and inserting colours and letting you test-run your program with a single click.

2. Code Explorer

The left-hand pane displays information about the program you're currently working on, including easy access to its main parts.

3. Coding Window

This is where you'll be spending most of your time. Geany includes:

- Code suggestion – the editor guesses what you're typing and offers to finish for you
- In-built reference – when you type the name of a Python statement, it shows what that function expects to follow it and how it works
- Syntax colouring – 'syntax' refers to the words and numbers that make up your code, and by automatically applying different colours to different types of syntax, Geany makes code easy to read and debug

4. Message Window

Geany displays messages and status reports in this window. You can also select the Terminal tab to get quick access to the LXTerminal.

Programming from the inside out

We help you understand the principals of programming, using examples from real life

WHAT YOU'LL LEARN

- Understand how compter programming works
- Learn about the input-logic-output model
- See the logic model in action with our examples

EXAMPLE 1 – A VAT CALCULATOR

Yes, it's boring but somebody has to write programs to carry out useful, mundane tasks such as this. A VAT calculator would ask the user to type in an amount; it would then work out the VAT on that amount and add that to the original value to arrive at a total. Finally, the program would display the result on-screen.
In this case, then, the amount entered by the user is the input, the VAT calculation is the logic, and displaying the result on-screen is the output. Bear in mind that the output could just as easily be to a printer or even a speech synthesiser; however, if that was the case, neither of the first two parts would be affected. Whilst this might make little difference on a tiny app such as this, on large corporate systems splitting the code into these three purposes makes it possible for different programmers to work on each and for the application to be easily ported from desktop to web to mobile, or to update individual parts easily.

▶ A simple calculator still works to the input-logic-output model

Computers, microcontrollers and other electronic devices are used for so many tasks that you might imagine they share very little in common. However, whether they're running on an Xbox, inside the dashboard of a car or controlling the Curiosity Mars Rover on the surface of the planet, most programs work in a fundamentally similar way: they take input, apply some sort of logic to it and then output the results.

Some very simple programs do this once each time they're run – for example, a calculator – but most applications go through this loop many times per second. As a programmer, almost every process you'll ever work with will fall into one of these three categories – and knowing how they work makes understanding how code is put together much simpler. Dotted around this article are a few examples to show how this works in practice.

Under the microscope

Most programs take input, process it using logic and then output it in some form; we can use this model as we design and write our applications. For example, let's say you've decided to create an old-school arcade game. In your mind's eye you see fruits falling from the top of the screen, some of them raspberries. The player uses a laser-gun that moves across the bottom of the screen to shoot the raspberries but miss all the other fruit. Without some sort of model, you'd struggle to work out where to begin and how to organise your thoughts. The ILO model gives you a template to get started.

Input

Let's begin by thinking about what inputs a game will take from the user. During the game, the player needs a way of controlling the laser gun, so we need to decide if that's going to be achieved via keyboard, mouse or touch. The choice depends largely on the platform we're aiming at. In the case of the Raspberry Pi, keyboard is best, so we're going to track the left and right arrow keys, along with the spacebar for firing laser bolts. Why space? Because it's the convention. How do you know? By playing games. If you ever needed an excuse for trying out as many games as possible now you have one! Other inputs will include buttons for starting, choosing levels, exiting and help.

Output

Think about how the user will experience the game. First they'll see the fruit, laser and bullets appear on-screen and then move. So we'll need to write code for displaying these graphical elements and animating them. The player also needs to see a score and any other status information – perhaps a time limit and basic instructions – so we'll need a way to display information in text format. And then we'll need to write code to play the obligatory bleeps of the classic arcade game.

But output isn't just what the player sees or hears. If we want to store the players' high scores, we need to save the data somewhere. This is output even though it isn't visible to the user.

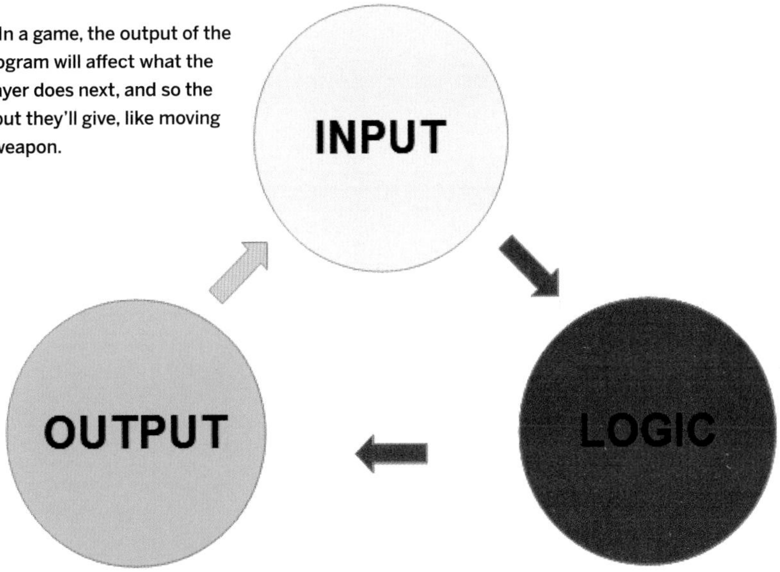

▶ In a game, the output of the program will affect what the player does next, and so the input they'll give, like moving a weapon.

EXAMPLE 2 – FORZA MOTORSPORT 4 FOR XBOX 360

In a driving game, the player uses a controller or steering wheel as input and the console then translates the directional changes and applies them to its calculations of the car's position using its logic code. Once it has done this, it generates and displays the output in the form of graphics on the screen. Given the frame rate of a modern console game, this is happening many times per second – not just for the visuals, but for the sound effects too. In that case, the input might be the controller buttons assigned to acceleration and braking, the logic involves applying the correct physics to the Xbox's model of the game world, and the output – along with the visual elements – includes the sound of a thrashed engine or screaming brakes. Together, the way the inputs are processed and the reactions to them are often described as the 'physics' of a game.

▶ A complex game will process input many times a second

Logic

Whilst a player might notice the quality of graphics and animations, or how well the laser gun responds to their keyboard presses, far more effort will go into the behind-the-scenes tasks our program must carry out to make sure the game works as intended. Logic is the glue that links input to output: without it you might have falling fruit and rising bullets but no way of connecting the two.

In most cases, you'll find yourself spending the majority of your time writing logic code. For example, we must constantly send new co-ordinates for all the objects on the screen to the output code so it can accurately reflect their positions. We must check for collisions, and when one is detected we must react accordingly by updating the output and scores – as well as checking whether the game has finished. By breaking all these jobs down into smaller and smaller steps, you eventually end up at the level of the single programming task.

Mirror mirror

Most programs interact with a user in some way. In a game, it's the user that's providing the input in the first place. In fact, the player and the program become part of a cycle: the user sees the fruit descending (input), decides where to move the laser gun (logic), and presses the keys accordingly (output). Put another way, the output of your program becomes the player's input, and vice versa.

If you're designing a program that interacts with a user like this, you must take account of the whole system. It's not enough to think about the best way for the code to accept input; you must also consider how the player will provide it. For example, when choosing keys for moving the gun left and right, it may be more convenient from a programming point of view to use A and B – but it makes much more sense for the player to use the left and right arrow keys. We've all used apps that have clearly been designed for the convenience of the programmer – try to avoid that in your own.

Modularise

So you've split the tasks your program needs to perform into input, logic and output: how does this translate into the real world of creating your game? It does this by helping you to work out how to organise your code. Imagine slicing a pie into equal parts. You could begin by cutting it into thirds, and then continuing to halve until you reach the optimum size. Input, logic and output are these thirds, which you then divide up into smaller units of programming. In Python these units are called Modules, Functions and Objects.

EXAMPLE 3 – THE MARS ROVER

Right now, around 225 million miles away, a robot the size of a Ford Fiesta is wending its way across the surface of Mars. Controlling the Curiosity Mars Rover is a computer less powerful than a Raspberry Pi. This computer, the RAD750, created by a subsidiary of British company BAE Systems, contains over 2 million lines of code written in C (although Python was used to create testing scripts).

This code controls everything from sensing the environment to navigating the Rover through the Martian landscape. Since radio waves take more than 12 minutes to travel between Mission Control and Mars, the Rover can't be driven like a remote-control car. So it includes software that uses its cameras (input) to determine where rocks and other obstructions are, calculates a safe path (logic) and turns the wheels (output). Bear in mind that human beings wrote the code, and they started programming with as little knowledge as you may have right now. The sky really is the limit!

▶ Millions of miles away, the Mars Rover has less computing power than a Raspberry Pi

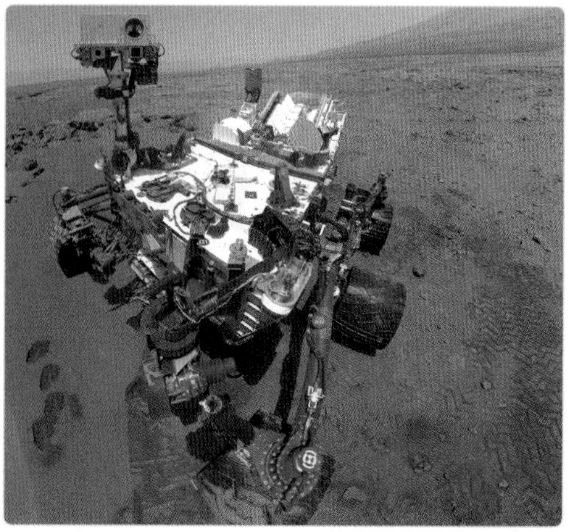

EXAMPLE 4 – OUR CLOCK

Finally, remember the tiny clock app we created in the last section? It took the current system clock time as input, converted it to a human-readable form (logic) and displayed it on-screen (output).

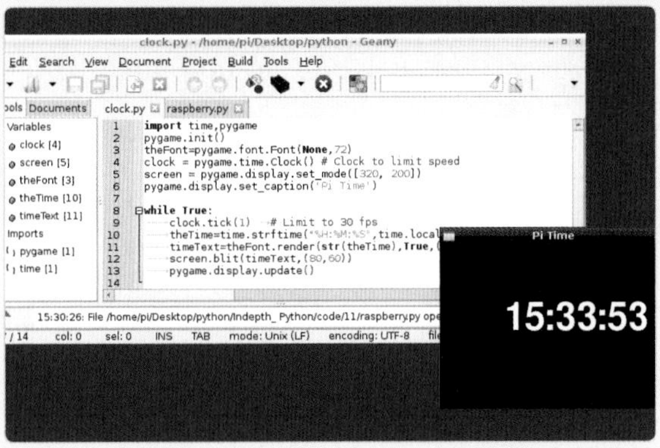

▶ **Our clock is simple, but it still shows how information flows**

> **“** Learning how to split your code up into modules, functions and objects will help you to program efficiently. **”**

Modules

To create a Python program, you type code into an editor and save it. The saved file is a module so, in a way, every Python program could be called a module, even our tiny clock. However, typing all your code into a single file is rarely a good idea unless the app is very simple. More typically, you create a main script file, then split the rest of the code into separate files, each of which is a module. For example, you might create a module for handling the display, one for saving the score and reading it back, and another to listen for the user's key presses. You would then make the code in those modules available to the main script by 'importing' them. Take a look again at the first line of the clock code:

```
import time,pygame
```

As you've probably guessed, time and pygame are modules. time is built into all Python installations and is, in effect, part of the standard language, whereas pygame is a specialised module that helps in the development of games. Importing your own modules is done in exactly the same way.

Functions

Modules divide into functions: blocks of code that perform a specific task and have their own unique name. For example, in the "display" module for our game, we might have a function for drawing a bullet, another for painting the animated background, and a third for exploding the fruit. Within these functions you'll find our actual lines of code – so functions are the smallest subdivision of your program.

Objects

Python is an object-oriented programming (OOP) language. This means the code that controls how parts of a program works is contained within those parts – as opposed to the procedural approach used by languages such as BASIC, which keep everything in a big central file. OOP makes it easier to build and maintain code, and it means we can effortlessly create multiple copies of objects.

For example, think about a game of Space Invaders. The invaders themselves are identical to each other and move left, right and down the screen. The procedural approach would be to draw each invader separately, one at a time, and keep track in memory of which one is where, whether it's been destroyed or has reached the bottom of the screen.

The object-oriented approach is to write code for one invader (this is called a Class) so that it keeps track of its own position and status, and then to create as many copies (called Instances) of that class as necessary. Once they're up and running, they each run independently.

As a rule, OOP means less code overall; programming that is much easier to understand (as you know that any code within the 'invader' class relates to the aliens); and, because of this simplicity, fewer bugs and better performance.

So, a Python program is usually made up of modules containing functions and classes (which also contain functions). Despite their somewhat intimidating names, modules, functions and classes are simply ways of organising code, and they're there to make life easier. With that behind us, it's time to dive into Python. ca

▼ **In a game, information is constantly flowing between user and program, each affecting the other**

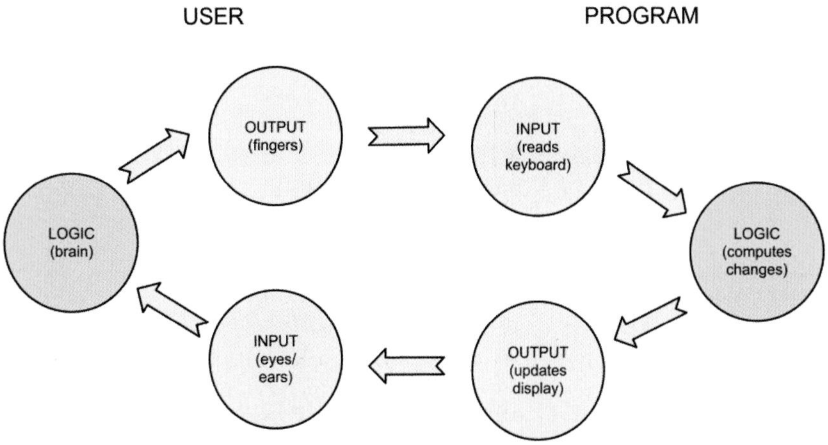

Introducing Python

Learning to speak another language has never been this easy

WHAT YOU'LL LEARN

- Find out how easy it is to program in Python
- Learn the dos and don'ts of programming in Python

You've set up the Raspberry Pi and you've got a basic grasp of the principles of programming under your belt. It's time to start learning the practical skills needed to create Python programmes.

In the next few sections of the book you'll find many code samples. These are all short and we strongly recommend you type them in by hand: doing so will help you gain familiarity with the structure of a Python program, and give you practice in using an editor and running programs. However, you will also be able to download much of the code from the web – we will provide you with link as we go along.

Don't worry if you struggle with some of the concepts introduced in this section; we're going to cover a lot of ground quickly so we can move onto programming larger, more rewarding projects as soon as possible. Whether you're aware of it or not, if you follow the examples, most of what you need to know will sink in and you'll then have plenty of opportunity to see how the fundamentals of Python work in action as we build the code for our projects in the following sections of the book.

Speaking in tongues

All programming languages have the same broad purpose: to provide a way for humans to control devices powered by a microprocessor. With most languages, code made up of letters, numbers and symbols is typed into an editor line by line before being run by the computer.

Python is a high-level language because the code itself is relatively English-like. Indeed, any competent programmer looking at a well-designed Python application should be able to work out what it is trying to achieve, whether or not they have ever learned the language itself. This makes Python a good first language and an excellent choice for a wide range of purposes. But how does it compare with English, for example? Let's have a look using this table.

English	Python	
Books	Programs	Books and programs tend to be about one thing – whether that's a story or a game.
Chapters	Modules	Books are split into chapters and programs into modules – the difference is that chapters are designed to be read in order whereas modules can be used multiple times.
Pages	Functions	Chapters are subdivided into pages but, again, they are presented in a linear order. Modules are made up of functions, each responsible for a specific task.
Paragraphs	Blocks	Usually blocks of code, within functions, are processed in the order they appear, just like paragraphs on a page.
Lines	Lines	Each line of a book contains one thought or idea, while each line of a program contains one complete action.
Words, numbers and punctuation, etc	Statements, commands, operators and separators, etc	The nuts and bolts of both human and computer languages. To become a French speaker, you must learn French words, and how they are put together using grammar. To write Python code, you learn the various statements that have meaning in the language, and how they are put together in meaningful ways.

So, both human and machine languages have much in common. Perhaps the biggest difference is that while you don't have to speak perfect German to make yourself understood to a native, computers are entirely unforgiving; if you don't get your language 100% correct, they won't understand what you mean. This is because, at their digital hearts, computers understand only two conditions – 1 and 0, right and wrong – so there can be none of the ambiguity or guesswork of human communication. Fortunately, Python is much easier to learn than French, for example; when you get it wrong, only you and your Raspberry Pi will know. And the Pi won't tell.

The basics

Python is what's known as an interpreted language. This means that when you want to run a program you've written, it must first be saved as a text file and then passed to another program called the Python Interpreter, which reads in your code and converts it, on a line-by-line basis, into low-level code that the computer understands. Without the Python Interpreter, the program can't run. You can contrast this with C, which is a compiled language: with C, before your code can be run, the text of the program is converted into a machine-readable form that doesn't need an interpreter.

All things being equal, compiled code runs more quickly than its interpreted equivalent, because it's ready to go when it's loaded; Python needs to first load its runtime engine – that is, the software the PC needs to run to convert the language from high level to low level – and then read in the text files and then, finally, run the program.

You might wonder why, in that case, we have interpreted languages. First, because the difference in speed is, for most real-world purposes, undetectable on modern hardware (even the Raspberry Pi). Sure, if you wanted to create a 3D engine for a first-person video game, you'd write it in C (or C++) rather than Python to get the best possible performance, but most games – and most other programs – run perfectly through a runtime engine.

Another important benefit of an interpreted language is that it eliminates a step from the development process. With Python you can write code, save it and immediately run it to see whether it works. With C, you must write, save and compile before you get results. The more code you write, the longer this process takes and the more time you save with Python.

We've described in the last chapter how the work a computer program does can be divided into input, logic and output processes. In practice, this means that Python programs tend to be made up of several text files that are usually saved with a .py extension. In most cases there is a central file, normally called main.py, which is the starting point; this is the text file that the interpreter is instructed to run.

The other files are linked to main.py using the import statement and, if you could slow down the interpreter to human reading speed, you'd be able to watch as it jumps in and out of those other files in response to your commands, but always returning back to main.py. Geany makes all this simple because it has a button on the toolbar for running the project – just make sure you have the main.py file in the edit window when you click.

The Python philosophy

Very few programmers stick to a single language, and as you gain experience of programming, you'll notice that different languages seem to have 'personalities' of their own. Quite often, you'll find you come to prefer one language over another because its personality appeals to you – so it's good news that Python is easy to like.

As you'd expect from a language that takes its name from a TV comedy series, Python doesn't take itself too seriously. Some languages seem to hoard their secrets and so attract fans who take great pride in overcoming their limitations: the harder it is to get something done, the more they

```
import pygame,random
pygame.init()
clock = pygame.time.Clock() # Clock to limit spe
WIDTH=600; HEIGHT=600; BLACK=(0,0,0)
screen = pygame.display.set_mode([WIDTH, HEIGHT]
screen.fill(BLACK)

def draw_circle(colour):
    x=random.randint(1,WIDTH)
    y=random.randint(1,HEIGHT)
    size=random.randint(1,5)
    pygame.draw.circle(screen,colour,(x,y),size)

def random_colour(minimum, maximum):
    red=random.randint(minimum,maximum)
    green=random.randint(minimum,maximum)
    blue=random.randint(minimum,maximum)
    colour=[red,green,blue]
    return colour

for n in range(100):
    clock.tick(25)
    colour=random_colour(100,255)
    draw_circle(colour)
    pygame.display.update()

raw_input("Press a key")
```

▲ Python is a simple language to learn . Read on and you'll soon be able to understand all of this code

seem to like it. Python takes the opposite approach and this has helped to build a community of fans eager to help others get into the language.

The Zen of Python

1. There is one right way to do it

Some languages encourage you to find your own way of achieving something, providing many different methods. Whilst Python has plenty of flexibility when it comes to organising your code (which is your business), when it comes to writing individual lines of code to carry out a task there's usually a single best way to go about it. If it feels as though you're going around the houses to get something done, there's almost certainly a better way.

2. Always choose simple over complex and complex over complicated

Python is built to make it easy for you to write simple code. This is good because it reduces bugs and makes it simpler to maintain your program, whether you're doing it or someone else. If you can't make it simple then make it complex, but keep it clear rather than complicated.

3. Get it done

Python is an incredibly productive language. It takes a remarkably small amount of code to achieve useful results. Whereas programmers using other languages boast about how many lines of code their application contains, Python programmers brag about how few lines it took.

4. Organise for readability

As we'll see, Python includes many ways of putting code into blocks to get things done. You can also put blocks within blocks (within blocks) but this leads to code that's difficult to understand. If this happens when writing Python code, think about how you can put the sub-blocks elsewhere (into modules, functions or objects for example) so that the main code remains simple to read.

5. Have fun

Whereas coding in some languages can feel as though you're wading through treacle to do the simplest things – Objective-C and Java, used for the iPhone and Android respectively, we're looking at you – using Python is a joy. If you don't have fun writing programs using Python then you might want to reconsider taking up programming. As with any new skill, learning to program is a challenge, but Python manages to make it as simple as possible whilst doing its best to demand little and deliver plenty. ca

NO CURLY BRACES

If you've seen programming code at any point, you've probably seen curly braces used to divide code into blocks. When the interpreter reaches an opening curly brace – "{" – it knows that everything that follows belongs together, until it gets to a closing brace. The problem with this approach is that you end up with a lot of curly braces.

Traditionally, programmers have used tab indenting to make a visual link: in other words, all the code that's indented by one tab stop belongs together. However, most languages use the braces to group code, so using tab stops is purely optional and anything that's optional tends to get forgotten by busy programmers. The end result is a mess of braces that can be very difficult to understand.

Python solves this problem by not using curly braces at all, and relying entirely on indentation. In other words, if you don't organise your code to be easy to read, it won't work; and code that does work is readable. Remember, then, to take care with indenting. It quickly becomes natural but it's also the biggest single source of errors by new coders, especially those transferring across from another language.

Learn Python basics

Put all the theory into practice by writing your very first lines of code

WHAT YOU'LL LEARN

- Create your very first programs easily
- Break down your code into easy-to-understand elements
- Learn all about strings, statements and expressions

We've looked at how programs are split, like a book, into smaller and smaller subdivisions. When you're planning a novel, you need to think about the overall plot, character and setting. But actually writing the book is done one word at a time, building up sentences, paragraphs, pages and chapters. Planning a program involves thinking about what you want to achieve through input-logic-output and how that's reflected in its modules, objects and functions, but it boils down to typing code letter by letter into an editor.

The programming equivalent of the sentence is a statement – the smallest chunk of code that makes sense on its own. Statements are usually made up of several expressions, which are similar to verbs in that they get things done. They achieve this by creating and using objects, whether these are built into Python or created separately (perhaps by you).

One of the main advantages of Python over lower-level languages is the range of pre-existing objects you can draw upon. If you were a C programmer you'd spend much of your time manually setting up objects; using Python allows you to bypass much of this and get on with making something useful quickly.

Start coding in Geany

We're going to look at some simple code, and the best possible way for you to learn is to follow along. To do this, start Geany and click the Terminal tab in the Message window at the bottom. If you don't see the Message window, click the View menu, and select the Show Message Window option. If Terminal is not amongst the tabs and you're using Linux, then open up a terminal window and type the following line to install it.

```
sudo apt-get install libvte9
```

Now, restart Geany and the tab should appear. If it doesn't then use LXTerminal (on the Raspberry Pi) or the Terminal app in other forms of Linux. If you're using Windows, you'll need to run the command prompt.

In all cases, now type python into the Terminal tab (or window) to start the Python interpreter. You should get a message reporting which version of Python is running, followed by the prompt >>>, which indicates that it's waiting for input. What's happening here is that you are talking directly to the interpreter rather than loading a text file into it. This means you can try things out instantly, which is what we're going to do now.

Note: in the code snippets that follow, if we want you to type code into the interpreter via the terminal/command prompt, we'll start the line with >>>. Lines that don't begin with the chevrons represent text the interpreter is 'printing' out and should not be typed.

Variables

In basic algebra, you swap numbers for letters to help solve problems. For example:

```
a × 3 = 6
```

In this case, a is equal to 2. Variables work in a similar way – they act as containers for values. These values can be numbers, letters or even objects – the variable works as a convenient way of working on a value and passing it from place to place.

Let's look at this by re-writing the above code as it might appear in a real program. Go to the Terminal tab in Geany (or a running terminal or command prompt) and type the following lines, pressing Enter after each (remembers – don't type the chevrons!):

```
>>> a=2
>>> print(a * 3)
6
```

The first line creates a variable called a and gives it a value of 2. The second line is a statement that contains an object (print) and an expression (a * 3).

What makes the last part an expression is that it returns a value that it has calculated. In this case, Python multiplies the variable a (which contains a value of 2 as set in the previous line) by 3 giving a result of 6. Note that in programming, we use the asterisk to indicate multiplication.

The result is sent to the print object which, as you'll have guessed already, simply writes the value to the message window. You should see the number appear on the next line.

Here's a variation:

```
>>> a = 2
>>> b = 3
>>> print(a * b)
6
```

You'll see the number 6 appear again, just as before. This time two variables were multiplied together.

Let's try a simple VAT calculator. Type the following and press Enter:

```
>>> beforeVAT=raw_input("Add VAT to this: ")
```

The raw_input part refers to a Python function that asks the user to type something in. In this case, we add a message asking them to tell us what figure they want us to add VAT to. This figure is then assigned to the variable beforeVAT.

When you see the prompt, type a number (for example, 100) and press Enter. Then type the following, pressing Enter after each line:

```
>>> afterVAT=float(beforeVAT)*1.2
>>> print(afterVAT)
```

The second line creates a new variable, afterVAT, which is the result of beforeVAT (the number you typed in) multiplied by 1.2 (which has the effect of adding 20%) and, finally, we print this new value out on the next line.

Now, that's all very well but what if we wanted to use this program again? Commands typed into the interpreter will be erased from memory when you shut down your computer or Geany; we're going to start creating files for our programs so we can keep and reuse them.

In Geany, select File|New (don't select a template) and type the following line (including the # symbol)

```
#my first program
```

Now save the file to a location of your choice, making sure you add the extension .py to the end of the file name. You should notice that your single line has turned red. This is because any line that begins with the # symbol is ignored by Python – it's used to make comments in your code so that when you come back to it you can understand what you were doing. Geany knows you're writing Python code because you added .py to the file name, so it's turned the line red to indicate a comment.

Retype all the lines of the VAT calculator into Geany. Notice that, as you type the first few characters of raw_input, Geany offers an autocomplete – press Enter to accept. It also shows you what information raw_input expects you to type in – this can be useful to help you learn the specific commands and also reduces bugs.

Once you've typed each line, save the file and then click the Execute button on the Geany toolbar (the cogs). After a short delay, LXTerminal will pop up and your prompt will appear. Type a number and Python will tell you what the total including VAT would be.

Now that the program has been saved, you can run it as many times as you like by loading it into Geany and clicking Execute.

Data

We've seen that we can use variables as containers and then do things with them. We've used numbers in the example so far, but Python provides several types that you'll be using a lot. Here are the most important:

Numbers

Which of the following are numbers?

```
3290, 3290.123, 3290e3, "3290"
```

We can find out by making use of the fact that Python is a strongly typed language. This means that if you try to multiply two variables that aren't both numbers, for example, it will report an error. PHP, which is another popular programming language, would do its best to work out what you meant – but this can often result in bugs. Go back to the Geany Terminal tab and type:

```
>>> a=3290; print(a*5)
16450
```

Python prints the answer we'd expect. Notice that semi-colon? It's there to allow us to put two statements on one line. Other languages use the semi-colon at the end of every line. In Python, we use it only when we want to use multiple statements on a single line.

Now let's try the next one:

```
>>> a=3290.123; print(a*5)
16450.615
```

This time, the number has a decimal point – in Python, numbers formatted in this way are called floats, because they have a floating decimal point. Numbers without points are called integers. Floats take up a little more memory than integers, so use them only if you need the extra precision. Note that when two number types are multiplied (the floating point 3290.123 and the integer 5), Python shows the answer in the most precise form – in this case, as a float. Go back to the terminal:

```
>>> a=3290e3; print(a*5)
16450000.0
```

This is another type of floating point number, except that this time we used e3 at the end: this is a convenient way of signifying 3,290 x 10^3 or, to put it another way, 3,290,000.

Now try:

```
>>> a="3290"; print(a*5)
32903290329032903290
```

That was unexpected! But completely logical – to Python. By putting quotes around the number, you told Python that the characters 3290 were intended to be treated as a string rather than a number. A string is a sequence of letters, numbers and symbols intended to be treated as text. When you multiply a string, as we did here, Python thinks you want multiple copies so it just repeats them.

To see Python throw a real wobbler, try this slightly different version (with a plus rather than a multiplication symbol):

```
>>> a="3290"; print(a+5)
```

What happens? Python shows an error message. This is because the + symbol is interpreted in different ways depending on whether it's dealing with numbers – where it means to add the numbers together arithmetically – or strings, where it means glue the second onto the end of the first. So, 'raspberry' + 'pi' becomes 'raspberrypi'; but faced with the expression 'raspberry' + 3.141592 (the number pi), Python is unable to perform the operation and will simply return an error.

Although Python has several other number types, most of the time you'll stick to integers and floats. As you've seen, to perform arithmetic on numbers, we use the * operator to represent 'multiplied by' and + to indicate addition. We can also process numbers in different ways using built-in functions and modules – the most useful being the math module.

We'll come across all of these later but, as a taster, here's a list of the main operators and functions you'll come across:

Operator/ function	What it does	Example
+	Numerical addition	>>> a=9; b=a+5; print b 14
-	Numerical subtraction	>>> a=9; b=a-5; print b 4
*	Multiply by	>>> a=9; b=a*5; print b 45
/	Divided by	>>> a=9.0; b=a/5; print b 1.8
%	Modulus (the remainder of a division)	>>> a=9; b=a%5; print b 4
int	Convert to an integer	>>> a=9.0; b=a/5; print int(b) 1
round	Round to the nearest float	>>> a=9.0; b=a/5; print round(b) 2.0
float	Convert to a float	>>> a=9; b=float(a)/5; print b 1.8

Of these, modulus is probably the only one that's not immediately obvious. That's partly because the percentage sign is commonly used to mean something quite different. The term may also be unfamiliar: it simply means the remainder that's left after performing a division. So, 11%2 gives a result of 1, because 2 goes into 11 five times with 1 left over.

You'd be surprised at how often this is used in programming: it's excellent for finding out if a number is odd or even, because any even number divided by 2 will have a modulus of 0, whereas any odd number divided by 2 always results in a modulus of 1. You might use this when shading the rows of a table alternately, for example.

The math module includes some additional useful and interesting functions, too. Python has two types of built-in function: those such as round that can be used as if they were part of the language; and those such as math.floor that can only be used if the appropriate module is imported first. Don't worry, it's very simple. Look at the following table. Remember, they're still all one line.

Function	What it does	Example
math.floor	Always rounds down to the nearest integer	>>> import math; a=9.0; b=a/5; print math.floor(b) 1.0
math.ceil	Always rounds up to the nearest integer	>>> import math; a=9.0; b=a/5; print math.ceil(b) 2.0
math.pi	Stores the value of pi	>>> import math; print math.pi 3.14159265359

Strings

String variables are used to store things such as usernames, text we're going to display on-screen (for example, the prompt we used earlier with raw_input), and other elements we might want to work with, such as database entries. To tell Python you want a variable to be a string, you can enclose the text in either double or single quotes – it makes no difference from the interpreter's point of view. These are equally valid:

```
>>> myName="Terry"
>>> myName='Terry'
```

The only thing you need to look out for is to use the same marks at the start and end of the string. If you try to use double quotes at the start and single at the end, Python will return an error. If the phrase itself includes speech marks or apostrophes, simply use the other punctuation mark to enclose it:

```
>>> myName="Terry's Terrifics"
>>> myName='Terry "Terrific" Travis'
```

In other words, if the string contains apostrophes, you simply need to surround it with double quotes, and vice versa. Given that apostrophes and single quotes turn up in text more often than speech marks, it makes sense to use double quotes by default.

Hold on – what if a piece of text contains both? In this case, simply add a backslash in front of the character you've used to enclose the string where it appears within the text. This tells Python that the character is to be taken literally. For example, here's how we might signal to Python that the internal apostrophe in a phrase is to be treated as part of our string, and not as an end-marker:

```
>>> myName='Terry\'s the "Terrific" Travis'
```

ARRAYS

If you've ever used another programming language before, you'll probably have come across arrays. And, in that case, you may have already worked out that lists and dictionaries are the equivalent structures in Python. Where you might have used a standard array sorted by index in PHP, for example, you use the list in Python instead. Dictionaries are the equivalent of associative arrays in other programming languages. If you've never programmed before, just bear this in mind when you look at the documentation for other languages – this is one particular aspect in which Python is quite unusual.

Things to do with strings

Once you've loaded some text into your variable to create a string, Python allows you to process it in all sorts of weird and wonderful ways. Python thinks of strings as being similar to Scrabble tiles – each character on its own tile – which makes it really easy to get at any letter or number, as well as dead simple to split the string into bits. There are dozens of functions designed to handle strings, but the selection below will give you an idea of how such functions work and how they might be used:

Function	What it does	Example
len	Tells us how long a string is (including spaces)	>>> print len("Terry Travis") 12
+	Add (concatenate) two strings together	>>> print "Terry " + "Travis" Terry Travis
String[position]	Return the character at that position in the string (the first position is zero)	>>> a="Terry Travis"; print a[0] T
String[p1:p2]	Return all the characters between two positions	>>> a="Terry Travis"; print a[5:12] Travis
replace(old,new)	Replaces an existing set of characters with another	>>> a="Terry Travis"; print a.replace("rav","ard") Terry Tardis
split	Splits a string into parts	>>> a="Terry Travis"; print a.split() ['Terry', 'Travis']

Lists

Strings and numbers contain single values: Python's list object lets you store multiple values in one variable. Imagine, for example, you had a database of names such as 'Terry Travis' and you wanted to write to everyone using their first name only. The names could be stored in a list object, then pulled out one at a time so that the split() function could be used to fetch the first name from each.

IT'S MATHS – BUT DON'T PANIC!

If the idea of having to deal with maths brings you out in a cold sweat, there's good news. Far from being the difficult-to-grasp subject you might have found it at school, maths is at the heart of all computer programming, so you'll see its practical use. Plus, the vast majority of the maths-related programming you'll ever have to do is based on simple arithmetic.

Here's how we might define that list of names. Note that because the line is longer than our margins can accommodate, we've used the symbol '»' to indicate that the code spills over to the next line. Don't press Return when you see this symbol, but keep typing to the end of the next line.

```
>>> list_of_names=['Andrew Ant','Charlie »
Childs','Martina Mongoose','Peter Purbrook', »
'Terry Travis','Vera Verity']
```

Once this list is entered, to pull out Terry we could do this:

```
>>> this_name=list_of_names[4]
>>> print "Full name="+this_name
Full name=Terry Travis
```

To isolate just his first name:

```
>>> first_name=this_name.split()[0]
>>> print "First name="+first_name
First name=Terry
```

In Python – and most other computer languages – when you're selecting elements from inside a variable, the numbering starts with 0, not 1 as you might expect. This number is called an index and the item it fetches is called an element.

In the case of a string, specifying a single index gives you one character from the string as its element; with a list, you get the whole element. So, "Terry Travis"[0] would return "T" (the first character) whereas list_of_names[0] would give you "Andrew Ant".

A list can contain a mix of variables, including other lists. For example, for a calendar divided into the weeks of the year, each week could be a list containing the dates. This is how that would look for the beginning of 2013:

```
>>> year_2013=[[31,1,2,3,4,5,6],[7,8,9,10,11,12, »
13] ,[14,15,16,17,18,19,20],[21,22,23,24,25,26,27], »
[28,29,30,31, 1,2,3]]

>>> week=year_2013[1]
>>> print week
[7, 8, 9, 10, 11, 12, 13]
```

Note how each of the nested lists is contained within square brackets. The second line fetches the dates for the second week in January (remember, list indexes start with 0); that is, a list within a list. You could extract the date for Wednesday of that week with week[2].

As you can see, lists allow you to pack a lot of data into a single variable. Don't worry if they seem a little complex right now. We'll be using lists a lot and you'll soon get to grips with them.

Dictionaries

You can think of dictionaries as super-lists. Like lists, they're collections of other objects; unlike lists, each element is given its own name so you can access the variable directly. Try this:

```
>>> family={'father':'Terry', 'mother':'Vera', »
'daughter':'Jane', 'son':'Jack'}
>>> print family['father']
Terry
```

As you can see, each pair is given a name and a value. We can then pull out any dictionary element by using that name. As you'd expect, this means that each name must be used only once per dictionary. You'll also notice that dictionaries use curly braces to indicate when they start and end, whereas lists use square brackets – this is how Python knows which of the two you mean to create.

You can change the contents of both lists and dictionaries during a program. If you typed in the family example above, you could change it like this:

```
>>> family['son']='Jak'
>>> print family['son']
Jak
```

You don't have to use literal values when you create a dictionary or list – you can use a variable instead.

```
>>> son="Jake"
>>> family['son']=son
>>> print family['son']
Jake
```

This time, we created a new variable called son and assigned it a string value "Jake". We can then use the variable to feed into the family dictionary. Not particularly useful as it stands, but imagine if we were reading a database of families: we'd then be able to change the son variable to the name of each son without having to type them manually. A final useful thing to know is that you can add a new

> “ Dictionaries and Lists are great ways of organising data in Python, and there are plenty of commands to work with them. ”

entry to a dictionary after it's been created. In this case, let's add grandparents:

```
>>> family['grandad']='Cyril'
>>> family['granny']='Edith'
>>> print family
{'daughter': 'Jane', 'grandad': 'Cyril', 'mother': »
'Vera', 'father': 'Terry', 'son': 'Jake', 'granny': 'Edith'}
```

Fortune teller

Remember those little plastic balls that presented a random answer to your questions when you shook them? Let's create our own fortune teller in Python – in just a few lines of code. We're going to want to run this more than once, so fire up Geany and type in the listing. Remember that the '»' on line 2 tells you to keep typing, rather than pressing Return to start a new line.

```
import random
fortunes=['Yes','Probably','Certainly','Outlook »
promising', 'Not sure','Ask again','Doubtful','No']
how_many_fortunes=len(fortunes)
raw_input('Think of a question, press Enter for »
the answer')
which_fortune=random.randint(0, »
how_many_fortunes-1)
print fortunes[which_fortune]
```

The code begins by importing the random module, which will produce the random numbers that allow us to pick an unpredictable answer each time the program is run. On the following line we create a list containing all eight of the possible answers – feel free to change them as you wish!

On the next line we use the len function to find out how many answers there are. This might seem odd, when we could count them (how_many_fortunes=8), but this way we can add and remove answers without affecting the rest of the code.

The following line uses the raw_input statement to pause the program, displays the prompt and waits for the user to press the Enter key.

Next, we use the randint function to generate a number. Notice the brackets after randint? Those are there to pass parameters to randint. Parameters are the information the function needs to work. In this case, we're telling randint to generate a number between 0 and how_many_fortunes-1. Given that there are eight fortunes in our example, this means randint will give us a number between zero and seven. That's because, in case you've forgotten, the first item in a list has an index of 0, not 1, so the last one has an index of 7, not 8. Don't worry if you find this rustrating: the zero-based indexing of lists and other objects catches out even experienced programmers from time to time.

Finally, on the last line of the program, we print the element from fortunes that has the index generated by randint.

Run the program a couple of times by clicking the cogs; you should receive a different answer pretty much every time (though of course things will repeat occasionally – that's the nature of randomness). Also have a go at changing the text in the answers and adding or removing some.

Congratulations! You have just written your most advanced computer program yet – a fortune-telling genie, in only six lines of code! If you're having problems typing in the code, you can copy and paste the finished code from ***www.snipca.com/9798*** to compare it with your own.

VARIABLE NAMES

You have plenty of flexibility about what you call your variables. You can use any letter and number (although the first character of a variable can't be a number – '1ucy' is invalid, for example) and also the underscore character. There are a few words that Python uses itself, such as 'else', which you can't use. Don't worry too much, though, it will soon tell you!
The Python community uses some conventions which, in the main, we'll follow in this book. In the end, however, whatever system you use needs to make sense to you. You can't use spaces in variable names as they must all be one word.
One way to get around this is to use the underscore character; another is to capitalise the first letter of words after the first – this is called camelCase. It's up to you whether you believe that my_variable is a better name than myVariable; Python doesn't mind – both are more readable than myvariable though. For now, just try to be consistent.

Variables, decisions & loops

Take your programming skills to the next level by learning to use decision-making structures

WHAT YOU'LL LEARN

- Find out how computers make decisions based on variables
- Discover how to run sections of code multiple times with loops
- Create a simple dice roll program to see variables, decisions and loops in action

Over 200 years ago, Joseph Jacquard demonstrated a new mechanical loom with a unique feature: it used punched cards to control the pattern of the textile. Each card contained several rows of holes in specific locations. As the card was fed through, row by row, small rods detected whether there was a hole. If there was, that particular thread would be used; if not, it wouldn't.

Since each row in Jacquard's system offered 25-30 positions for holes, very complex patterns could be created with minimal human involvement. Loading up another set of cards yielded a completely different pattern.

This invention (building on earlier work by others) was such an efficient way to create textiles that it's still in wide use today. It also gave rise to two important concepts that formed the foundation of computing: the idea that you can program a series of operations in advance and, secondly, that a machine can be given more than one purpose by simply changing its 'software' (or 'paperware' in this case).

Another similarity between Jacquard's system and modern computing becomes apparent if you take one row from a set of Jacquard cards, and represent a hole with a 1 and the absence of a hole with 0. You might get a sequence like this: 1111100 110000011001110011111111. In other words, Jacquard used a 19th-century implementation of binary notation – the 'language' at the heart of all digital computers. The looms used mechanics in place

▲ Programming is nothing new - Jacquard's loom was an early example of how to create a sequence of commands

of programming languages but, essentially, they worked in a similar way. If a 1 was encountered in any particular position, a certain action was taken; if it wasn't then either a different action was taken or nothing happened.

Jacquard's system had only one variable type (a binary number), whereas Python has many (including its equivalent of the binary type, namely the Boolean). We've covered the most important of these – numbers, strings, lists and dictionaries. Now it's time to move onto the coding equivalent of the mechanics that decide what to do with those variables.

If-then-else

The ability to make decisions based on the contents of variables and then take actions depending on the results is what separates computers from calculators, and if-then-else is the most important decision-making structure. In the case of the Jacquard loom, each position on the card where there might be a hole is a simple if-statement. In English, this could be written as:

> If there's a hole here use blue thread,
> otherwise use yellow thread.

In Python, that statement might be represented as:

```
if hole==1:
        thread=blue
else:
        thread=yellow
```

The first thing you'll notice is how clear this code is – we mentioned earlier how easy Python is to understand – and this sort of readability is one of the main aims of the language. We begin with the if keyword, and we follow this with the condition that's being tested.

In this case, if the hole variable (a number) is equal to 1 then the program moves immediately to the next line. You'll notice that this line is indented and Python will now carry out all lines at that indentation (in this case, there is only one). If the hole variable is not 1 then the interpreter skips down to the line containing else and executes the code beneath it.

Python uses a colon to indicate the start of a block of code and then continues until the indentation changes. In practice what this means is that you add the colon, then hit the Enter key to start a new line. You then hit tab once (Geany does this automatically after a colon) and type your first line – every other line that's also tabbed once will be executed one after another. The interpreter will stop when it spots a different indentation.

This is really important – Python is the only mainstream language that relies entirely on indentation to mark blocks of code. The benefit of this is that your code is much clearer, as we explained earlier, but it takes a little getting used to. Let's look at a slightly more involved chunk of code to help you understand. Don't type in the line numbers in the left-hand column – these are just for reference. We've left some blank lines between sections, which helps to follow the structure more easily. In this case we have also colour-coded some of the lines too, to help make it even easier.

```
1   input_name=raw_input("What is your name?")
2   name_length=len(input_name)
3   average_name_length=5
4
5   if name_length>average_name_length:
6           result="longer"
7           conjunction="than"
8   elif name_length<average_name_length:
9           result="shorter"
10          conjunction="than"
11  else:
12          result="the same"
13          conjunction="length as"
14
15  response=input_name+", your name is "+result+" "+conjunction+" "+"average"
16  print response
```

The program above asks the user to type in their name. It then works out how many characters their name contains. The if block compares this with the average length of a first name (the average_name_length variable) and puts together a response depending on the result.

At line 5 – the start of the red section – the length of the user's name is compared to the average. If their name length is greater than the average (we use the mathematical > symbol), then the following code in red is carried out. Once Python reaches the end of the red text, it jumps out of the if statement and straight down to line 15.

If their name length is not greater than average, the interpreter skips the red text and then evaluates line 8. elif is short for 'else if' – in other words, 'now check whether this is true'. Here, we ask if their name length is less than (<) the average.

If it is, the code in blue is carried out, then Python jumps to line 15.

If the user's name is neither larger nor smaller than the average, it must be the same length. So, we use else as a catch-all: it means 'if none of the others is true, then do this'. Note that Python will only arrive at this line if it hasn't already been diverted by one of the other if statements. This time it will carry out the instructions in green before jumping to line 15. Give it a try with names of different lengths to make sure it works.

We've now met three different ways to compare two variables: equals (==), less than (<) and greater than (>). The complete list of commonly used comparison operators is shown here:

Operator	What does it do?	Example
==	Are the two values the same?	if a==b:
<	Is the first value less than the second?	if a<b:
>	Is the first value more than the second?	if a>b:
>=	Is the first value greater than or equal to the second?	if a>=b:
<=	Is the first value less than or equal to the second?	if a<=b:
!= or <>	Is the first value not equal to the second?	if a!=b:

In other words, when used in an if statement, if the answer to the question is yes then Python executes the code immediately following. If not, it skips to the next block. Finally, in case you were wondering, we use == rather than = for 'equals' in conditional statements because Python assigns values to variables using =. Watch out for this – it'll trip you up sooner or later!

Repeating yourself

Using only if-then-else structures leads to very short programs. Remember our fortune teller app? Every time you wanted to ask a new question, you were forced to run the program again. The Jacquard Loom, conversely, kept on going because the cards were constantly fed into the machine via a loop mechanism; otherwise it would have only created one line of thread.

Similarly, we can create loops in our programs, to run sections of code multiple times. Almost every useful Python program will include loops.

For..in

If you want to do something a specific number of times, the 'for' loop is the tool to pick. Let's take a look at a very simple for loop in action:

```
input_name=raw_input("What is your name?")
for c in input_name:
        print c
```

Give it a go. Create a Python file in Geany, type in those three lines and run it. When prompted, enter your name. You'll find that Python then prints each character of your name one at a time, each on a separate line.

The structure of a for loop is this:

```
for [iterator] in [collection]:
```

Collection means any variable that can be split into parts. Lists and dictionaries are often used but, in this example, it's a string. Iterator is just the name we give to each bit as it's pulled out. Put into English, our example would be 'for each letter in input_name', and it means that the next line will be repeated until it gets to the end of the collection (the name you typed in, in this example).

So, let's say you typed 'Jo Bloggs' at the prompt. Collection is therefore 'Jo Bloggs' and the loop will start. The value of our iterator will be 'J' to begin with and so the print line will output that letter. Python now checks to see if we've reached the end of the collection and, since we haven't, moves to the next letter and prints 'o'. Bear in mind that if there were several lines after the for statement, Python would execute them all as part of the loop – until it got to a line that wasn't in the same tab position, at which point it would go back to the for and start again.

What do you think would happen if you were to replace the first line with the code below? Give it a try.

```
input_name=("Jo", "Bloggs")
```

You should find that, this time, Python prints 'Jo' on one line and 'Bloggs' on the next, rather than each word on its own line. Why? Because input_name is now a list, not a string, so the iterator is now each element in the list, not the individual characters in the string. In fact, it's much more common to iterate over a list than a string, largely because lists are so useful.

If you've studied any other programming language, you've probably come across a for structure that iterates a fixed number of times. In BASIC this would be written as for n=1 to 10, which would create a loop that ran ten times. Whilst this might seem simpler, in practice you nearly always iterate through a collection, so the Python approach is much more efficient. If you do need to loop a fixed number of times – for example, if you wanted to create a specific number of objects – the

Python equivalent of that BASIC statement would be:

```
for n in range(10):
```

Again, below this statement, simply place the code you want to be run ten times (in this case), indented by one tab stop.

While

Most Python programs, especially games, include the 'while' loop. In English, this loop means 'while a particular condition is satisfied, keep looping'. For example, in a game you'll usually have a main loop that keeps repeating until the Escape key is pressed:

```
import random
user_roll=raw_input("What number did you roll?")
my_roll=0
how_many_rolls=0

while my_roll != int(user_roll):
        my_roll=random.randint(1,6)
        how_many_rolls+=1
        print my_roll

print "it took "+str(how_many_rolls)+" rolls"
```

This little program asks you to roll a die and input the number. It then works out how many rolls it took to get the same number (on average it should be around six). As you can see, we need to begin by importing the random module. We also create two number variables and set them to zero.

When Python gets to the while loop, it checks its value for my_roll (remember, we set it to zero when we created it) and compares that to the number you entered. The != comparison means 'does not equal' so, if my_roll does not equal the user's number then Python will move into the block. Since you will have typed a number from one to six, my_roll will not equal user_roll the first time, so Python will always run the loop at least once.

We then set my_roll to a randomly generated number between one and six to simulate our die roll. On the next line we increase the how_many_rolls variable by one to keep track of the number of rolls it took to get the same number the user rolled. The += characters are used as a shorthand to increase (increment) that value by one.

We then print the randomly generated die roll, and Python jumps back to the while line. This time my_roll will not be zero, it will be a number from one to six. Python checks whether this randomly generated number matches whatever the user typed in earlier. If it doesn't, it moves into the loop again. This continues until they do match, each time generating and printing out a new random number. When it does match, Python jumps to the final line and prints out the number of attempts it took.

You'll notice that the while statement includes the int function. This is because, when we use raw_input, the user's input is treated as a string, even if they've typed in numbers. Python can't compare a number with a string (even if that string contains only digits), so we use the int function to convert the string into an integer (a number without a decimal point) that the while statement can use to compare. Similarly, on the final line, we use the str function to turn the how_many_rolls number variable into a string so it can be incorporated into the print statement.

Decisions, loops, nesting and breaks

Loops and if-then-else structures are at their most powerful when they work together. You can also create loops within loops (this is called nesting) and ifs within ifs – and any combination of both. Indeed, a program of any complexity at all will involve these sorts of combinations and it can be tricky to work out where you are at any one time.

But this is where Python's clear structure pays off: you know that all lines at the same tab stop are at the same level. This is much easier than the approach other languages use of employing curly braces – in that case, unless you've been hyper-careful making sure your tabs line up, you'll end up counting braces to see where you are. In Python, if you don't line up your tabs, the program won't work so you're forced to get it right. This is a good thing!

Occasionally, you will want to break out of a loop before it has completed. If you'd created a Space Invaders-type game, for example, and were using a while loop to update the position of the invaders several times a second, you might want to exit to another part of the program if the user pressed F1 for help. In that case, you use the break statement; this exits the loop immediately and proceeds as if it had completed.

The continue statement, on the other hand, skips straight back to the start of the loop, preventing Python from executing the remaining lines in that cycle. Combining all these, you create the logic that determines how your program behaves. ca

> "Decisions, loops and breaks are the building blocks that let you tell the computer how to behave."

Organising your code

Discover ways to simplify your code and make it more manageable

WHAT YOU'LL LEARN

» Make your own code easier to understand

» Find out what functions, objects and modules are and how to use them

We've covered Python's most important nuts and bolts – variables, decisions and loops – enough to create simple programs. However, to create a useful application, you need a way to organise your code. Otherwise it would end up as one long, indecipherable block of Python.

Functions

Going back to our book analogy, functions are the equivalent of paragraphs: a chunk of lines with a specific purpose. Functions can exist on their own or within objects or modules. They're the smallest unit in the Python universe. A function is a block of code with a particular purpose. By organising your code this way, it can be used as many times as you like from within your program. For example, you might have a function that reads the system clock every second to update the elapsed time in a game. Rather than having several lines of code to do this within the main program, this can be isolated into a function to be called as often as you like. This has the added benefit of making our main code much simpler and easier to understand because it isn't so cluttered. Each function can be named, which, again, makes the program as a whole much easier to understand.

Let's get straight into a practical example that uses functions and modules. Type the listing below into Geany and run it (it continues over the page).

```
import pygame,random
pygame.init()
clock = pygame.time.Clock() # Clock to limit speed
WIDTH=600; HEIGHT=600; BLACK=(0,0,0)
screen = pygame.display.set_mode([WIDTH, HEIGHT])
screen.fill(BLACK)

def draw_circle(colour):
	x=random.randint(1,WIDTH)
	y=random.randint(1,HEIGHT)
	size=random.randint(1,5)
	pygame.draw.circle(screen,colour,(x,y),size)

def random_colour(minimum, maximum):
	red=random.randint(minimum,maximum)
	green=random.randint(minimum,maximum)
	blue=random.randint(minimum,maximum)
	colour=[red,green,blue]
	return colour

for n in range(100):
	clock.tick(25)
```

```
23        colour=random_colour(100,255)
24        draw_circle(colour)
25        pygame.display.update()
26
27    raw_input("Press a key")
```

This simple program fills a black window with randomly generated circles. You'll remember that when we created if-then-else, while and for..in blocks, we started the block with a colon and then indented the code that is to be run. Functions work in exactly the same way.

We use the 'def' keyword to define a function. You can see that, in this code, we have two functions, which we've called draw_circle and random_colour – we can use any name that makes sense to us and follows the rules for naming variables.

When the program is run, Python will begin at line 1 and immediately carry out the instructions through to line 6. Note the two variables WIDTH and HEIGHT are in capitals – this is the convention for variables whose values remain the same throughout ('constants'). When it gets to line 8, it comes across the first function: rather than being immediately run, the code within the function is loaded into memory to be used later. The same happens with the second function (random_color).

The Python interpreter arrives at line 21 and finds a for..in loop. In this case, it's a loop that will run exactly a hundred times, since this is how many circles we want to generate. In other words, Python carries out the code from line 22 to line 25 one hundred times before the loop ends. The interpreter then jumps down to line 27, which waits for a key to be pressed before ending the program.

To run the code in a function, we call it – you can see the two ways to do this on lines 23 and 24. The purpose of many functions is to carry out a task and send back the result. Take a wild guess at what line 23 is doing:

```
colour=random_colour(100,255)
```

Yes, we're creating a variable called colour and assigning it the value sent back by the function random_colour. Note that every single element in this statement was named by us, not Python, so we can choose words that make sense to us so that our code is easy to understand.

But what about the set of brackets at the end? Well, have a look at the function definition on line 14. Immediately after we name the function, we also indicate what information the function needs in order to run: in other words, which parameters must be passed to it. In this case, we need a minimum and maximum value for the colour (see the box entitled Mixing Colour on page 80 for an explanation of how colour works in Python).

Since our background window is black, we don't want colours that are too dark. Look back at line 23 and you'll see we're passing 100 to the function as the first parameter (minimum) and 255 as the second parameter (maximum).

Each of the first three lines of this function (starting at line 14) generates a random number between minimum and maximum (100 to 255 in this case). The variable names have been chosen to make clear what they represent. However, red, green and blue at this point are just number variables and nothing more; their names are to help us remember their purpose.

In line 18, we create a new list variable called colour containing each of these random values. Again, it's just a list with a convenient name containing three numbers of between 100 and 255 each. Finally, on line 19, the return command sends the list back to the line that called it (line 23).

Scope

Hold your horses – why does the variable colour appear twice? Surely that can't be right? It is right, because variables, by default, only exist inside the function that gives birth to them. This is what we call their scope. So, the variables within the random_colour function (red, green, blue, colour) can be accessed only by lines of code also inside that function. The colour variable defined at line 23 is not inside random_colour, so this part of the program can't 'see' the one at line 18: this is why we must return it.

Having said that, if a function contains another function, then variables declared in the parent are accessible in the child. This is why screen, which is declared in the main code, can be used in draw_circle.

On the face of it, you might think it would make more sense to allow every part of a program to see and use variables from every other part, but there are two reasons why this isn't a good idea.

Firstly, each variable takes up memory and, since the variables within a function are there purely to help the function to perform its task, it would be wasteful to keep them 'alive' once that task is complete. In fact, it might cause a program to run out of memory entirely.

Secondly, by keeping variables 'local' to their function, we can reuse the variable name in other functions without causing a naming clash. This isn't just a matter of convenience: it also means that we can use reuse functions across lots of programs (including functions written by other people) without having to worry about accidentally duplicating variable names.

Occasionally, you do need to have access to a variable throughout the program. You can achieve this simply by using the global keyword in the line that originally defines the variable:

```
global my_var = 999
```

For the reasons given above you should only use global variables when absolutely necessary, and this is very rarely. There is usually a better way to do it that avoids the problems they create. So, back to our program. The random_colour function generates a list with red, green and blue colour values and sends this list back to line 23. What happens next? On line 24, we call our other function draw_circle. This time the parameter is the colour we just received back from random_colour. On lines 9 and 10 we create random numbers between 1 and the width or height of the program window.

Most programming languages use a coordinate system, with the point at the top left-hand corner being 0,0. The x axis is left to right so, on line 9, we generate a horizontal position for our circle. The y axis is top to bottom, so line 10 generates a vertical coordinate. Line 11 generates a random number between 1 and 5, which will be the radius of the circle, and line 12 uses a function from the Pygame module to actually draw the circle on the screen.

When the interpreter reaches the end of line 12, it will see that there is no next line at the same tab level and go back to line 25 – there is no return statement this time because, well, there's nothing to return!

To make sure you understand, follow the order of the lines executed by the interpreter as it goes once through the loop from line 21:

```
21,22,23,14,15,16,17,18,19,24,8,9,10,11,12,25
```

Each of these iterations generates and displays one circle. Python repeats this until 100 have been generated, then drops down to line 27 to finish.

It's quite possible that, at this moment, your brain is smouldering – but don't worry! It all becomes natural very quickly, and this program contains most of the key concepts you need to understand to become a coder. From here on in, it's a question of broadening your knowledge and applying it to more sophisticated (and more useful) apps.

Modules

Modules sound intimidating, but they're simply groups of functions saved in a separate text file and accessed by the interpreter as needed. In fact all Python files are modules, and the usual approach is to have one main module and one or more other modules with specific jobs. So, a word processor might – in addition to its main module – have modules called print.py, save.py and spellcheck.py.

Python comes with a range of standard modules – random and math are two that we've used already – and there's a huge selection of third-party modules, including pygame.

You might wonder why Python doesn't include all these functions in the main language. It's for efficiency: not all programs need random or maths functions, so the code is kept lean by only including modules necessary for a particular task.

Python's built-in modules are available automatically; use the import statement and they become usable. Third-party modules either have to be specially installed (as with pygame) or saved as .py files where the interpreter can find them. In practice, this usually means including them in the same folder as your code. Let's look at how we might refactor (improve) our colour circle program using modules. Here's the main module, which we've called snow.py:

```
import pygame, display
pygame.init()
clock = pygame.time.Clock() # Clock to limit speed
screen=display.setup()

for n in range(100):
        clock.tick(45)
        colour=display.random_colour(100,255)
        display.draw_circle(colour,screen)
        pygame.display.update()

raw_input("Press a key")
```

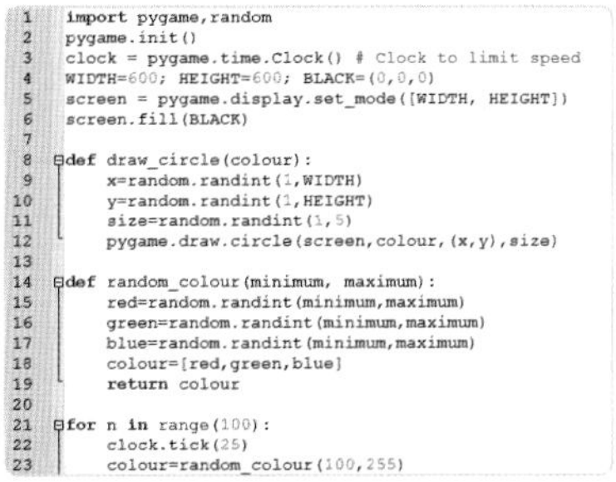

```
1  import pygame,random
2  pygame.init()
3  clock = pygame.time.Clock() # Clock to limit speed
4  WIDTH=600; HEIGHT=600; BLACK=(0,0,0)
5  screen = pygame.display.set_mode([WIDTH, HEIGHT])
6  screen.fill(BLACK)
7
8  def draw_circle(colour):
9      x=random.randint(1,WIDTH)
10     y=random.randint(1,HEIGHT)
11     size=random.randint(1,5)
12     pygame.draw.circle(screen,colour,(x,y),size)
13
14 def random_colour(minimum, maximum):
15     red=random.randint(minimum,maximum)
16     green=random.randint(minimum,maximum)
17     blue=random.randint(minimum,maximum)
18     colour=[red,green,blue]
19     return colour
20
21 for n in range(100):
22     clock.tick(25)
23     colour=random_colour(100,255)
```

▲ Geany will highlight and colour your code, to make it easier to follow on screen

Now we're going to create a secondary module. Let's call this one display.py:

```
import pygame, random
WIDTH=600; HEIGHT=600

def setup():
        BLACK=(0,0,0)
        screen = pygame.display.set_mode([WIDTH, HEIGHT])
        screen.fill(BLACK)
        return screen

def draw_circle(colour, screen):
        x=random.randint(1,WIDTH)
        y=random.randint(1,HEIGHT)
        size=random.randint(1,5)
        pygame.draw.circle(screen,colour,(x,y),size)

def random_colour(minimum, maximum):
        red=random.randint(minimum,maximum)
        green=random.randint(minimum,maximum)
        blue=random.randint(minimum,maximum)
        colour=[red,green,blue]
        return colour
```

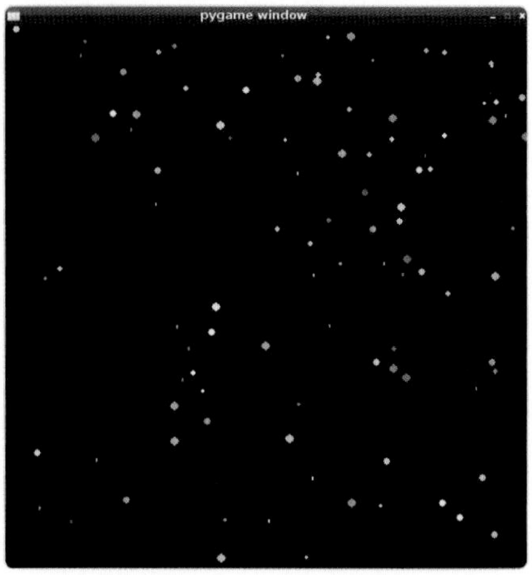

▲ **Our code draws random circles on the screen, and only needs about thirty lines of code.**

In a nutshell, we've moved everything to do with drawing to a new module called display.py, by creating a new Python file in Geany and pasting the existing functions into it. We've added import statements for pygame and random at the top, since they're needed by these functions, and moved the WIDTH and HEIGHT variables to this module, too. The only major change we made is moving all the screen setup code into a function called setup.

Back in our original file (our main module), having moved code to display.py, we need to make some changes. Firstly, we import our new module on line 1 (and we've removed 'random' as it isn't used here anymore). Secondly, we need to call the setup function in display.

There are a few things to notice. Firstly, if we want to call a function in another module, we add the module name to the beginning so that Python can find it. Secondly, if a function has no parameters, we add empty brackets. Finally, note that the setup function returns a screen variable: this is because it is needed by draw_circle. When we created our setup function, we put screen inside it, so it's no longer accessible by draw_circle, and we must return it from setup to the main program, then pass it as a parameter to our draw_circle code.

Whilst this might seem a lot of work, take a look at snow.py now. By moving the display code to another module, it's much shorter and very clear.

The more sophisticated your program, the more you will gain from splitting the code into modules. It's a good habit to get into right from the start. CA

MIXING COLOUR

In Python, colours are made up by mixing red, green and blue, with each component colour assigned a value representing how strong it is. The possible values range from 0 to 255; in other words, there are 256 possibilities. This may seem odd – to a human it would make more sense if the range were set to 0-100, for example – but doing it this way makes complete sense to a computer.

Remember that, at their heart computers use binary notation. In binary, 255 is 11111111; or, put another way, 2^8. In other words, it's the largest number that can be written in eight bits or one byte of data. So, 0 represents none of that colour, and 255 represents 100% of it.

For our circle, the colour is written as a list of the three channels. Pure black would be [0,0,0] – in other words 0% of red, green and blue – and pure white is [255,255,255], with mid-grey being [128,128,128]. Pure red would be [255,0,0], pure green [0,255,0] and a pure blue would be [0,0,255].

To get other colours, you simply mix the channels. Magenta is [255,0,255] and yellow [255,255,0], whereas [128,64,0] makes brown. Geany has a colour mixer built in, to help you work out the best values.

Object-oriented programming

Use advanced programming techniques to produce reliable, reusable code

WHAT YOU'LL LEARN

- Find out how to create and use 'classes'
- Create self-contained objects that you can reuse elsewhere
- Make your code much more efficient

Many introductory books avoid explaining object-oriented development because it's seen as an advanced topic. But it's an essential part of modern-day programming, and something you'll need to understand if you're to do serious coding, let alone have a career in programming.

Fortunately, it's a pretty simple concept to get your head around – and it's very useful, especially for creating games, so we're going to tackle it head on. We'll leave some of the nitty-gritty to later on. For now the point is to understand what we're doing when we use object-oriented programming (OOP) techniques and why.

The basics

We introduced objects in the article on page 60. Procedural programming is like writing code to directly control a puppet. Object-oriented programming is more like placing the code inside the puppet itself, so you can simply tell it what to do and it will go off and do it independently.

The code for an object is contained in a class. You can think of this as a blueprint. Each time a new object (sometimes called an instance) is needed, Python uses the class as its model for that object. In other words, if you needed lots of on-screen puppets, you could write just one class, then create a for..in loop to create hundreds at once.

One of the main benefits of OOP is called encapsulation. This means that everything an object needs to know is contained within its own code. You could, in theory, take an object and use it in another program without having to change it at all. And that means that objects are often an important part of any big programming project.

In this way, objects are similar to modules, and they're made up of functions, just as modules are (functions are often called methods when they're inside classes). Objects can sit within the main code, within modules, or in a file of their own. The more reusable they are, the more likely you'll want to store them separately.

Perhaps the most powerful feature of OOP is inheritance. Writing a single class for puppets is all very well, but marionettes come in many forms and the code for creating a Pinocchio would be different to that used for creating Mr Punch. Inheritance lets you define a generic class containing the code that applies to all puppets, and supplement it with child classes to define more specific cases.

So, let's say the generic class includes code for drawing a head, arms and legs. When we come to create the Pinocchio child class, we can simply write new code to add support for his extending nose. Mr Punch doesn't have standard puppet legs, so his child class might override the draw_legs function of the generic class with his own draw_legs function, whilst keeping all the rest of the code intact.

This approach means you, as a coder, only have to write the minimum code. It also becomes very easy to create new child classes, since most of the work is already done. And each change you make to the generic class is immediately inherited by all child classes, making bug fixing much simpler.

A simple class

Let's have a look at how we can revise our circle drawing program to use object-oriented principles. First we'll write the main module, as below:

```
import pygame, circle
pygame.init()
clock = pygame.time.Clock() # Clock to limit speed
WIDTH=600; HEIGHT=600
screen = pygame.display.set_mode([WIDTH, HEIGHT])
BLACK=(0,0,0)
screen.fill(BLACK)
circles=[]

for n in range(100):
    clock.tick(45)
    circles.append(circle.Circle(screen,WIDTH,HEIGHT))
    pygame.display.update()

clock.tick(1)

for c in circles:
    clock.tick(45)
    c.clear_circle(screen)
    pygame.display.update()

raw_input("Press a key")
```

Now we'll add a module containing a class called circle, as below:

```
import pygame, random

class Circle:
    _minimum=100; _maximum=255
    _colour=None
    _properties=[]

    def __init__(self,screen,width,height):
        self.random_colour()
        self.draw_circle(screen,width,height)

    def draw_circle(self, screen, width, height):
        x=random.randint(1,width)
        y=random.randint(1,height)
        size=random.randint(1,5)
        self._properties=[x,y,size]
        pygame.draw.circle(screen,self._colour,(x,y),size)

    def random_colour(self):
        red=random.randint(self._minimum,self._maximum)
        green=random.randint(self._minimum,self._maximum)
        blue=random.randint(self._minimum,self._maximum)
        self._colour=[red,green,blue]

    def clear_circle(self,screen):
        pygame.draw.circle(screen,(0,0,0),(self._properties[0],self._properties[1]),self._properties[2])
```

> “Objects are a powerful tool for programmers, and can be re-used in different projects very easily.”

Should you need to, you can also download the finished code for both of these in a zip file from ***www.snipca.com/9799***. The circle class completely replaces our display module. This in itself demonstrates object-oriented thinking: rather than creating a module that draws circles over the screen, we instruct each circle to draw itself. That's why we name the class this way.

You'll see immediately that two of the functions of the display module are present, largely unchanged, in our circle class. We begin with the keyword class, which is used to define the block containing all the code relating to that class. You can see that every line within the block is indented; again, this is how Python knows it belongs to the block.

Creating a class makes a special type of function available, which is always called __init__ (with two underscores either side of the name). This is short for 'initialise' and, as you might imagine, is run when the object is first instantiated (created). In this case, the __init__ function automatically runs the two functions we created for the display module, so as soon as it's created our circle is drawn. This isn't always the case: the __init__ function is often used to set up the object for later use.

You may have spotted that the main difference in the code is the addition of the 'self' keyword. This is critical to understanding how objects work. As you'd expect, self refers to the specific circle object being created at that moment. Remember the loop that runs 100 times in our main module? Each time it runs, it will create a new object, each of which has its own self. It's just as if you met 100 children: you might struggle to tell them apart, but each would themselves know who they were. So, each function has a self parameter that's used to refer to itself.

Finally, the other main change is that a new function called clear_circle has been created. Guess what this does? We've added a new variable to the object called _properties (note: it's a convention to use the underscore before the names of class variables, but it isn't compulsory) into which we save the x and y coordinates of this particular circle, along with its size.

Now go back to our main module. First, we replace display in the import statement with circle. You'll see that we've moved the initial setup code

> “Objects contain all their own code - they ‘know’ how to behave, so you can just tell one to display itself on screen, like a puppet.”

back here, because it doesn’t make sense for it to be within the Circle object. We also create an empty list called circles. Our main loop has become even simpler, and line 12 is the critical one. Just as with the display module, if we want to refer to a function within an imported class we must start with the name of the import – circle – followed by a full-stop and then by the name of the function.

In this case, because we’re creating a new object, we simply refer to it. By convention, class names start with a capital letter, and our class name is Circle so that gets us to circle.Circle. This will run our __init__ function, requiring three parameters of screen, WIDTH and HEIGHT. So now we have circle.Circle(screen,WIDTH,HEIGHT). Finally, so that we can use our objects later, we load them into a list using the append method; this simply adds one to the end. We’ll end up with a list that’s 100 objects long.

So the effect of line 12 is to create a new object based on the Circle class (which results in a circle being drawn on the screen), and to add that object to a list. If we were just showing the circles, then the list wouldn’t be needed but, as you can see in the second for..in loop, we also want to erase them.

Line 17, then, says “for every circle in the list”; line 18 sets the speed and then line 19 calls the clear_circle function in the class. So, it’ll pull out each circle object, beginning with the first and, because each circle knows where it was painted on the screen and how big it was, we can use this self-awareness to paint a black circle on top, effectively erasing it.

The old-school way of doing this would have been to keep track of all of this within the main program. That’s not as neat for a simple program such as this, and the more sophisticated a class is, the more useful it is to have objects look after themselves. It also makes it possible to reuse your code and objects elsewhere since they’re fully self-contained.

Run the program (always run the main module, not the class) and you should see the random field of circles appear, pause for a moment, and then just as sedately disappear in reverse order.

This program has been an exercise rather than a functional application. For example, there’s no user input at all. However, by adding input it could be turned into something more useful. Imagine if you painted circles across the whole screen and then paused the program. If you noted the position of the mouse pointer, you would be able to tell when it moved and respond by removing the circles using the code from line 17. What would you have? A simple screensaver – in fewer than 50 lines.

Again, don’t worry if not all the principles of object-oriented programming have fully sunk in. The aim of this introduction is simply to start you thinking in an object-oriented way. You’re now equipped with all the main concepts you need to build a career, or simply personal expertise, in programming. The rest of this section will help firm up what you’ve learned and show you how it works in practice as we create a working game. ca

NEVER DO IT TWICE

As a programmer, one of the most important attitudes to develop is a distaste for writing the same code twice. Whenever you find yourself repeating chunks of code, it should send a shiver down your spine; this is your warning that you should be finding a better way of doing it. For example, could you spin the code out into a function? This is marginally more hassle the first time you do it, but it pays dividends once you’re able to use that function the second, third and fourth time.

In fact, most programming takes this organic form. You spot an inefficiency in your code and tidy it up by creating a function. Let’s say, for example, that you find yourself asking the system to provide the current time repeatedly. This takes several lines of code because you want it returned in a specific way. You decide this would be better in a function so you create one.

Later, you find yourself doing a similar thing for the date or, perhaps, implementing a countdown timer. You create functions for each and then realise they could be organised together into a separate module called time_lib. This is great, but then you realise that you need to have multiple countdowns running at once – so you decide to take that particular function and turn it into a class. Later, you can re-use the class in another program.

Extending Python

Explore some of the essential third-party modules available for Python

WHAT YOU'LL LEARN

- Find out about the extra functions Pygame adds
- Learn about ways to store and retrieve your data
- Understand how database systems work

We've already seen that Python has a number of built-in functions – for example, those that handle strings, lists and dictionaries – as well as a range of modules that are supplied with the language but must be imported before being used, such as those containing operations for random numbers and time. However, part of Python's great versatility comes from the huge library of free third-party modules out there. These range from very popular mainstream libraries, such as Pygame, to those aimed at niche uses, such as connecting a Raspberry Pi to a robot.

Let's take a quick look at some of the most important modules – especially those we're going to use in our game and project.

Pygame

Don't be fooled by the name: Pygame can do much more than help you develop games. Remember our clock widget, the first thing we coded to test our setup was working? We used Pygame to display the window and display the text. Most of our examples so far have used Pygame, even though we haven't started coding a game. Pygame functions include:

- **Display** – Create windows, or allow games and projects to run full-screen
- **Draw** – Draw a whole range of basic shapes such as rectangles, polygons, lines, ellipses, circles and arcs (and optionally fill them with colour)
- **Surface** – Draw objects in memory, then paint them to the display in one go – essential for games with lots of graphics
- **Font** – Embed fonts into your project, so you can display them without relying on the end user having the same font installed on their system
- **Image, Transform** – A wide range of image manipulation functions that might be used to create specialised picture-processing applications
- **Sprite** – Create self-aware sprites with built-in collision detection, making complex games much simpler to create
- **Mixer, Music, Movie** – Add sound and video to your projects
- **Event** – 'Listen' for player action such as key presses or mouse movements

Pygame is written mainly in C, so it gives good performance in games (remember that one of Python's strengths is its ability to use properly prepared C libraries). It's also available for a wide range of platforms: you can create games and apps for every mainstream desktop platform, and a few not-so-common ones!

Saving data

It's important to be able to save data between sessions, and load it back in as required – whether you want to allow users to save their position within a game, store records to a database or exchange information with a web server. Python offers a whole range of methods for achieving this, but the main ones – in order of increasing complexity – are: the File object, pickle and sqlite3.

File

The File object lets you create, save to, read from and delete text files. Anything you save is converted to text so, essentially, you're reading and writing strings. That doesn't mean you can't use File to handle sophisticated data, though. Let's take a very simple example. Type the listing over the page into Geany and save it as file1.py:

```
1   first_name=raw_input('Type your first name...')
2   second_name=raw_input('Type your surname...')
3   savefile=open('data.dat','w')
4   savefile.write(first_name+'\n')
5   savefile.write(second_name+'\n')
6   savefile.close()
7   print('Saved')
8   first_name=None
9   second_name=None
10  openfile=open('data.dat','r')
11  name=openfile.read().split()
12  first_name=name[0]
13  second_name=name[1]
14  print first_name+" "+second_name
```

Should you need to, you can also download the finished code for this example from ***www.snipca.com/9806***. Clearly, the first two lines ask the user to type in their first and second names. The interesting stuff begins on line 3, where we create a new variable using the file object's open method (remember, 'functions' are called 'methods' when inside objects). We pass in the name of the text file: this can be any name we choose as long as it's valid for our operating system (if the file doesn't exist, it will be created by Python at this point). The 'w' parameter means that we want to write to the file; in other words, we want to save some data.

In line 4 we write the first name. By appending '\n' we add a new line. This is the file equivalent of pressing the Enter key – essentially we're using a file to organise text by line, so by inserting a \n at this point the surname will appear separately a line below. You could also simply add a delimiter to each saved record – the pipe symbol '|', for example – but you must choose a character that you would never use within a record.

Having written the second name to the file, we then close it. This tells the operating system to save the file, together with its new contents.

We're now going to open it up again and read the contents back in. Lines 9 and 10 clear the name variables, so we can be sure we've read in the file and not simply kept what the user typed. On line 10 we create a new file object, using the same name, but this time with the parameter 'r', which reads in the contents of a file but leaves it unchanged. Since files only contain text, openfile is a string at the moment: this means we can use the split() function to take this text and create from it a list with each of the lines as a separate element.

For example, if the user's name was Jo Bloggs, printing name would result in:

```
['Jo','Bloggs']
```

To retrieve the first name we use name[0]; for the surname we use name[1]. Run the program and you'll see your name reappear in the terminal. There's an even better test, however: find the file data.dat (if you've used the same name) and open it in a text editor. You should see the names one per line. The file object is the workhorse of Python file input/output; it's pretty simple to use.

Pickle

The great benefit of pickle is that, unlike file, it can take any data form and save it to a file. It can also "unpickle" the data back to exactly its original form. In fact, pickle is specifically built to augment the built-in file object and make it more useful. Again, this is best understood through a short example, which we'll call pickleExample.py:

```
import pickle
save_data={'username':'Joe Bloggs', 'score':9234,'max_level':5}
save_file=open("savedata.dat","wb')
pickle.dump(save_data,save_file)
save_file.close()
#zero variables, read file back in
progress_file=open("savedata.dat","rb')
progress_data=pickle.load(progress_file)
print "Dear "+progress_data['username']+ ", your data \n"+str(progress_data)
```

Note that we must begin with an import statement – pickle is part of the standard Python install but, because it isn't quite as basic an object as file, it must be explicitly added to the code. You don't have to install anything, however, if you're using Linux (including Raspbian), Windows or Mac.

On line 2 we create a dictionary containing basic data, including the user's name, their current score and the furthest they've reached in our imaginary game. Next, we create a file object with the parameter 'wb', which stands for 'write bytes'. Pickle uses its own storage format, so we need to specify that it's writing bytes of data, not text. This means the file it creates will look like gobbledygook if you open it in a text editor.

Line 4 uses the pickle.dump method to save the data – passing it the data itself (it could be any variable type, we're using a dictionary) and the file object. We then close the file.

In a real game, you'd probably want to read this data back in later or, indeed, in a later game session. The code from line 7 achieves this. We create a new file object, this time with the 'rb' parameter because we're reading bytes back in. On line 8, we create a new variable and use it to receive the data from pickle using the load method. Line 9 prints it out.

Pickle is a very powerful and widely used module. Its main advantage over the simpler file object is that you don't need to write code to parse (read and convert) the saved data when you want to retrieve it: pickle simply gives it back to you in the same format you used to save it. If you think about the amount of information you're likely to want to save in your game (a leaderboard, for example), you can appreciate how much simpler pickle makes this – not only saving time, but reducing the chances of bugs creeping in.

SQLite3

If you get into commercial programming then you'll encounter SQL (Structured Query Language – and no, it is not pronounced 'sequel') pretty quickly. This is a database system that's ideal for starting large amounts of structured data – such as for a customer database, or a football league manager game.

The main advantage of relational databases (the sort of databases SQL is most often used with) is that they make the retrieving of data lightning-quick. After all, if you have a large database of Conference League footballers and you want to list all players for sale, this needs to happen in the blink of an eye to avoid your game appearing slow.

SQLite is a halfway house between the ease of use and versatility of pickle and the full-fat power and complexity of, for example, MySQL (the database software used by a large percentage of websites). It's a cross-platform standard, represents data in a flat form similar in concept to card indexes. It isn't good at cross-indexing data but it's very good at simple retrieval – for example, it would make mincemeat of our 'players for sale' query.

Python's SQLite3 module allows you to create, edit, read and write SQLite files and, if you intend to find work as a programmer, it's a good place to start learning about SQL whilst also being very useful. SQL itself is standard across its many forms so your experience of SQLite3 with Python would give you a head start when faced with learning any other mainstream database.

To do things with SQL databases, you write queries and then execute those queries using your chosen SQL engine. So, our Conference League player search might look something like this:

```
SELECT * FROM players WHERE league = 'conf'
AND status = 'for sale'
```

It really is that straightforward – but since this isn't a book about SQL, we'll move along. The key point to bear in mind is that it's nothing to be frightened of. You can carry out most database functions with a small range of commonly used techniques.

Congratulations

So far in this book you've seen how to set up your Raspberry Pi and your coding environment. You've learnt how to think like a programmer. And you've had a whistle-stop tour of the basics of Python and object-oriented programming, so you now know the most useful variable types; how to create and use functions, modules and objects; and how to structure your code using decisions and loops. You've also learnt about the extra functionality Pygame adds, and explored the various ways to store and retrieve data using Python modules.

The best way to reinforce this knowledge and make sure it sticks is to put it into practice; so in the coming chapters we're going to cover, in great detail, the development of three very different projects. You've learned a lot so far, but don't worry if you don't remember everything we've covered – even the most experienced programmer considers Google to be their best friend. Programming is much more about technique and knowing which tool to use in a given situation than about remembering the specifics of how Python, or any other language, implements that tool.

Once you've completed the projects, you should have a very good idea of which situations call for a loop, which require a decision, and when it's best to spin out your functions into separate objects. This only comes through practise, so once again it's time to roll up your sleeves and get stuck in.

SECTION 4

Program your own game

Go beyond the theory by using your newfound programming skills to create a simple but effective game that your friends will love

In the previous section of this guide you will have learned a lot about the principles of programming and written your first few lines of code. Now we're going to take all that theory and put it into practice with a project that will see you putting together a game from scratch. Don't worry if you still feel unprepared – we will guide you through every step of the way and provide you with all the resources you need to complete the project. And, once you've finished, we'll show you how to share your work with others. We guarantee your homemade game will impress your friends and family!

IN THIS SECTION

Design a game

Take some time to consider your options before you start

WHAT YOU'LL LEARN

- How to plan your project before you start
- Find out where to get music and images for your game

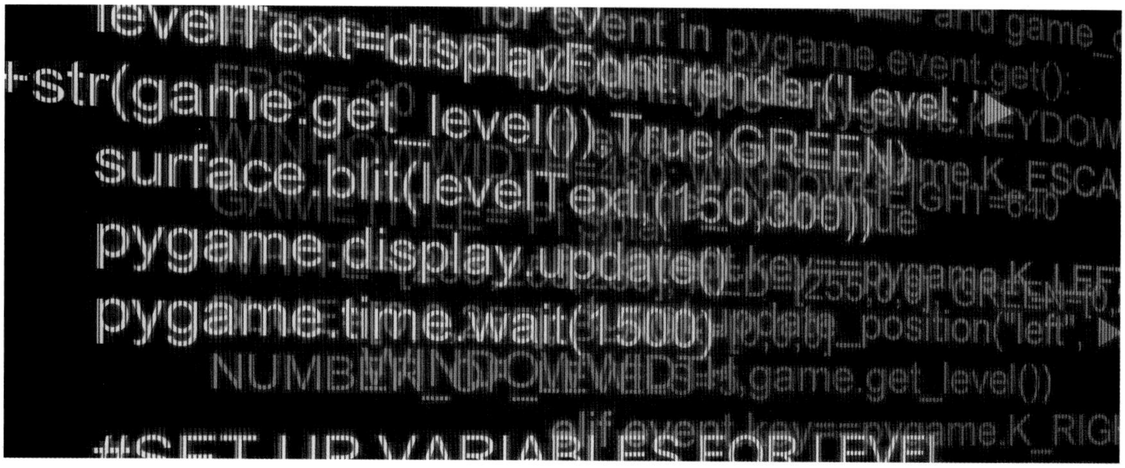

In this section we're going to build on what we've learnt to design and create a simple game. By doing this, not only will we create an end product that will be fun to play, but we'll also explore many of the general programming skills you'll be able to transfer to future projects.

To get the most from this section, we strongly recommend that you type in the exercises as we go through. This way, you'll better understand what each line and statement does within the game. However, if you need to save time or check your work, the resources can also be downloaded from *www.rpilab.net/code.*

Fools rush in

However simple the game, you shouldn't just sit down at your computer and start coding right away – such an approach will result in nothing but chaos and frustration. You need to begin by thinking carefully about exactly how your game is going to work and, from that, generate a list of the tasks both you and your code will need to complete.

Genres of games

According to Wikipedia, there are 13 major genres of game, including action, role-playing, strategy, sports and puzzle. One way to come up with game ideas is to look through the genres and think about examples from each. Another option is to play plenty of games – on a phone, console or computer – and think about what you enjoy most. Don't bite off more than you can chew, though. A Space Invaders clone is certainly achievable by a new programmer, whereas a first person shooter inspired by Call of Duty probably isn't a realistic ambition – not as a first project, at least!

SPECIFICATIONS

If you follow a career in programming, you'll quickly come across the concept of the 'specification'. This is a document that is created before programming starts and fully details what the application does, how it works and what it looks like. Different programming teams use different specifications and many now adopt a more rapid development approach called 'agile', which minimises the up-front work and focuses more on smaller work units that evolve as the project progresses. For a simple game, our specification will be brief.

The concept

In this case, we're going to choose a simple shoot-'em-up called Pi Splat. We're using the Raspberry Pi as our inspiration so, naturally, our targets are going to be fruit. The concept can be summarised as follows:

We're being invaded! Several types of fruit fall from the top of the screen – but beware, most are poisonous. Use a mobile gun platform to destroy poisonous fruit, but allow raspberries through to reach the ground. When enough raspberries have landed, the planetary defences will be activated and the population will be saved.

Okay, it isn't exactly the most original concept but it's simple and fun – two excellent traits for our first game. Our next job is to decide on the rules for our game, and the victory conditions.

Rules

In real life there's nothing to stop you creating your own card game and making up the rules as you go along. However, the computer needs to know what to do in every conceivable situation. In this case, the game rules are simple.

1. Fruit appears randomly and drops vertically down the screen, disappearing if it reaches the bottom.
2. The gun turret can be moved left and right along the bottom of the screen. Pressing the Fire button launches a bullet up the screen.
3. If a bullet collides with a fruit, the fruit is destroyed.
4. If the destroyed fruit is not a raspberry, the player receives points.
5. If the destroyed fruit is a raspberry, the player loses points.
6. If a raspberry reaches the bottom of the screen, the player receives points.
7. If any other fruit reaches the bottom of the screen, the player loses points.
8. Once a set number of raspberries have reached the bottom, the level ends.
9. As levels pass, the speed of the falling fruit increases.

Victory condition

A game needs to have an aim. In games that have multiple levels, there is often one victory condition for the levels and a different, overall, aim for the game as a whole. For our game, the aim of each level is to collect the prescribed number of raspberries. The aim of the game as a whole is to clear 5 levels.

Now we have our rules and our victory condition, it's time to design the game, according to the principles of input, logic and output.

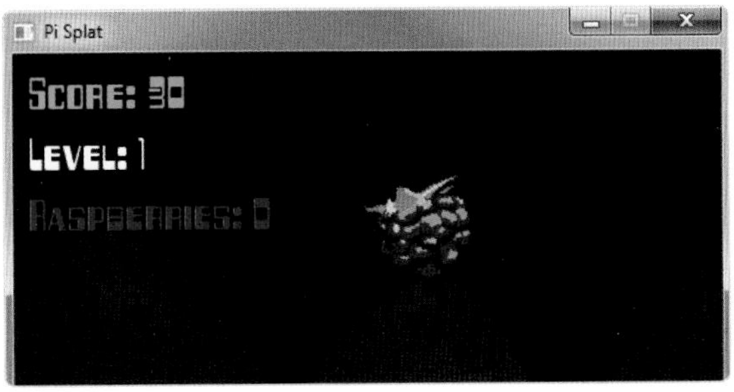

◀ **Our simple game will involve shooting fruit - but keep the raspberries safe!**

WHERE TO FIND GRAPHICS AND SOUNDS

You can download a huge quantity of graphical and audio resources from online libraries – but check the terms of use, especially if you intend to edit them. You can find free graphics at the Open Clip Art Library (***http://openclipart.org***), which you can normally edit and use as you wish. Fotolia (***http://en.fotolia.com***) provides top-quality graphics and photos for a small cost: for the best results, download the vector format of the image and edit it in a suitable program. A good source of free sounds is ***http://freesound.org***. You'll find everything here from music loops to special effects, freely reusable.

Input

The user needs to control the gun. This means we'll have to set up a way for the player to move it left and right, as well as firing. Keyboard control works best for a game of this sort, so we need to write code to specify which keys the player can use to control their gun turret and more code to 'listen' for those key presses.

We'll also want the user to be able to save their progress so they can exit the game and resume later. So, when the game loads, it needs to check whether there's any progress data and, if so, read it as an input.

Output

We'll need to create (or find) graphical images for each of the fruits that's going to appear in our game, and we'll need to write code to move them down the screen. To add a bit of visual interest, we'll also want to create an explosion effect for when the fruits are hit.

In addition, we'll need a turret graphic and bullets for the player – and this is also the right time to consider screen decorations for the background, over which we might display text for game instructions, score reports and so forth. In all we'll need the following graphics:

- Fruit (raspberry, cherry, strawberry, pear and banana)
- Player graphics (turret and bullets)
- Background graphic
- Splash screen

Sound is also a form of output, so we should also at this point consider whether we might want to include some in-game music and sound effects. Lastly, as mentioned opposite, we will also be saving the player's progress data to the hard disk – another form of output.

Logic

Our logic code will check whether bullets have collided with fruits, and update the score accordingly. It will also keep track of which level is being played, and when the game is over. ca

Create the basic game

Put together the first building blocks of your game's code

WHAT YOU'LL LEARN

- How to organise your code into modules
- What types of files to use for graphics and sound
- How to test code as you go along

Now we've done our large-scale planning, you can finally open up your editor and start typing. We haven't yet worked out the fine details of how we're going to implement everything, but that's all right. Creating a game is a completely different process to building a real-world object such as a house. In that case you need a detailed blueprint before you dig the first hole. Programming is more like building a house out of Lego: you select from a toolset of pre-created blocks and build one part at a time, experimenting and amending along the way. It's an iterative and organic process, in which you focus on the building blocks of the program – writing, testing and editing code to create each function, module and class – before bringing them together to make the final product.

Getting started

We'll begin by creating a simple template for our game, then fill in the code to get the game working. To create the template, we need to think about how our code will be organised in terms of graphics, sounds and Python files – and we do this using the familiar structure of input, logic and output from the previous chapter.

Broadly speaking, you should expect to create a class for each of the game's visible objects. You could add the code for each of these classes in the main Python file, but it makes more sense to have each in its own file: this is clearer and easier to understand, and removes clutter from the main program code.

1. Main.py

Create a folder to contain your Python game. Now, in Geany, create and save a file called main.py. Type in the code in the listing overleafk and save it.

2. Classes

Create Python files named bullet.py, fruit.py, turret.py and game.py. The first three are straight out of our design document and represent visible objects. The game class is there to hold information about the game as a whole. For example, it can keep track of the player's score and level number, and can be conveniently reused across multiple projects

Add the following text to the top of each of the class files:

```
class Bullet():
        def __init__(self):
                pass
```

...replacing Bullet with the name of each class. The pass command is simply a placeholder – it doesn't do anything, but if we didn't provide it Python would report an error since it isn't valid to define a completely empty function.

3. Images

Finally, in your project folder, create a subfolder called 'images' and copy all the game's graphic files into it, so they're in a convenient place for us to access later.

PICTURE AND SOUND FORMATS

The images used in this game are saved in PNG (Portable Network Graphics) format. This is because PNGs can have transparent backgrounds; if you used the popular **JPEG** format, for example, you'd see a white edge around each of the fruits. When developing games for the Raspberry Pi, you need to choose the best format for each graphic, and for those with transparent backgrounds the **8-bit** PNG format with alpha transparency works well.

As you'll remember, an 8-bit image can include a maximum of 256 colours (a 32-bit PNG can contain millions of colours), so this also gives the Pi less work to do when it's painting each screen.

When it comes to sound, **WAV** is a good format for short noises. Although the file size is larger than **MP3**, files in this format aren't compressed, so your computer doesn't have to do any unnecessary work to play them.

Main.py – the 'boilerplate' of our program

```
1	import math,random,pygame,sys
2	from fruit import *; from game import *;from turret import *; from bullet import *
3
4	##TOP LEVEL CONSTANTS
5	FPS = 30
6	WINDOWWIDTH=480; WINDOWHEIGHT=640
7	GAMETITLE="Pi Splat"
8	WHITE=[255,255,255]; RED=[255,0,0]; GREEN=[0,255,0];
9	BLUE=[0,0,255]; BLACK=[0,0,0]
10
11	def main():
12		#set up initial display
13		pygame.init()
14		clock=pygame.time.Clock()
15		surface=pygame.display.set_mode ([WINDOWWIDTH,WINDOWHEIGHT])
16		pygame.display.set_caption(GAMETITLE)
17
18		#MAIN GAME LOOP
19		game_over=False
20
21		while game_over==False:
22			for event in pygame.event.get():
23				if event.type==pygame.KEYDOWN:
24					if event.key==pygame.K_ESCAPE:
25						game_over=True
26			print pygame.time.get_ticks()
27			pygame.display.update()
28			clock.tick(FPS)
29
30	if __name__ == '__main__':
31	  main()
```

USING EXTERNAL RESOURCES

You can find the code, images and other resources for this game at ***www.snipca.com/9811***. The finished game can be downloaded in its entirety from ***www.snipca.com/9812***, though obviously it's much better to type all the code yourself. You'll find specific information about Pygame functions at ***www.pygame.org/docs*** and documentation for Python 2.7 is at ***http://docs.python.org/2/index.html***.

We're not going to go into detail about every single command used in this code. Where a command or function is new we'll explain what it does; but we expect you to use the documentation to learn the detail, as a skilled programmer would.

You'll also notice our code doesn't include many programming comments (explanatory text following the # symbol). This is to keep our listings clean and short. The downloadable code (which you should look through after completing the chapter) is heavily documented.

The initial 31 lines of our program comprise the "boilerplate", or standard structure, which hardly varies from game to game. Line 2 imports our classes. We then set a series of constants: variables whose values will not change during the game. Unlike many other languages, Python doesn't have a separate type for constants, so we name them using capital letters so we can identify them later.

On line 11 we set up a function called main, which is where our program will begin. Lines 13-16 use pygame functions to draw the initial window for the game. Lines 21 to 28 constitute the main loop: this is the code used to draw the screen many times per second as the game is being played.

We set up a variable called game_over in line 19 and give it the value False. We then start a while loop that will keep repeating until game_over becomes True. The for loop at line 22 asks Pygame if any events have taken place. In this case, we're interested in keyboard events so, in line 23, we cycle through all the events in the queue and, if a key has been pressed, we then ask if that key was "Esc". If it was, we set game_over to True, causing the game to exit.

Line 27 updates the display (we haven't yet added anything visual, but will do soon) and line 28 tells Pygame to make sure the loop doesn't cycle more quickly than 30 times per second. Finally, lines 30 and 31 are used to make sure that the main function will be accessed only if this was the file open in Geany when we clicked the cog button. In other words, if we accidentally imported this module into another, main would not be called.

Once you've entered and checked all this code, click the cog icon (or press F5). You should see a series of numbers running down the terminal window: these are generated by line 26 and are simply the number of milliseconds since the program started, proving that you've typed everything correctly and are ready to move on. If you see any error messages in the terminal window, you need to correct them before continuing.

Add graphics to your game

Create the visuals for your game and define their behaviour

WHAT YOU'LL LEARN

- How to create object classes and use inheritance
- When and where to use constants
- Basic image manipulation

```
1   import pygame, random
2   class Fruit(pygame.sprite.Sprite):
3
4           def __init__(self,WINDOWWIDTH):
5                   pygame.sprite.Sprite.__init__(self)
6                   self._species=random.choice(["raspberry","strawberry","cherry","pear","banana"])
7                   self.image=pygame.image.load("images/"+self._species+".png")
8                   self.rect=self.image.get_rect()
9                   self.rect.y=0-self.rect.height
10                  self.rect.x=(random.randint(self.rect.width/2,(WINDOWWIDTH-self.rect.width)))
11
12          def update_position(self,speed,WINDOWHEIGHT,game):
13                  if self.rect.y<(WINDOWHEIGHT):
14                          self.rect.y+=speed*5
15                  else:
16                          if self._species=="raspberry":
17                                  game.update_score(50)
18                                  game.update_raspberries_saved()
19                          else:
20                                  game.update_score(-10)
21                          self.kill()
22
23          def shot(self,game):
24                  if self._species=="raspberry":
25                          game.update_score(-50)
26                  else:
27                          game.update_score(10)
28                  self.kill()
```

Open up fruit.py in Geany and type in the code above. Now it's time to make the fruit appear and drop down the screen. We'll start by setting up the fruit object, so let's look at the code in a little more detail.

We begin by importing the pygame library and the random module. Take a look at line 2 – you can see that we've added pygame.sprite.Sprite to the class definition. This is an example of class inheritance in action: this line tells Python to create a new object based on Pygame's Sprite class, so Python will assume that this object is a sprite in all its behaviours and properties – except where we explicitly specify otherwise. A sprite is a specialised object that's based on an image and which can be easily moved around the screen. It contains all the functions needed to handle the visual side of our fruit.

The __init__ function is run when the main program creates a new instance of the Fruit class. In other words, when we want a new fruit to appear and fall down the screen. In line 6 we create a property of the sprite that we've named _species. In reality it's just a variable like any other, but the convention is to call variables that are inside objects 'properties'.

The self keyword in front of a variable name tells the object that this variable is part of its unique identity and should be remembered. So every Fruit instance will remember which species it was set to for as long as it's alive; this is a very useful feature of objects, as we'll see.

In line 7, we use Pygame's image functions to load an appropriate picture into the sprite from the images folder we created on page 92. The next line makes sure that the size of the sprite matches the size of the image just loaded. Line 9 sets the y (vertical) position to zero minus the height of the image. So if the picture was 50 pixels tall, the top-left corner of the fruit will be drawn at -50, so it's just off the top of the screen.

Line 10 looks a little bit more complicated, but it simply specifies a random horizontal (x) position for the fruit. The random.randint function takes two parameters, to set the range between which you want it to generate a number. Our first

▲ Our Raspberry Pi game is built up from re-usable objects

parameter – the lower bound – is:

```
self.rect.width/2
```

In other words, we want the lowest possible horizontal value to be half the width of the image from the left. This ensures the fruit will never be drawn either wholly or partially off the left edge of the screen. The second parameter, specifying the upper bound, is:

```
WINDOWWIDTH-self.rect.width
```

In this case, the maximum right-hand position will be the width of the window minus the width of the image. So with a WINDOWWIDTH of 480 pixels and a fruit width of, say, 72 pixels, we'd be asking random.randint to provide a number between 36 (72/2) and 408 (480-72). That would be used to place each fruit in a different horizontal location.

The __init__ function sets things up, but we need to add more functions to make things happen. These will vary depending on the purpose of the class, and in this case the most obvious attribute of our fruit is that it moves down the screen, so we'll begin with a function called update_position. Unlike __init__, this function will only run when it's called (in this case, by the main program).

The function definition in line 12 includes four parameters that it must be passed. self is part of all class definitions, but the others are our own variables. WINDOWHEIGHT is self-explanatory, game is the game object (we haven't created it yet) and speed is a parameter we'll set in main.py.

The function is pretty simple. On line 13 we check to see if the vertical position of the fruit is still less than the height of the window (if it isn't, then the fruit must have dropped off the bottom). If it is, then in line 14 we increase its y position by an amount related to the speed.

If the fruit has dropped out of the window then Python will execute the code after the else in line 15. In this case, it's another if statement: it's very important to understand that code between lines 16 and 21 will only be executed if line 13 is false.

So, on line 16 we check to see if the current fruit is a raspberry. Remember that the point of the game is to allow raspberries to reach the bottom of the screen, so, in that case, we are going to increase the score and increment the number of raspberries saved so far (the game ends when this number gets to ten). Note that we haven't actually added any code to the game object yet, but we now know which functions to create.

Line 19 translates as "if the fruit is not on-screen (because it's reached the bottom) and it's not a raspberry then execute the next line". In this case, line 20 decreases the score because the player has allowed one of the other fruits to reach the bottom.

Finally, line 21 deletes the object. Look closely at the indentation to make sure you understand when this line will be executed: the self.kill function is not inside the if structure starting on line 16, so if the object has fallen off the bottom of the screen it will be "killed" whichever fruit type it represents. Although the fruit is no longer visible, it makes sense to clear it and stop it updating: otherwise it will continue to fall, even though we can't see it, pointlessly wasting computing power and memory.

Finally, since the object of the game is to shoot fruit (except raspberries), we add a function called shot. A quick look over the code should be ample for you to see what it does. ca

WHY USE VARIABLES FOR CONSTANTS?

You'll have noticed that once we've set the value of WINDOWWIDTH in main.py, it stays the same throughout our game – that's why we call it a constant and why, conventionally, we write it all in capital letters. So why do we bother with it? Why don't we just specify the value 480 directly when we need to refer to the width of the window?

We do it this way for two reasons. Firstly, because this allows you to create a new game – with a different width – by doing nothing more than changing a value once at the start of the program, rather than having to find and alter every occurrence of 480.

The second reason is that it makes reading your code much simpler. By using WINDOWWIDTH rather than 480 in a calculation, you know exactly what that number represents.

Constants are often used to make configuring a script easy. By grouping them all at the start of the main code, you can change all the settings very easily.

Setting up the game

Refine, edit and update your game code

WHAT YOU'LL LEARN

- How to create your game's main logic loop
- Controlling speed and performance
- How to use Pygame's sprite functions

```
class Game():
        def __init__(self):
                self._score=0
                self._raspberries_saved=0

        def update_score(self,amount):
                self._score+=amount

        def get_score(self):
                return self._score

        def update_raspberries_saved(self):
                self._raspberries_saved+=1

        def get_raspberries_saved(self):
                return self._raspberries_saved
```

Having written our Fruit class, we now know what we need (initially, at least) to include in our Game class (above – save it as game.py). Remember that this is a different sort of class to Fruit; it doesn't relate to a visible object on-screen. It's simply a convenient wrapper for code and variables that relate to the game as a whole.

The class definition doesn't contain anything between the brackets because we're not basing Game on a pre-existing class. The __init__ function initialises two variables – the score and the number of raspberries we've saved – so we can use them later. update_score takes the amount sent to it and adds that to the running score (see line 17 of fruit.py to see this function called). Meanwhile, get_score uses the return keyword to send back the score. So, we could write a line of code like this to print the current score to the terminal:

```
print game.get_score
```

The final two functions fulfil the same purpose for the raspberries_saved variable, so our program can easily check this value too.

Updating Main.py

It's time to fill out the 'boilerplate' code we created earlier, to accommodate the additional features needed to work with our fruit sprites. Update your main.py module as follows:

```
import math,random,pygame,sys
from fruit import *; from game import *; from turret import *; from bullet import *

##TOP LEVEL CONSTANTS
FPS = 30
```

```
6   WINDOWWIDTH=480; WINDOWHEIGHT=640
7   GAMETITLE="Pi Splat"
8   WHITE=[255,255,255]; RED=[255,0,0]; GREEN=[0,255,0]; BLUE=[0,0,255]; BLACK=[0,0,0]
9   SPEED=0.5
10
11  def main():
12      game=Game()
13
14      #set up initial display
15      pygame.init()
16      clock=pygame.time.Clock()
17      surface=pygame.display.set_mode([WINDOWWIDTH,WINDOWHEIGHT])
18      pygame.display.set_caption(GAMETITLE)
19
20      #MAIN GAME LOOP
21      game_over=False
22      live_fruit_sprites=pygame.sprite.Group()
23      ticktock=1
24      while game_over==False:
25          for event in pygame.event.get():
26              if event.type==pygame.KEYDOWN:
27                  if event.key==pygame.K_ESCAPE:
28                      game_over=True
29
30          if ticktock % (FPS/SPEED)==1:
31              if len(live_fruit_sprites)<10:
32                  live_fruit_sprites.add((Fruit(WINDOWWIDTH)))
33
34          surface.fill(BLACK)
35          for sprite in live_fruit_sprites:
36              sprite.update_position(SPEED,WINDOWHEIGHT,game)
37
38          live_fruit_sprites.draw(surface)
39
40          pygame.display.update()
41
42          ticktock+=1
43
44          clock.tick(FPS)
45
46  if __name__ == ‘__main__’:
47      main()
```

You'll see we've made quite a few changes. We've added a new constant called SPEED at line 9; and at line 22 we create a sprite group. This is essentially a list of all the fruit sprites so we can easily handle them later.

The if statement beginning at line 31 checks if there are fewer than ten fruits on the screen, and if so creates a new fruit object and adds it to the sprite group. You'll notice we created a variable called ticktock on line 23, and we use it on line 30. This is needed because the main loop (beginning at line 24) runs at 30 frames per second (see line 44). Without the code at line 30, all the fruits would be added almost instantly rather than spread out.

At line 42, ticktock increments each loop, so it'll be worth 30 after one second, 60 after two seconds and so on. Line 30 says that if you divide ticktock by the number of frames per second (30 in this case), divided by the speed variable (0.5 at the moment), and get a remainder of 1 (that's what the % or modulus means), run line 31 and add a fruit if there are fewer than ten. It's a bit of a brain-melter, but if you think it through, you'll see that there will be a remainder of 1 when ticktock is worth 61, 121, 181 and so forth. The effect, then, is to run line 32 every two seconds or so – which is exactly what we want. Alternatively, we could use Python's time functions, but doing it this way keeps things in sync if the computer struggles to keep up for any reason.

Line 34 fills the window with black. Line 35 cycles through every fruit (if there are any) and in line 36, we calls the Fruit class's update_position function we just created, moving each one down the screen or deleting it. Finally, we run Pygame's draw function, which will paint every fruit to the screen in one go. Give it a try. Make sure main.py is in your Geany window and press F5 or click the cog. You should see fruit appear at the top and move smoothly down the window. Stop the program then add a hash symbol (#) to the start of line 34; this "comments out" the line so that Python ignores it. Press F5 and you'll see you should see a very different result.

Enter the code below and save it as turret.py:

```
1   import pygame
2   class Turret(pygame.sprite.Sprite):
3           def __init__(self,WINDOWWIDTH,WINDOWHEIGHT):
4                   pygame.sprite.Sprite.__init__(self)
5                   self.image=pygame.image.load("images/turret.png")
6                   self.rect = self.image.get_rect()
7                   self.rect.x = (WINDOWWIDTH-self.rect.width)/2
8                   self.rect.y =WINDOWHEIGHT-self.rect.height
9
10          def update_position(self,direction,WINDOWWIDTH):
11                  if direction=="left" and self.rect.x>10:
12                          self.rect.x-=10
13                  elif direction=="right" and self.rect.x<(WINDOWWIDTH-10):
14                          self.rect.x+=10
15
16          def get_gun_position(self):
17                  position={}
18                  position["x"]=self.rect.x+(self.rect.width/2)
19                  position["y"]=self.rect.y-(self.rect.height/2)
20                  return position
```

This class is similar to the Fruit class, with lines 7 and 8 positioning the turret graphic at the centre of the screen's bottom edge. At line 10 we set up the update_position method, which takes the direction and the width of the window as parameters and either deducts from the turret's horizontal (x) position to send the graphic left, or adds to send it right. See if you can work out how we stop the turret from disappearing off the side of the screen.

Finally, starting at line 16, we add a function to send back the position of the gun in the centre of the turret, so we can make bullets appear like they're emerging from the gun. Here's the code for the last class, bullet.py:

```
import pygame
class Bullet(pygame.sprite.Sprite):
        def __init__(self,position):
                pygame.sprite.Sprite.__init__(self)
                self.image=pygame.image.load("images/bullet.png")
                self.rect = self.image.get_rect()
                self.rect.x=position["x"]
                self.rect.y=position["y"]

        def update_position(self):

                if self.rect.y>=-self.rect.height:
                        self.rect.y-=5
                else:
                        self.kill()
```

In the __init__ function, we send the gun position from Turret. The function update_position is very simple; since bullets go up the screen, their y value gets smaller as they move. Once they go off the top, we destroy the sprite.

Main.py – the fully working version

Now we've set up the code to handle our turret and bullets, we simply need to make a few last changes to main.py to tie it all together and finish the first version of the game.

```
import math,random,pygame,sys
from fruit import *; from game import *;3 from turret import *; from bullet import *


##TOP LEVEL CONSTANTS
FPS = 30
WINDOWWIDTH=480; WINDOWHEIGHT=640
GAMETITLE="Pi Splat"
WHITE=[255,255,255]; RED=[255,0,0]; GREEN=[0,255,0]; BLUE=[0,0,255]; BLACK=[0,0,0]
SPEED=0.5

def main():
    game=Game()

    #set up initial display
    pygame.init()
    pygame.key.set_repeat(1, 75)
    scoreFont=pygame.font.Font("256BYTES.TTF",32)
    clock=pygame.time.Clock()
    surface=pygame.display.set_mode([WINDOWWIDTH,WINDOWHEIGHT])
    pygame.display.set_caption(GAMETITLE)

    #MAIN GAME LOOP
    game_over=False
    live_fruit_sprites=pygame.sprite.Group()
    bullet_sprites=pygame.sprite.Group()
    other_sprites=pygame.sprite.Group()
    turret=Turret(WINDOWWIDTH,WINDOWHEIGHT)
    other_sprites.add(turret)
    ticktock=1

    while game_over==False:
        for event in pygame.event.get():
            if event.type==pygame.KEYDOWN:
                if event.key==pygame.K_ESCAPE:
                    game_over=True
                elif event.key==pygame.K_LEFT:
                    turret.update_position("left",WINDOWWIDTH)
                elif event.key==pygame.K_RIGHT:
                    turret.update_position("right",WINDOWWIDTH)
                elif event.key==pygame.K_SPACE:
                    bullet=Bullet(turret.get_gun_position())
                    bullet_sprites.add(bullet)

        if ticktock % (FPS/SPEED)==1:
            if len(live_fruit_sprites)<10:
                live_fruit_sprites.add((Fruit(WINDOWWIDTH)))

        for sprite in bullet_sprites:
            sprite.update_position()

```

```
52                  collisions=pygame.sprite.groupcollide(live_fruit_sprites,bullet_sprites,False,True)
53
54                  if collisions:
55                      for fruit in collisions:
56                          fruit.shot(game)
57
58                  surface.fill(BLACK)
59                  bullet_sprites.draw(surface)
60                  other_sprites.draw(surface)
61
62                  for sprite in live_fruit_sprites:
63                      sprite.update_position(SPEED,WINDOWHEIGHT,game)
64
65                  live_fruit_sprites.draw(surface)
66
67                  scoreText=scoreFont.render('Score: '+str(game.get_score()),True,GREEN)
68                  surface.blit(scoreText,(10,10))
69                  pygame.display.update()
70
71                  ticktock+=1
72                  if game.get_raspberries_saved()>=10:
73                      game_over=True
74
75                  clock.tick(FPS)
76
77              #handle end of game
78              surface.fill(BLACK)
79              scoreText=scoreFont.render('Game over. Score: '+str(game.get_score()),True,GREEN)
80              surface.blit(scoreText,(10,200))
81              pygame.display.update()
82
83              raw_input("press any key")
84
85          if __name__ == '__main__':
86              main()
```

Line 17 calls a Pygame function that sets the repeat interval on a keypress to 75 milliseconds, so the player can hold down the spacebar to fire a stream of bullets. Line 18 imports a custom font (***www.1001freefonts.com*** is a good source) that we'll use to show the score. In lines 26 to 29, we create two new sprite groups: one to hold the bullets, and a second for any other sprites we're adding.

Lines 37 to 40 respond to the arrow keys, updating the turret's position. Lines 41 to 43 create a new bullet when the spacebar is pressed and add it to the group. Lines 49 and 50 cycle through all the bullets currently visible and trigger the update_position function for each in turn.

Line 52 is a bit of Pygame magic. This one line checks whether any bullet has collided with any fruit. If one has, Pygame generates a list of those fruits that have collided. All we have to do is pass in the two sprite groups we want to check (hence our maintaining separate groups for bullets and fruit), along with parameters indicating whether Pygame should kill colliding sprites. For the fruit, we send a False parameter because we want to update the score before killing them manually. For the bullets, it's fine for Pygame to kill them.

In lines 54 to 56, we iterate through any collisions and run the shot function of the fruit that was hit. Lines 59 and 60 draw the new groups to the screen.

On line 67 we use Pygame's font.render to create a picture that displays the score in green with a transparent background. Line 68 paints the score onto the screen using the blit function.

Lines 72 and 73 let us break out of the main game loop once we've saved 10 raspberries, then lines 78 to 83 clear the screen, draws the final score and wait for the user to press a key.

Once your code matches our listings, save and press F5 to play the game. Whilst it's basic, you now have a fully working, playable, arcade game in fewer than 200 lines of code. Not bad!

Completing the game

Add the all-important finishing touches to your first game

WHAT YOU'LL LEARN

» How to use pickle to save a game's progress

» Boost your game with extra levels

To add a bit of depth to Pi Splat, we might add levels that become progressively harder. While we're at it, we should also implement the additional input and output functions we planned at the start: adding a splash/instructions screen at the start of the game, and giving the player the ability to save and restore the player's progress. We'll also smooth out a few rough edges to give the game a more professional polish.

The finished code

Rather than typing in all the code that follows, we recommend you download the complete version of the game from ***www.snipca.com/9812***, load it into Geany and follow the discussion.

Most of the remaining work takes place in main.py. This makes sense, as adding levels doesn't affect the way individual objects such as fruits or bullets behave.

On line 1, we add two new modules: pickle and os. Both are needed so that we can save the user's progress. We remove the SCORE constant and replace it with NUMBER_OF_LEVELS, which we're setting to five. You can change the number of levels in your version of the game by altering this number.

Starting at line 23, we've added some code to create a splash screen. This has been created as a single graphic. It might have been more flexible to add the text at runtime, but a static image is fine for a simple game such as this.

```
1   import math,random,pygame,sys,pickle,os
2   from fruit import *; from game import *; from turret import *; from bullet import *
3
4   ##TOP LEVEL CONSTANTS
5   FPS = 30
6   WINDOWWIDTH=480; WINDOWHEIGHT=640
7   GAMETITLE="Pi Splat"
8   WHITE=[255,255,255]; RED=[255,0,0]; GREEN=[0,255,0]; BLUE=[0,0,255]; BLACK=[0,0,0]
9   NUMBER_OF_LEVELS=5
10
11  def main():
12          game=Game()
13
14          #INITIAL SETUP
15          pygame.init()
16          pygame.key.set_repeat(1, 75)
17          pygame.mouse.set_visible(False)
18          displayFont=pygame.font.Font("256BYTES.TTF",28)
19          clock=pygame.time.Clock()
20          surface=pygame.display.set_mode([WINDOWWIDTH, WINDOWHEIGHT])
```

```
21      pygame.display.set_caption(GAMETITLE)
22
23      #SPLASH SCREEN
24      splash=pygame.image.load("images/splash.png")
25      surface.blit(splash,(0,0))
26      pygame.display.update()
27      game_over=False
28      start_game=False
29
30      while start_game==False:
31          for event in pygame.event.get():
32              if event.type==pygame.KEYDOWN:
33                  if event.key==pygame.K_ESCAPE:
34                      game_over=True
35                  elif event.key==pygame.K_RETURN or event.key==pygame.K_KP_ENTER:
36                      resume=False
37                      start_game=True
38                  elif event.key==pygame.K_LSHIFT or event.key==pygame.K_RSHIFT:
39                      resume=True
40                      start_game=True
41
42      if resume==True: #if they want to pick up a saved game
43          if os.path.exists("savedata.dat")==True:
44              game.load_game()
```

▲ A splash screen displays instructions

At line 24, we load the splash screen and blit it to the surface on line 25, before refreshing the screen so it becomes visible. We've moved the game_over variable to this point so the user can exit even when a game isn't underway.

Lines 30 to 40 wait for the user to press a key, and respond when he or she does. The instructions tell them to press Enter to start a new game or Shift to resume an existing one. Since there are two physical Enter keys (the one under Backspace and the one alongside the numeric keypad), we have to handle this in line 35. Similarly, there are two Shift keys: line 38 captures this and sets the resume variable to True.

On line 42, we check to see if they chose to continue an existing game, but we first need to check if a save file already exists (there won't be one if it's the first time they've played the game). This is achieved through the os (**operating system**) module function. On line 44, we run a yet-to-be-created function of the game object. The code continues:

```
45
46      #MAIN GAME LOOP
47      while game.get_level()<=NUMBER_OF_LEVELS and game_over==False:
48
49          #SHOW LEVEL NUMBER
50          surface.fill(BLACK)
51          levelText=displayFont.render('Level: '+str(game.get_level()),True,GREEN)
52          surface.blit(levelText,(150,300))
53          pygame.display.update()
54          pygame.time.wait(1500)
55
56          #SET UP VARIABLES FOR LEVEL
57          game.save_game()
58          live_fruit_sprites=pygame.sprite.Group()
```

```
59          game._raspberries_saved=0
60          bullet_sprites=pygame.sprite.Group()
61          other_sprites=pygame.sprite.Group()
62          turret=Turret(WINDOWWIDTH,WINDOWHEIGHT)
63          other_sprites.add(turret)
64          ticktock=1
65          level_over=False
```

We've added a new loop that runs while the current level is less than or equal to the total number of levels and the user hasn't pressed Escape. Before each level begins, we want to display a text message, so on lines 50 to 54 we erase the splash screen (by filling it with black) and set up a font. We've changed the name of this variable from scoreFont because it now has a more general use.

We then use Pygame's time.wait() function to pause for 1.5 seconds, after which we start the code for each level (remember, the code after line 47 runs each time a new level is started). On line 57 we run another function of game – one we haven't yet written – to save progress. Why save it now? Because we want the user to come back at the start of the level they were playing when they exited, so we save the state before it begins. The only other changes to this block of code are that we zero the variable game._raspberries_saved before the level starts and we create a new variable level_over.

```
66
67          #PLAY INDIVIDUAL LEVEL
68          while level_over==False and game_over==False:
69                  for event in pygame.event.get():
70                          if event.type==pygame.KEYDOWN:
71                                  if event.key==pygame.K_ESCAPE:
72                                          game_over=True
73                                  elif event.key==pygame.K_LEFT:
74                                          turret.update_position("left", WINDOWWIDTH,game.get_level())
75                                  elif event.key==pygame.K_RIGHT:
76                                          turret.update_position("right", WINDOWWIDTH,game.get_level())
77                                  elif event.key==pygame.K_SPACE:
78                                          bullet=Bullet(turret.get_gun_position())
79                                          bullet_sprites.add(bullet)
80
81                  if ticktock >=120:
82                          ticktock=0
83                          if len(live_fruit_sprites)<10:
84                                  live_fruit_sprites.add((Fruit(WINDOWWIDTH)))
85
86                  for sprite in bullet_sprites:
87                          sprite.update_position()
88
89                  collisions=pygame.sprite.groupcollide (live_fruit_sprites,bullet_sprites,False,True)
90
91                  if collisions: #if there are any
92                          for fruit in collisions:
93                                  fruit.shot(game)
94
95                  background=pygame.image.load ("images/gameBoard.png")
97                  surface.blit(background,(0,0))
98                  bullet_sprites.draw(surface)
99                  other_sprites.draw(surface)
```

```
100 for sprite in live_fruit_sprites:
101     sprite.update_position (game.get_level(),WINDOWHEIGHT,game)
102 live_fruit_sprites.draw(surface)
103
104 scoreText=displayFont.render ('Score: '+str(game.get_score()),True,GREEN)
105 levelText=displayFont.render ('Level: '+str(game.get_level()),True, WHITE)
106 raspberriesText=displayFont.render ('Raspberries: '+str(game.get_raspberries_»
    saved()),True,RED)
107 surface.blit(scoreText,(10,10))
108 surface.blit(levelText,(10,50))
109 surface.blit(raspberriesText,(10,90))
110 pygame.display.update()
111 ticktock+=game.get_level()
112
113 if game.get_raspberries_saved()>=10:
114     game.update_level(1)
115     level_over=True
116 clock.tick(FPS)
```

You'll notice that all of this code has been indented by an additional tab (do this in Geany by highlighting the lines you want to indent and pressing Tab once). If you think this through you'll see that we've done this because, at the end of each level, we want to loop back to line 47 to see if we've reached the final level.

You'll also see that on line 68 we're testing two conditions: the level will play if level_over isn't True and if the user hasn't pressed Escape. The event-handling code is unchanged, but we've simplified the code for adding new fruits to the screen: we're now doing this every time ticktock reaches 120, which, for level 1, will be 4 seconds (30 frames per second into 120).

On lines 95 and 96 we load a more interesting background, as an 8-bit PNG. The code then remains unchanged until line 101 when we add a new parameter to the update_position function of the Fruit class. We'll come to this when we look at the changes to that class.

Lines 104 to 110 have been enhanced to add extra player information. And on line 114 we call a new function of the game object to increment the level if ten raspberries have reached the bottom of the screen. We set level_over to True so that the level exits and Python loops back to line 47.

The only change to the last few lines (which we haven't reproduced here) is to add a summary to the final screen showing the player's overall score.

Game.py

```
import pickle
class Game():
    def __init__(self):
        self._score=0
        self._raspberries_saved=0
        self._level=1

    def update_score(self,amount):
        self._score+=amount*self._level

    def get_score(self):
        return self._score

    def update_raspberries_saved(self):
        self._raspberries_saved+=1

```

▲ **Our game module now includes code to save and restore progress, using pickle**

```
17      def get_raspberries_saved(self):
18          return self._raspberries_saved
19
20      def update_level(self,amount):
21          self._level+=amount
22
23      def get_level(self):
24          return self._level
25
26      def save_game(self):
27          save_data={'score':self._score,'level':self._level}
28          save_file=open("savedata.dat","wb")
29          pickle.dump(save_data,save_file)
30
31      def load_game(self):
32          progress_file=open("savedata.dat","rb")
33          progress_data=pickle.load(progress_file)
34          self._score=progress_data['score']
35          self._level=progress_data['level']
```

The main change to game.py is to add the code for saving and loading the player's progress. So, on line 1 we import the pickle module. We've also added functions to update the score – on line 9 we multiply the amount the score changes by the level number, so the further through the game you get the bigger the rewards for hitting the right fruit (and the deductions for shooting a raspberry!). We also add functions to update and get the level numbers.

The interesting stuff starts at line 26. The code here is very similar to the examples in the section on Python libraries. On line 27 we create a dictionary containing the data we want to save (just score and level numbers for this game, but we could include the player's name for example). We open a file to save the data (if it doesn't exist, Python creates the file) and then dump it to save.

The load_game function is almost exactly the reverse. If the user had reached level 3 with a score of 1,234 when they pressed Escape, on restarting the game, pickle would load that data and game._level would now be 3. game._score would be 1,234, exactly as if they had never exited.

Fruit.py

```
import pygame, random
class Fruit(pygame.sprite.Sprite):

    def __init__(self,WINDOWWIDTH):
        pygame.sprite.Sprite.__init__(self)
    self._species=random.choice(["raspberry","strawberry","cherry","pear","banana"])
        self.image=pygame.image.load("images/"+ self._species+".png")
        self.image=pygame.transform.rotate(self.image, random.randint(-35,35))
        self.rect=self.image.get_rect()
        self.rect.y=0-self.rect.height
        self.rect.x=(random.randint(self.rect.width/2,(WINDOWWIDTH-self.rect.width)))

    def update_position(self,level,WINDOWHEIGHT,game):
        if self.rect.y<(WINDOWHEIGHT):
            self.rect.y+=2+level
        else:
            if self._species=="raspberry":
                game.update_score(50)
                game.update_raspberries_saved()
```

```
20              else:
21                  game.update_score(-10)
22
23              self.kill()
24
25      def shot(self,game):
26          if self._species=="raspberry":
27              game.update_score(-50)
28          else:
29              game.update_score(10)
30
31          self.kill()
```

▲ By using the game's level to make the falling fruit speed up, we make things more exciting

We've made only a couple of minor changes to fruit.py. Line 8 rotates new fruit images by a random value between -35 and 35 degrees, making their appearance a little more varied. You could add code into update_position to have them gently swing as they fell if you wanted the full effect!

Otherwise, the only change is on line 13, where we replace the speed parameter with level. Then, on line 15, we use that to change the position of the fruit. Effectively, that means that as the player progresses through the levels, the fruit falls faster, making the game harder.

Turret.py

```
import pygame
class Turret(pygame.sprite.Sprite):
    def __init__(self,WINDOWWIDTH,WINDOWHEIGHT):
        pygame.sprite.Sprite.__init__(self)
        self.image=pygame.image.load("images/turret.png")
        self.rect = self.image.get_rect()
        self.rect.x = (WINDOWWIDTH-self.rect.width)/2
        self.rect.y =WINDOWHEIGHT-self.rect.height

    def update_position(self,direction,WINDOWWIDTH,level):
        if direction=="left" and self.rect.x>10:
            self.rect.x-=10+level
        elif direction=="right" and self.rect.x<(WINDOWWIDTH-10):
            self.rect.x+=10+level

    def get_gun_position(self):
        position={}
        position["x"]=self.rect.x+(self.rect.width/2)
        position["y"]=self.rect.y-(self.rect.height/2)
        return position
```

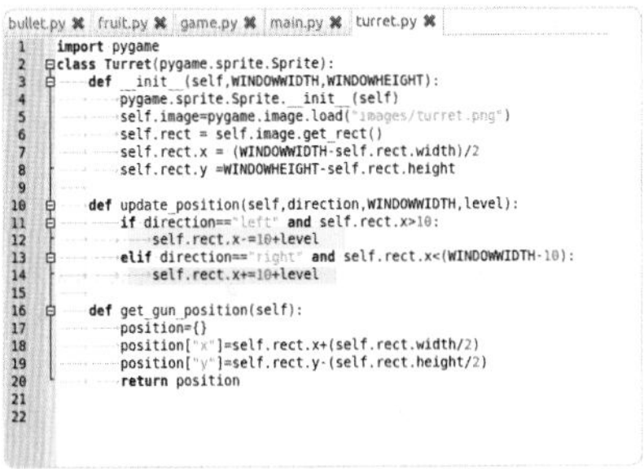

▲ To help catch all the fruit, the gun turret moves faster in higher levels of the game

The final change we've made is to add the level number to the amount the turret moves each cycle. This has the effect of speeding it up as the levels get higher; otherwise, as the gameplay accelerates, the player would struggle to get across the screen in time to shoot the fruit.

Run the game and you should find you can play multiple levels and get a final score. It may not be of commercial quality but it's a complete, working game, and strangely addictive!

Targeting the Raspberry Pi

If you've been using a PC to create your game for the Pi, the last step is to test it on real Raspberry Pi hardware to ensure it performs acceptably.

Pi Splat could certainly be enhanced – with animations and explosions, for example – but it isn't currently possible to access the Pi's full graphics capabilities from Python. Once support is added, you'll be able to include spectacular effects with little impact on performance. ca

Sharing your game

You've finished your game – now find out how to share it with others

WHAT YOU'LL LEARN

» How to prepare your game for sharing

» How to compile Python programs on Windows

Once you've polished your masterpiece, you'll want to share it. Exactly how you go about that depends on your target audience.

Sharing with Raspberry Pi and Linux users

Every major **Linux** distribution, including Raspbian, comes with Python installed, and Raspbian also has Pygame as part of its default installation. If you share your game with users of other distributions, they may need to install Pygame.

Zip it up

To share a Python program with other Linux users, you can simply compress the files into an archive (on Windows, these are called ZIP files) and send it. To do this on the Raspberry Pi, right-click on the main folder containing your game and select Compress. Then choose a file name and type for the package. If you're sharing with other Linux users then you can leave the type as .tar.gz. (If you want to share your file with Windows users, you'll want to change it to .zip – in this case, there are other some steps you'll need to take too, which we'll discuss below.) When the recipient receives this archive, they'll be able to extract your files, load main.py into Geany (or their preferred Python environment) and launch the game.

Clearly it would be nicer if the player could simply double-click a file to run the game. We can achieve this by creating a script file that tells the computer how to launch and run it. Here's how to do this in Linux:

Start by navigating to the folder containing your main.py file, then right-click and select Create New Document|Empty Document. Give it the name start.sh. Now, right-click and select 'Open with Geany'. Then, in Geany type the single line:

```
python main.py
```

...and save the file. This is the same line you would type in at the terminal to run a Python file. We now need to tell Linux that it should execute this command when the text file is double-clicked. To do this, open a terminal window and type the following:

```
cd Desktop/Pi_Splat
```

The cd part is the Linux command for 'change directory' and it simply tells the terminal that we want to work in the folder containing the game. Replace Desktop/Pi_Splat with the location of your game if you've saved it somewhere different. Now, in the terminal type:

```
chmod +x start.sh
```

The chmod command changes the 'mode' of the file; in this case, the +x makes it executable. So, for example, instead of launching a text editor, the operating system knows that it can load the file as if it's an application, and then run the command it contains. To see this in action, double-click the start.sh icon and select Run.

▼ You can turn your Python code into a Windows app

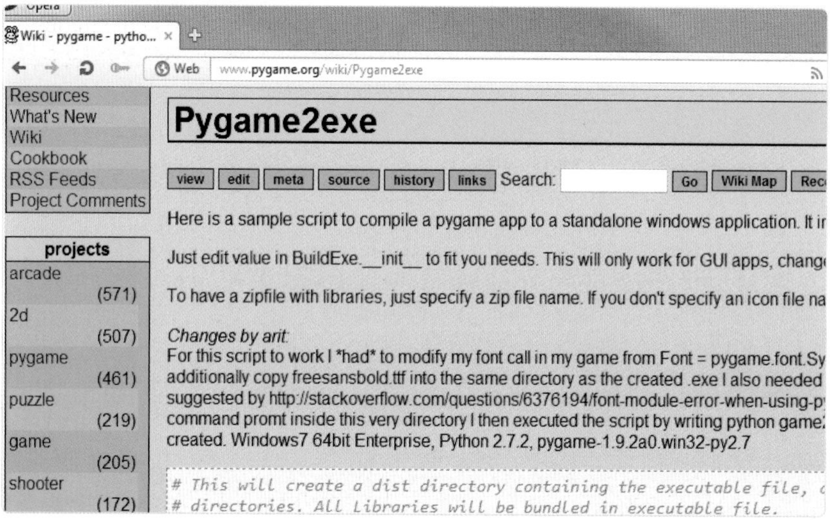
Wiki - pygame - pytho...
Web
www.pygame.org/wiki/Pygame2exe
Resources
What's New
Wiki
Cookbook
RSS Feeds
Project Comments
Pygame2exe
view
edit
meta
source
history
links
Search:
Go
Wiki Map
Here is a sample script to compile a pygame app to a standalone windows application.
Just edit value in BuildExe.__init__ to fit you needs. This will only work for GUI apps,
To have a zipfile with libraries, just specify a zip file name. If you don't specify an icon file
Changes by arit:
For this script to work I *had* to modify my font call in my game from Font = pygame.font.
additionally copy freesansbold.ttf into the same directory as the created .exe I also needed
suggested by http://stackoverflow.com/questions/6376194/font-module-error-when-using-
command promt inside this very directory I then executed the script by writing python game
created. Windows7 64bit Enterprise, Python 2.7.2, pygame-1.9.2a0.win32-py2.7
This will create a dist directory containing the executable file,
directories. All Libraries will be bundled in executable file.
projects
arcade
(571)
2d
(507)
pygame
(461)
puzzle
(219)
game
(205)
shooter
(172)

Sharing with Windows users

Windows doesn't come with Python installed as standard, so you can't simply send a Windows user an archive of your game and expect them to be able to play it. If they had to download and install Python just to try out your program, there's a good chance that they simply wouldn't bother - no matter how good it is.

An easy solution to this problem is a tool called Py2Exe, which can compile your game into a single executable file that a Windows user can run with a double-click. The process feels convoluted the first time, but needs doing only once – and the person you're sharing with doesn't need to do anything at all.

To begin, head over to ***www.rpilab.net/links*** and download Py2Exe. Next, we need to delve into the bowels of Windows to make sure Py2Exe can find Python. To do this in Windows 7 or 8, press the Windows key, type **edit environment variables** into the Search box, then press Enter. Open the Settings dialogue that comes up, click the Environment Variables button, and then, in the System Variables list, find the entry Path and click the Edit button. Now, assuming you've installed Python 2.7 to the default location, simply add the following entry to the text in this box (making sure the entry before it ends in a semi-colon):

```
c:/Python27;
```

Save these settings and then reboot the PC.

When Windows comes back up, go to ***www.pygame.org/wiki/Pygame2exe*** and copy and paste the text in the white box on that page into a Geany window. This is a template specifically written for using Pygame with Py2Exe, so, to get it to work for our project, we need to change the following lines:

45. change filename to main.py

48. Change project name to PiSplat

54. change project version to 0.1

57. change licence to GNU General Public License (sic)

65. change description to A simple shoot-em-up

71. change the self.extra_datas list to include images so that the game images, in a subfolder of that name, will be bundled into the resulting file.

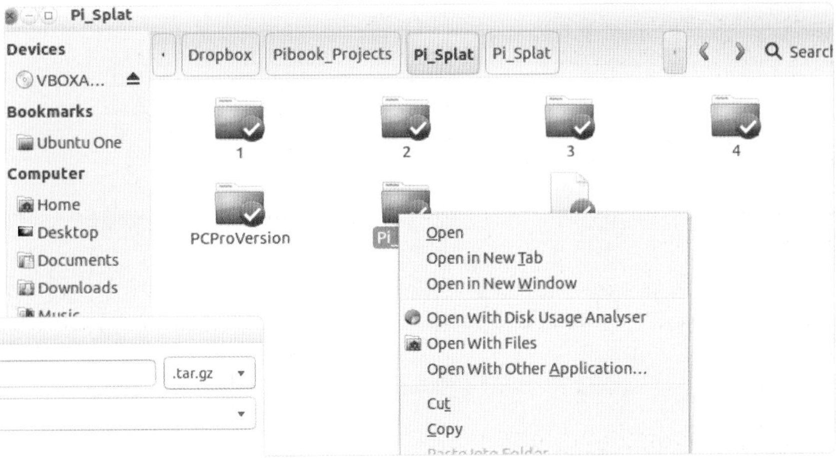

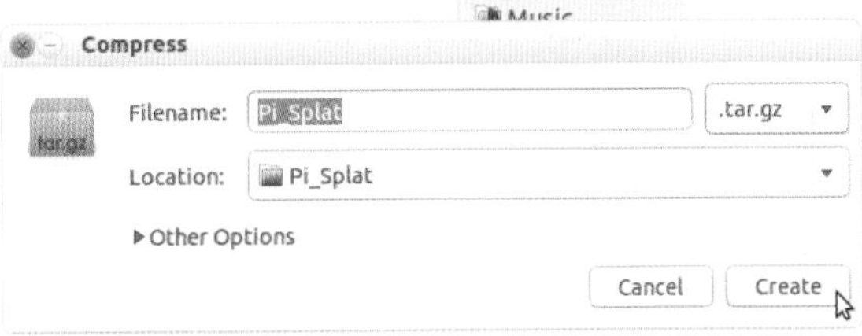

▲ To share your Python code with Linux or Mac users you just need to turn it into an archive

When you're done, save the file as compile.py, then open a Windows command prompt and navigate to the folder containing your game using the cd command.

So, for example, if you've been saving the program files into a folder on your desktop, you might type:

```
cd Desktop\pi_splat
```

Now, to compile your EXE file type:

```
python compile.py
```

At the end of the process, you'll find a new subfolder called dist that contains all the files you need to distribute for your game to run. Double-click the file with the EXE extension and your game should now run.

To share the game, all you need to do is zip up and distribute the contents of the dist folder. Now, the people you send your game to can just click the file and start playing – effectively all the bits of Python they need have been wrapped up ready for them to use.

So that's your first game done, dusted and out of the door. For more of a challenge, turn the page. **ca**

▼ By compiling your code, it will run on any WIndows PC

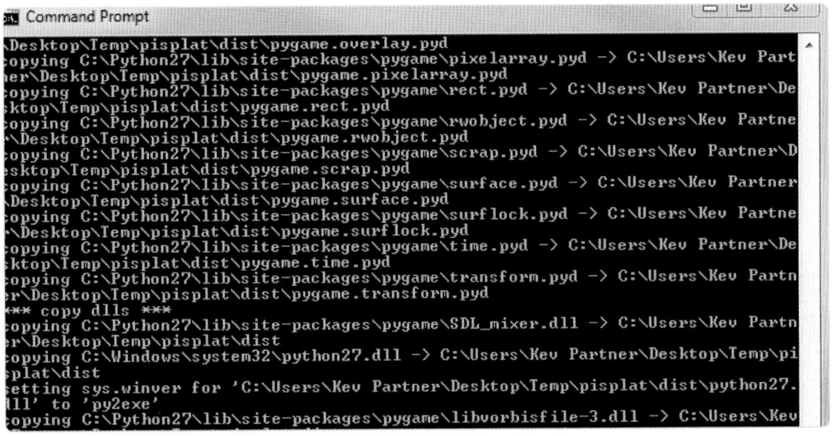

Create a polished game

In the previous chapters we made a simple game – now let's make a commercial-quality game that could have been produced professionally

WHAT YOU'LL LEARN

- How to plan a large project effectively
- Optimise your program to run efficiently
- Creating complicated objects

Back in the mid-1990s, Russian programmer Eugene Alemzhin released a game called Shariki in which the player scored points by matching three or more circles of the same colour.

Shariki was the basis of many popular games including the hugely successful Bejeweled series by PopCap Games and current favourite Candy Crush Saga by King.com. Together, this genre has become known as match-three games.

In this chapter, we'll look at a Raspberry Pi version of this game called Fruit Pi. Although (in principle) match-three games are relatively simple, creating a commercial-quality game is a more involved task than Pi Splat, our simple shoot-'em-up.

With that in mind, we're going to take a look behind the scenes at the game halfway through its development. That way, we can discuss the game's design phase, the programming techniques used so far and what remains to be done before it can be released. The code can be downloaded from *www.snipca.com/9819*.

How the game works

As with Pi Splat, the first step is to look at the game from the user's point of view: what do they expect from a match-three game? Here are the basic rules, which are shared by most games of this type:

- The player sees objects arranged in a grid, usually eight down by eight across
- These objects are randomly drawn from a limited selection. In the case of an 8x8 grid; there are usually six. Too small a selection would lead to too many matches, while too large a selection would result in too few matches.
- The aim is to swap adjacent objects so that, in their new configuration, they form a pattern of three or more identical objects either vertically or horizontally. If no swap is possible, the objects return to their original place.
- The initial board for each level should contain no matches (this is why it is pseudo random rather than truly random).
- When a pattern is formed, the objects are then removed from the board and points are awarded.
- The objects directly above then drop into that space. Random fruits are added at the top of the grid to keep the whole board populated.
- If this change in configuration causes matches, the game processes them and awards points.
- The level is complete when a pre-determined score threshold is reached.
- Different versions of the game add extra features such as "power-ups" or rewards for matching the same object type more than once in succession.

This is a comparatively brief list of rules – it's not like learning chess. However, translating these simple requirements into a computer program is a different matter. Once again, we'll start by breaking the rules down into the familiar categories of input, logic and output to arrive at an initial set of tasks.

Input

The user needs a way to indicate which objects they wish to swap. In a computer-based game, this will usually mean by using a mouse. The final game will also need a way of reading in any saved progress data or stored game preferences.

Logic

The code must generate a pseudo-random set of objects with no matches for the initial board. When the player starts swapping objects, it must check for matches. When a match is made, the logic must identify which objects to delete as a result, move existing objects down the grid, and add new objects at the top to replace them. Our game logic must keep track of game data, such as the player's current score and which level has been reached.

Output

From the player's perspective, the graphics, animations and sounds are what generate the experience of playing the game. So the game design, and the code we create to implement it, must include:

- Drawing attractive graphics
- Loading them into appropriate classes
- Animating them onto the screen
- Indicating which fruit has been selected during swapping
- Displaying the score and other game information
- Saving game progress and preference information to a file
- Playing in-game music and sounds

It's quite a list – and each of these tasks breaks down into many smaller programming jobs. Ultimately, we could be looking at hundreds or even thousands of lines of code. But don't be intimidated: as we mentioned earlier, many successful games have been developed by very small teams or individuals.

Fruit Pi

As with Pi Splat, we'll aim to get a single level running before going on to add multiple levels and the various other features that make for a complete, professional game. Aside from sourcing the fruit images for our game, we need to make several decisions, namely:

1. The size of the playing area. We've decided on a width of 1,024 **pixels** and a height of 768. This stretches the Pi's capabilities whilst still being large enough to make for a good visual experience.
2. How we will indicate which fruit is selected. The player needs a visual indicator. This might be that the fruit increases in size when clicked, for example. We've opted for a simple rectangle over the selected fruit.
3. How we will animate fruit. Many games make use of metaphor. We present the fruit as if they've been poured into the top of the computer screen from left to right, so we need to reflect this in the animation.
4. How we will present user information. Our 1,024 x 768 window leaves room for us to display information alongside the play area. We've opted to put the board on the right and the information on the left.

> “Our Fruit Pi game has much in common with some of the most popular mobile games available today.”

The game background is an **8-bit** PNG file, and we've created a graphic for the board that's placed on top. We can refresh just this area when fruits move, saving processing power. We'll use sounds from ***www.freesound.org*** as before, but before implementing them we'll focus on getting the game mechanics and graphics working well on the Pi.

Programming approach

As with Pi Splat, each fruit will be based on a Fruit class, which will remember what type of fruit it is and where it's located on the screen. It will be capable of updating its own position and following rules about when to stop moving. We'll also once more organise our code into modules. The main module contains the game loop; most of the logic is contained in a logic module and most of the output code will go in a module called display.

Fruit Pi follows a structure that's typical of games, and in particular those games created in Python. The central module, main.py, contains the core of the game – the main loop – with most of the work of generating and displaying the visual objects and handling user interaction undertaken by an array of modules and classes summarised in the diagram over the page.

This structure provides good examples of the differences between modules and classes. You can see that each of the classes defines an object that has a clear, individual, identity. The Fruit and Cursor classes are graphical objects and the Game

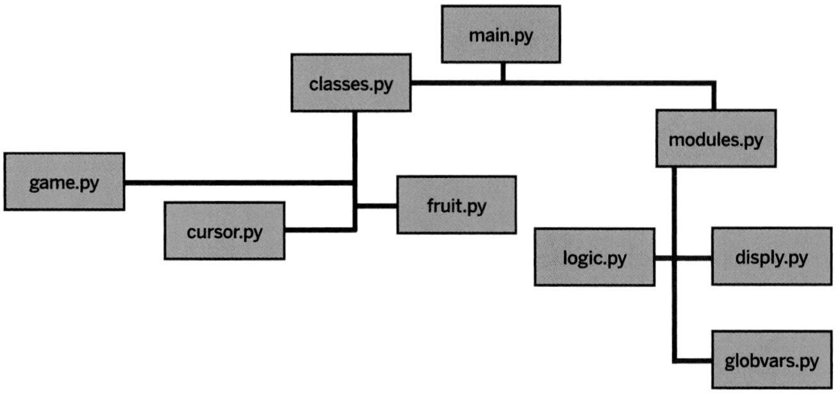

▲ Our new game is divided into modules and classes, to make coding and testing much simpler

class is used to hold information about the game currently being played (including score and level).

The modules, on the other hand, are simply blocks of code organised according to their purpose. The file logic.py, for example, doesn't define a sort of object: it's a set of functions that handles the program's decision making.

Similarly, the functions in display.py deal with the visual aspects of the game – including creating and handling the fruit objects. To use a juggling analogy, the class defines the balls and the module describes how the juggler throws them. We'll see this working in practice as we look at the code.

Modules, then, are mainly used to organise code into logical units, and they also make it easier to share code across projects. You could dump the entire contents of each module into the main.py file and it would still work, but it would be ungainly, impossible to reuse and hard to manage.

You'll have noticed that the module names are influenced by our input, logic and output approach (display.py representing the last of these). The only reason there isn't a discrete input module is that, for this game, user input amounts to little more than clicking a pair of fruits, so it can be easily handled within the other modules.

The way you organise your code must make sense to you (and your team if you have one). And, above all else, it must be practical. If you ever feel restricted by the structure you've created, then you've created the wrong structure!

So, from our thoughts on design and using our input, logic, output approach we can quickly generate structure for our game; we know from the start which objects we're likely to need and which modules to create. We may add or remove classes or modules as we go, but we have a starting point.

You'll notice one module that doesn't fit this rule: globvars.py. As its name suggests, this module contains all our global variables. Now, mention global variables to programmers of a certain type and they'll throw up their hands in horror because, used inappropriately, they can cause problems.

However, it makes sense to use globals for variables that need to be accessed by all modules, especially where they are constants. We do this by defining them in a separate Python file and then importing it into all modules and classes. Here's the relevant code:

```
import pygame
###TOP LEVEL VARIABLES
FPS = 30 # frames per second to update the screen
WINDOWWIDTH = 1024  # width of the program's window, in pixels
WINDOWHEIGHT = 768 # height in pixels
BOARDLEFT=300 #the position of the board, from the left
BOARDTOP=50 #the position of the board, from the top
CELLWIDTHHEIGHT=82 #the width of individual cells
CELLIMAGEWIDTH=68 # the width of the image files
BOARDWIDTH = 8 # how many columns in the board
BOARDHEIGHT = 8 # how many rows in the board
NUDGE=(CELLWIDTHHEIGHT-CELLIMAGEWIDTH)/2+4 #because the cell image is smaller than the
speed=30
WHITE=[255,255,255]; RED=[255,0,0]; GREEN=[0,255,0]; BLUE=[0,0,255]; BLACK=[0,0,0]

pygame.init()
displayFont=pygame.font.Font("256BYTES.TTF",28)


```

In the case of this game we're defining variables including the height and width of the game window, the position of the game board within that window, and the height and width of the cells within the board. We also define some common colours and a typeface.

The main loop

Let's look at the structure of a typical main loop for a game. Broadly speaking, this will be all that main.py contains, with all the other work being done by the modules and classes. We might characterise the structure of operations as:

```
#Import modules and classes
#Define variables
#Draw the background
#Game Loop
        #Level Loop
```

So, when the player first launches the game and the background has been drawn, they enter the game loop. Unless they've continued a saved game, they'll be at level 1, so the player enters a level loop that handles everything that happens next – fruit dropping into view, swapping, deleting and so on.

Once the level is completed, the player is sent back to the game loop (as the level loop is inside it). This checks to see whether the player was playing the final level and, if not, starts a new iteration of the level loop. This continues until the levels run out or the player exits the game. Let's take a look at how this works in practice.

Imports

We start by importing the various Python libraries we want to use on line 1:

```
1  import pygame, random, time, math, sys, copy
2  from pygame.locals import *
3  from game import *
4  from fruit import *
5  from logic import *
6  from display import *
7  from globvars import *
8  from cursor import *
9
```

Pygame is the only one of these libraries that isn't included in a standard Python install (although it is included on the Raspberry Pi). Lines 3 to 8 import our custom classes and modules. With these we use a slightly different syntax:

```
from [module/class name] import *
```

The from keyword is mainly used to allow us to import part of a module. For example, the following line would import only the randint function from the Random library:

```
from random import randint
```

This is a more resource-efficient way of doing things, because Python doesn't have to import any unnecessary code – but it means that if you subsequently want to use another function from the library, you'd have to go back and add it to the from line. By specifying an asterisk we import everything, exactly as if we'd used the import keyword. This may seem to defeat the object of using from; but by doing it in this way we can refer to the functions within the module by just using their function name, rather than having to also add the module name. So, if we use the from keyword with an asterisk as above, we can turn this line:

```
my_number=random.randint(0,5)
```

... into the simpler:

```
my_number=randint(0,5)
```

In other words, once you've imported a function using the from syntax, you can use it as if it were built into the language rather than imported. This saves typing and, in many cases, is just as clear as explicitly naming the module.

There's one caveat to this approach, though. If multiple functions in separate modules have identical names then this will cause an error, so it needs careful handling. One way to do this is to use only the from method of importing with your own classes. This means that game=game.Game() becomes game=Game(). The first one must indicate which file the class is contained in; the second doesn't have to because we've used from.

If your code is to be easy to understand, either by yourself or another programmer, you can either prefix all module functions with their name by using import or, if you use the shorter form, have a logical structure to the modules that makes it obvious which one a function belongs to. For example, you could reasonably expect to find a function called animateFruits in the display module; you wouldn't expect to see it in logic.py.

Let's look now at the heart of the game – the level loop. This loop runs many times per second and carries out the following instructions during each cycle:

1. If fruits are falling (both at the beginning and when fruit is removed) draw the animation before moving on.

2. If not:
  a. Check whether any keys have been pressed or whether the mouse button has been clicked.

  b. If a fruit has been clicked on then:
  i. If it's the first of a pair, draw the cursor.
  ii. If it's the second of a pair, check whether the two fruits are neighbours (if not, they can't possibly match).
  iii. If so, run the matching algorithm and:
    1. If they do match, swap the fruits, update the score, delete the fruits, regenerate the board in its new configuration and animate into place.
    2. If they don't match, move the fruits back.
  iv. If the two fruits were not neighbours, set the second fruit to be the new position for the cursor and await a second click.

3. If no animation is taking place, refresh the screen.

This level loop continues to run until a pre-determined score is reached for the level, at which point it exits back to the main game loop. Most of the lines within the level loop call functions from modules or classes that carry out the actual work. For example, consider this line:

```
animateFruits(board,DISPLAYSURFACE,fruit_»
sprite_group, BOARD_AREA,board_graphic)
```

This single statement calls a 34-line function in display.py. Using functions in this way makes it easy to reuse the function elsewhere in this program, and it helps keep the code clear and easy to understand.

Without knowing any of the detail of how animateFruits works, another programmer could look over the main module and instantly understand what the line does. So, main.py is, in a sense, a road map showing the primary route the program takes, with each module serving as a street atlas providing the detail.

Loading fruits

Before each level begins, the game must create a valid board. To do this we must first decide how the board will be represented; that is, what sort of variable can we use to store it? Fundamentally, the board is simply a table with eight rows and eight columns, and once you're used to Python you'll immediately realise that the humble list is the ideal variable type to store this. We might create a list for the bottom row of the playing area that looks like this:

```
('strawberry','strawberry','pear','banana','pear',»
'cherry','raspberry','raspberry')
```

To deal with the fact that we have eight different rows to handle, we'll make use of the fact that a list can contain other lists. In other words, we'll store the play area as a list of eight lists, each of which represents a row. We can then access the value of, say, the second fruit on the bottom row via the statement below. Remember that all lists are zero-indexed!

```
Fruit=board[7][1]
```

In practice, we rarely need to do this: it's easier simply to pull the whole row out and then access it in the normal way.

Now we've decided how our board will be represented, we can write a function that will create a new valid grid of fruits. The game loop runs this command before each level:

```
loadFruits(board,fruit_sprite_group)
```

As you'd expect, this function is found in display.py: here's how the relevant code looks:

```
16  def loadFruits(board,fruit_sprite_group):
17      cell_number=1
18
19      if len(board)>0:del board[:] #clear the board if there are any fruit objects already there (ie this is level 2+)
20
21  ####### CREATE FRUIT OBJECTS AND LOAD THEM INTO THE LIST BOX
22
23      for row in range(8):#run once for each of the 8 rows
24          thisrow=[] #each row is a separate list
25          y=row*CELLWIDTHHEIGHT+BOARDTOP+NUDGE #set the vertical position for the whole of the row
26
27          for column in range(8):#run once for each of the 8 columns in each row
28              exclude_fruits=[] #list of fruits that musn't be picked because they'd make an immediate match
29
30              if column>1: #check that the two fruits to the left do not match each other (not a prob for the first 2 columns)
31                  if thisrow[column-2]._name==thisrow[column-1]._name: #if the two to the left are the same as this one
32                      exclude_fruits.append(thisrow[column-1]._name)
33
34              if row>1: #now check whether the previous two rows hold the same fruit in this column
35                  if board[row-2][column]._name==board[row-1][column]._name:
36                      exclude_fruits.append(board[row-1][column]._name)
37
38              fruit_name=logic.get_fruit(exclude_fruits) #now get a fruit from the valid choices
39
40              x=column*CELLWIDTHHEIGHT+BOARDLEFT+NUDGE #set the left position of each fruit
41
42              this_fruit=Fruit(fruit_name,x,y,row,column,speed,BOARDWIDTH,BOARDHEIGHT) #create a fruit object
43
```

The use of two for..in loops such as this is very common when you want to represent two-dimensional structures such as a table in code. Line 23 runs eight times, once for each row – during which line 27 runs eight times, once for each cell in the row.

Line 25 sets the vertical position of the row, using the global variables to do so. By doing it this way we could replace the existing board with one of a different size by simply changing the values of those global variables.

Remember that one of the rules for the initial board is that it mustn't contain any immediate matches, so the if statements at lines 30 and 34 check whether a pair of the same fruit already exists to the left of the current cell or immediately above it. If so, then we can't use that fruit for this cell. So, we make a list called exclude_fruits, specifying those fruits we mustn't choose this time. We then call the get_fruit function in the logic module, which will send back the name of a randomly generated valid fruit. Here's the relevant section of logic.py:

```
120 def get_fruit(exclude_list=[]): #however many fruits there are, send back one randomly
121     fruit_names=["banana","blueberry","cherry","pear","raspberry","strawberry"]
122
123     for rottenfruit in exclude_list: #if any of the fruits are invalid
124         if rottenfruit in fruit_names: fruit_names.remove(rottenfruit) #remove them from the list of choices
125
126     fruit_name=randint(0,len(fruit_names)-1) #pick a fruit from the list of valid choices
127     return fruit_names[fruit_name]
```

Take a look at the parameters for get_fruit. You'll see that we specify exclude_list as you'd expect, so that display.py can send a list of fruit names we mustn't choose. However, most of the time this list will be empty. By setting exclude_list=[] we're telling Python that if we aren't sent a list, we can assume that there are no fruits, and to therefore use an empty list in this function. This is a default setting – it can be very useful if you aren't sure which parameters will be passed to a function.

We then create a list with the complete set of fruit names and, in line 123, cycle through the list of excluded fruits, removing them from the list of fruit names in line 124. The if statement in line 124 is needed because if, say, there are two raspberries to the left and two above, then exclude_list would contain "raspberry" twice – and Python would throw an error if we tried to remove it when it had already been deleted.

Lines 126 and 127 pull a random fruit out of the remaining candidates and send it back.

Once we have that name, we can create a new Fruit object for this cell. We then add this fruit to the row and, once we have a whole row, we add it to the board.

```
this_fruit=Fruit(fruit_name,x,y,row,column,»
speed, BOARDWIDTH,BOARDHEIGHT)
```

This calls the initialisation routine in the Fruit class and sends it the information it needs in order to create a fruit object. In this case, this means it will load the correct graphic and set its final position on the board. It also sets a variable called _moving, which the code will use later to work out if the fruit is still animating or whether it's arrived in place.

The other functions contained in the Fruit class illustrate how self-aware it is. calculate_new_position works out where the fruit should be the next time it's drawn to the screen. It takes account of whether it's travelling down the screen (as it would be initially), across or up (in the case of a swap), and also works out when to change the _moving variable to False so that the game can then ignore it during animation. In traditional procedural programming, you'd need to write a complicated nested list to track each fruit from within the level loop; here we leave it to the object itself to do this.

The calculate_neighbours method records the fruits above, alongside and below this fruit (where applicable). This is used later by the level loop when determining whether fruits can be swapped.

change_image is used when we swap fruits – this is because we're actually changing their image rather than directly swapping objects. This is a much simpler approach because it means that each object can retain its x and y positions in the grid for the entire level, and simply needs to update its fruit graphic to reflect the state of play. This function handles all the changes necessary when a fruit changes.

Finishing the game

One particularly distinctive aspect of games such as Bejeweled and Candy Crush Saga is the way the objects – gems, sweets or, in our case, fruit – fall onto the screen. When designing a routine for this, the first step is to write a set of rules for displaying the objects. Our rules are simple enough: first, the fruit appears from the top and fills the board from the bottom upwards. Then, fruit fills from the right-hand side of the row.

In other words, when building an empty board, the bottom right-hand cell is the first to be filled with fruit, and the top-left-hand cell the last. The implication of this is that we have to build a routine that not only adds fruit from bottom to top but also from right to left.

Remember, at this point we have a list called board containing eight sub-lists representing the rows and each containing eight fruit objects, one per cell. Our job now is to animate them onto the screen rather than simply plonking them there in one go (even though that would be much simpler to program!). To make matters more difficult, the row should fill from right to left rather than the whole row appearing at once.

The animateFruits function is contained in display.py, as you'd expect, and is called from the level loop whenever the re_paint variable is set to True. This will be the case at the start of each level as the board fills up and each time fruit is removed by swapping.

Here's the line that calls it:

```
animateFruits(board,DISPLAYSURFACE,fruit_ »
sprite_group, BOARD_AREA,board_graphic)
```

What do we send to animateFruits? The board (the list of fruits organised by row), the Pygame surface onto which we're drawom, the sprite group into which the fruits will be placed, a global containing a rect of the board area (that is, its x, y, height and width), and a reference to the graphic itself.

The structure of animateFruits is similar to that of loadFruits in that we're iterating over rows and columns. This time, however, we're altering the position of the fruit each cycle.

```
51 def animateFruits(board,DISPLAYSURFACE,fruit_sprite_group, BOARD_AREA,board_graphic):
52     #global speed
53     ##### SHOW THE ANIMATION OF THE FRUITS FALLING IN STAGGERED FASHION
54     clock=pygame.time.Clock() #create a game clock for limiting the frames per second
55 
56 
57     falling_fruits=[] #create a copy of the board nested list
58     for fruit_row in range(8):
59         falling_fruits.append(list(board[fruit_row]))
60 
61     current_row=0
62 
63     for fruit_row in reversed(falling_fruits): #the "reversed" keyword starts at the end of the list and works up
64 
65         fruit_sprite_group.add(fruit_row) #add all the fruit objects from this row to the sprite group ready to be displayed
66         n=0
67         for fruit in reversed(fruit_row): ##stagger initial positions
68             fruit._speed=speed
69             fruit._current_y+=n #add n to the starting position of the fruit
70             n-=speed #makes n smaller (negative numbers) so the starting position goes up the screen off the page
71 
72         while len(fruit_row)>0: #while there are any fruits still in fruit_row (ie still in motion)
73 
74             for fruit in fruit_row: #for each fruit in the row
75                 fruit.move_me() #move it
76                 if fruit._moving==False: # if it's reached the bottom
77                     fruit_row.remove(fruit) #remove it from fruit_row
78 
79             shrinking_board_area=(BOARD_AREA[0],BOARD_AREA[1],BOARD_AREA[2],BOARD_AREA[3]-(CELLWIDTHHEIGHT*(current_row-1)))
80 
81             DISPLAYSURFACE.blit(board_graphic,shrinking_board_area) #only blit the bit of the board over which the fruits are falling
82 
83             fruit_sprite_group.draw(DISPLAYSURFACE) # draw the sprites in their new positions to the surface
84             pygame.display.update(shrinking_board_area) # update only the animated part of the display
85             clock.tick(60)# Limit to 60 fps
86         current_row+=1
```

The above code shows the relevant part of display.py. We begin by making a copy of the board list – we'll see why later. In line 63 we begin the row by row loop; the reversed keyword specifies to start at the end of the list (the bottom row) and work upwards. On line 65, we add the entire row to the sprite group; then we work through each fruit (again using reversed; this time to work from right to left) progressively raising the vertical position as we go. This gives a staggered line with the left-hand fruit further off-screen than the right.

We then run each fruit in the row's move_me function, which launches the calculate_new_position function we covered earlier. We check whether the fruit's _moving property is False – indicating that it's arrived at its final position – and if so, we remove the reference to that row from fruit_row. Thus, we use fewer resources as each fruit stops moving, and we can use the len function in line 72 to check if the row has completed. If we'd been using the actual board variable, it would end up containing no fruits. This is why we copied it.

Line 79 calculates the minimum area the fruit will pass over as it falls. As the rows build up from the bottom, we don't need to redraw the settled rows every cycle, so this area becomes smaller and smaller. We feed this calculation into line 81's blit operation, which draws the board. We draw the fruit sprite group in one go but only update the shrinking board area. We could redraw the whole board each cycle, but this more efficient approach helps the Pi to keep up.

Once the board has been drawn, the program waits for the user to click on a fruit. Just as with key presses, Pygame can listen for mouse events, such as MOUSEBUTTONDOWN. Working out which fruit the mouse pointer was over when the button was clicked is handled in the logic.py function which_fruit:

```
def which_fruit(board,position): #work out which fruit is under th
    for fruit_row in board:
        for fruit in fruit_row:
            if fruit._rect.collidepoint(position):
                return fruit
```

This code takes advantage of a Pygame function called collidepoint, which receives as a parameter the event.pos returned by MOUSEBUTTONDOWN (this is actually two numbers, namely the x and y positions). Our loop simply iterates through each fruit in turn, checking whether collidepoint is True for that fruit. When it is, we know we're dealing with the fruit that's located under the mouse pointer, so we return this object.

```
56                  if clicked_fruit: #if the mouse has been clicked over a fruit
57                      if pair_of_fruits['source']==None:
58                          pair_of_fruits['source']=clicked_fruit
59                          decoration_sprite_group.add(cursor)
60                          cursor.moveMe(clicked_fruit._rect)
61                      else:
62                          result=check_for_neighbour(pair_of_fruits['source'],clicked_fruit)
63                          is_it_a_neighbour=result[0]
64                          direction=result[1]
65                          if is_it_a_neighbour:
66                              pair_of_fruits['dest']=clicked_fruit
67                              board=swap_fruits(pair_of_fruits,direction,board)
68                              result=handle_matches(board,pair_of_fruits)
69                              if result[0]==True: #if there were matches
70                                  pair_of_fruits['source']=None
71                                  game.update_score(result[1])
```

Back in main.py, we now check whether this was the first fruit to be clicked in a pair by establishing whether pair_of_fruits['source'] already contains a fruit. If it doesn't, we assume this is the first click, move the cursor over this fruit and wait for the player to click again.

Otherwise, the else at line 61 is triggered and we check whether the second fruit is a neighbour of the first. If it isn't, we consider this a "new" first click, since we assume that the player has found a match elsewhere on the board. If the second fruit is a neighbour of the first then we must check whether there is a match and, if so, increment the score and update the screen. If not, we swap the fruits back to their original positions and go back to square one.

Finishing the game

So far, we've seen how the code builds a playing board, animates the pieces into place and handles the player's attempt at matching fruit. The next thing we need is some code to check that two selected fruits really are a valid match. The first step here is to check whether the selected fruits are neighbours. The code that handles this can be found in logic.py.

This code is pretty simple: remember that when we created each fruit object, we ran a function that established its immediate neighbours. Take a look at line 32 and consider how this would translate into plain English: "If both fruits are on the same row and the second fruit's column number is the same as the first fruit's neighbour on the left, then they must be neighbours."

We then check the same on the right; then, in lines 36 and 38, we work out whether they are neighbours above or below. If any of these tests returns a True result, we immediately return this, along with the direction. If none of them returns True, we return False because we've established that the selected fruits can't be neighbours.

Assuming they are neighbours, our next task is to work out whether, by swapping the fruits into the place the player intends, a vertical or horizontal line of at least three fruits would be formed:

```
4  def check_for_matches(board,pair_of_fruits):
5      copy_board=copy.deepcopy(board) #we make a copy so that we can work on it without affecting the original
6  
7      #first check for row matches
8      any_matches=False #use this to track if there were any matches at all
9      row=0
10     for fruit_row in copy_board:
11         col=0
12         for fruit in fruit_row:
13             if col<6: #we only need to check the first 6 fruits in the row
14                 if fruit_row[col+1]._name==fruit_row[col+2]._name==fruit._name:
15                 #are the two fruits to the right the same as this one?
16                     any_matches=True
17                     fruit._delete=True; fruit_row[col+1]._delete=True; fruit_row[col+2]._delete=True
18             if row<6: #again, we only need to check the first 6 fruits in a column
19                 if copy_board[row+1][col]._name==copy_board[row+2][col]._name==fruit._name:
20                     #are the two fruits below the same as this one?
21                     any_matches=True
22                     fruit._delete=True;copy_board[row+1][col]._delete=True;copy_board[row+2][col]._delete=True
23             col+=1
24         row+=1
25 
26     return_parameters=[any_matches]
27 
28     if any_matches==True:
29         return_parameters.append(copy_board)
30 
31     return return_parameters
```

The actual business of finding matches is pretty straightforward. We begin by making a copy of the board, so we can work on it without changing the original.

We then use our familiar double for..in structure to go through each row and column in turn. Note that at line 13 we only need to check the first six fruits in a row: this is because any pattern that begins in the seventh would be too short to be valid (the same applies to columns, of course). For each fruit, we check to see whether the two fruits to its right are of the same type. If so, we set the _delete property to True for all three fruits. This has no immediate effect – it simply marks the fruits for deletion later, when we process all the updates for the board.

We repeat this for the columns from line 18, and send back both the any_matches variable (True or False), and, if True, we also return the updated copy of the board that we've been working with.

This version of the board contains copies of all the fruit objects, with those that are part of a matching pattern having their _delete property set to True, which makes it very easy to process all the changes, as you can see in the code at the top of the next page.

```
58 def delete_matches(copy_board,board):
59     #now assemble a list of all the fruits that are to be deleted
60     delete_fruits=[]
61     extra_fruits_needed=[0,0,0,0,0,0,0,0]
62     last_affected_row=[0,0,0,0,0,0,0,0]
63 
64     row=0
65     for fruit_row in copy_board:
66         column=0
67         for fruit in fruit_row:
68 
69             if fruit._delete==True:
70                 extra_fruits_needed[column]+=1
71                 last_affected_row[column]=row
72                 delete_fruits.append(fruit)
73             column+=1
74         row+=1
75 
76     #generate the new board
77     row=0
78     col=0
79     for number_of_new_fruits in extra_fruits_needed:
80         if number_of_new_fruits>0:
81             lastrow=last_affected_row[col]
82             for thisrow in range(lastrow,number_of_new_fruits-1,-1):
83                 board[thisrow][col]._current_y=board[thisrow-number_of_new_fruits][col]._y
84                 board[thisrow][col].change_image(board[thisrow-number_of_new_fruits][col]._name,\
85 board[thisrow-number_of_new_fruits][col]._x,board[thisrow][col]._current_y)
86                 board[thisrow][col]._moving=True
87                 board[thisrow][col]._direction="down"
88 
89             y=-80
90             for thisrow in range(0,number_of_new_fruits):
91                 board[thisrow][col]._current_y=y
92                 board[thisrow][col].change_image(get_fruit(),board[thisrow][col]._x,board[thisrow][col]._current_y)
93                 board[thisrow][col]._moving=True
94                 board[thisrow][col]._direction="down"
95                 y-=60
96         col+=1
97 
98     number_of_fruits_matches=len(delete_fruits)
99     return (number_of_fruits_matches,board)
```

The above code implements the delete_matches function – arguably the most important function in the entire program. This section of code removes fruits that have been found to be part of a matching set, and generates a new board with all the necessary changes made. It begins by creating two lists, both of eight elements (one for each column of the board).

Each element of the first list, extra_fruits_needed, represents the number of new fruits that need to be generated for that column. The second list contains the number of the last row that is affected by the changes, again by column. This enables us to simply ignore the rows that remain the same.

At this point, we need to think about how we're going to handle fruits disappearing and being added. From the player's perspective, when a gap appears, the fruit above drops to fill the gap.

As we've mentioned, it's easiest to handle this by updating the objects in the relevant positions. So, if three raspberries disappear and the fruit above the gap is a cherry, we can simply change the bottom raspberry to a cherry. This starts at line 79, above. To provide a better visual effect, however, we don't want the cherry to instantly jump down into place. Instead, we want it to fall from its old position to the new one. We can achieve this by temporarily changing the y position of each affected fruit to the same as that of the fruit whose variety it has stolen. Then we animate it moving back to its original position.

Lines 90 to 94 deal with adding new fruits to the board – or, to be more precise, assigning new fruit names as needed, to fill the gaps where fruits have fallen down. We generate random names for the relevant slots, load in the graphics and set the new fruits above the board so they can be animated into place, in the same way as when we originally filled it at the start of the level.

There's one final eventuality we must deal with: what if, after the player has matched a line of fruits, and the board has been updated, the resulting updated board itself contains new matches? This is easy to handle: once the fruits have animated back into position, we run the check_for_matches process again. The function doesn't care whether the board it's working on was created by a user swapping fruits, or is the result of being regenerated. Either way, it will check through and report any matches. Because we've used modular code, we're able to reuse the animate_fruits and check_for_matches procedures to handle both the initial board and all subsequently generated boards with no additional work.

TIPS FOR PROGRAMMING GAMES

1 Get each part fully working before moving on
For this game, the first step is to create the initial game board – so this was implemented before animation was considered. That was completed before the interactive features were added. This approach can mean updating code when you move to the next stage, but you're always building on a fully working foundation.

2 Code, test, code, test...
Remember that coding is done in small steps: you write a line (or a short block) and you test it. It almost never works first time, so amend and test again. Only move on once it's working.

3 Write it down!
Don't be afraid to pull out a pen and paper if you get stuck. Sometimes, by drawing a rough representation of what the player will see, you can work out the consequences of your code.

4 Use the terminal
If you're unsure of how a piece of code works, type it into the Python interpreter to see what happens.

5 Use the documentation
Python has excellent documentation at python.org, and on third-party sites such as ***www.stackoverflow.com***. There's no need to struggle – the Python community is very helpful.

6 Write the documentation
Use the # symbol to document your code as you go. The examples in this guide don't include many, for reasons of space, but our online samples are heavily commented.

7 Take a break
If you find yourself struggling with a problem, take a break. It's amazing how often a solution can pop into your head when you've rested.

8 Enjoy yourself
Give yourself a pat on the back when you get each part of the game working. There is nothing quite like working hard on a piece of code, running it and seeing it work on-screen.

Final steps

We now have a fully working single level. The next step is to implement multiple levels, along with a splash screen, instructions and a function to save progress. The graphics and animations will need a little extra polish and sound effects are more or less mandatory. However, adding additional pizzazz will impact performance. So it's important to thoroughly test the game on the Raspberry Pi, and optimise the basic version for this slow platform before adding anything else. If your game is intended only for more powerful computers you can omit this stage, but you're narrowing your audience. The best approach is to optimise as far as you can and add only a minimum of extra graphical overhead to the final game – that way, it should work well on all platforms. ca

SECTION 5

Going further

Discover even more possibilities with these advanced Raspberry Pi upgrades, secrets, projects and ideas

If you've worked through this guide, then by now you should have mastered not only the Raspberry Pi itself but the Python programming language too. You'll have even produced your first few programs. But it doesn't need to end there. The Raspberry Pi offers almost limitless ways to extend your experience and learn new skills. In this final section of our guide, we'll be looking at some of the ways to expand your little computer, adding new functions and abilities. We'll also offer some troubleshooting advice, reveal some of the Pi's innermost secrets and show you some of the amazing projects that other people have put together using their own Pi computers.

IN THIS SECTION

Expand, upgrade and mod your Raspberry Pi

Accessorise your Pi with the ultimate selection of useful extras, colourful cases and amazing add-ons

We've seen that the Raspberry Pi offers plenty of possibilities for creating your own programs and projects. But it doesn't stop with the basic kit. When you're ready get more ambitious, there's a whole range of accessories and upgrades available that can add extra capabilities to the Pi.

On these pages we'll look at a selection of useful and inspirational add-ons. Some of them are simple, such as snazzy cases and mounts; others are more technically advanced, such as cameras and infrared sensors. Don't be put off – all of these expansions are easy to set up and use, in keeping with the Raspberry Pi ethos. Even better, they won't break the bank. Most of the accessories in this page can be had for under £20, so it should be possible to soup up your Pi without too much scrimping and saving.

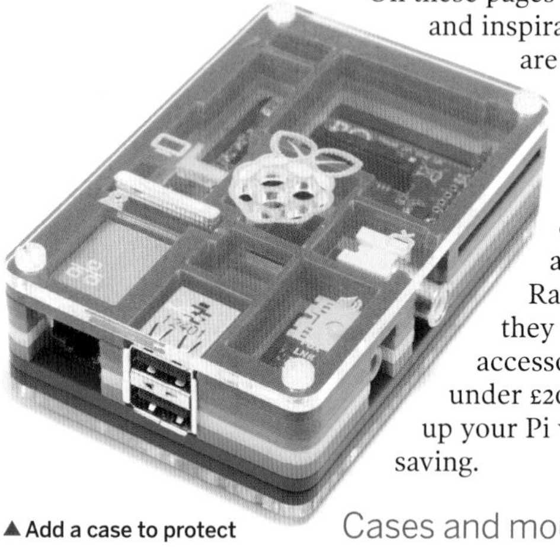

▲ Add a case to protect your Rapsberry Pi

Cases and mounts

Some people love to gaze upon the bare circuitry of the Raspberry Pi; but if you prefer, there are plenty of customised cases that can give it a cool, distinctive look, as well as affording some protection against accidental drinks spillages. The website ***www.modmypi.com*** offers a selection of cases in bright colours, eye-catching rainbow designs and stylish translucent plastic. Prices start at £6 and go up to £12 for the funky PiBow series, which fit together out of seven stackable layers.

Another sort of case you might consider is what's called a VESA monitor mount – a case that's designed to hook onto the back of a TV or computer monitor. If you're using your Raspberry Pi as a media centre, or as an alternative to a desktop PC, this tucks it neatly out of the way. Again, ***www.modmypi.com*** offers the mounts for just £3.

If you want to get really creative, you could even install your Raspberry Pi on a case that roams around the house. The PicoBorg motor controller costs £9 and lets you control up to four motorised devices directly from your Pi; affix four motorised wheels (available for £6 each) and you have a computer that can really go places – with a little programming, of course. The only catch is that if

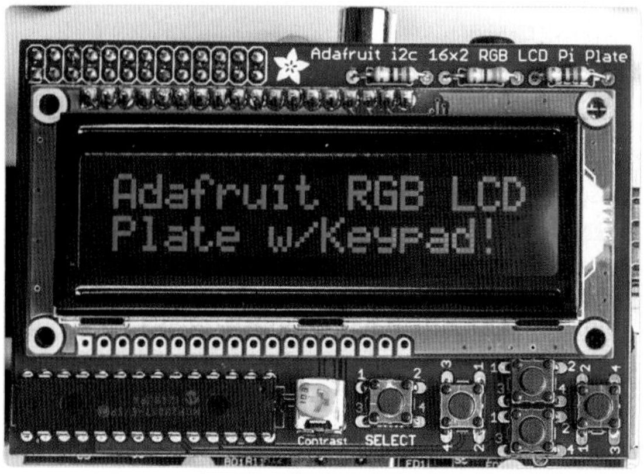

▲ The Pi Plate gives you simple controls and a two line display

MAKING THE CONNECTION

Some of the add-ons we've discussed on this page connect to the Raspberry Pi's USB ports, or plug directly into internal connectors. Many of them, however, come in the form of 'breakout boards': extra circuit boards that need to be wired to the Raspberry Pi's GPIO connectors. The easiest way to handle these is by investing in a 'breadboard': a plastic board with hundreds of electrically-connected holes in it. You connect components together by pushing their wires or connectors into holes, so once you've got the board connected to your Pi you can hook up electronic components with no need to enlist the help of a grown-up and a soldering iron. Breadboards themselves can be had for just a few pounds from many electronics suppliers, and the hardware to connect one to the Pi is cheap too: Adafruit's GPIO Cobbler kit costs just £4.50 from **www.modmypi.com.** Be warned, when you first receive the kit it will need putting together by an adult – it's a 15-minute soldering job.

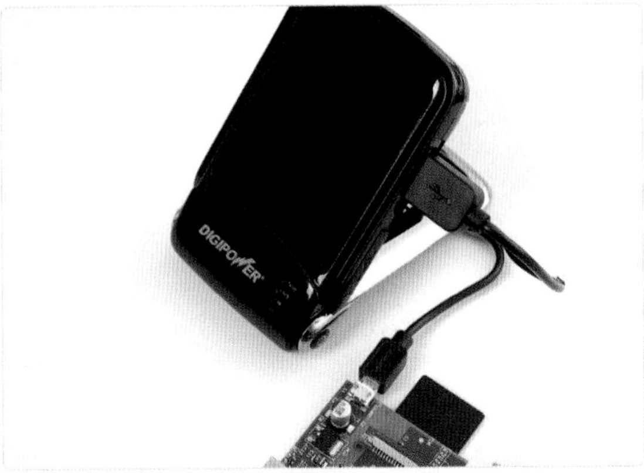

◀ A portable power pack will keep your Pi running when it's away from the mains

you want your Raspberry Pi to get more than a few metres from the power socket, you'll need to find another way to power it. A 2200mAh rechargeable battery pack supply can be had for £17 from ***www.thepihut.com***, and should power your Pi for around eight hours between charges.

Screens and input devices

When you're creating and testing your Pi projects, it can be a pain to have to keep hooking up a monitor or a networked display to check what's going on. Why not equip your Raspberry Pi with its very own LCD? For £20 the Adafruit Pi Plate and LCD equips your Pi with a small display capable of showing 32-character messages. It needs a bit of soldering to put together, so some adult help is required, but once in place it can be easily programmed in Python. The Pi Plate has five built-in push-buttons too, so you can control your programs with no need for keyboard or mouse.

Another way to control your Raspberry Pi is by hooking up a touch sensor: for just £5, ***www.modmypi.com*** will send you a small sensor that you can wire up to the Pi (see the box above); when someone touches it, a signal is generated that your program can pick up and respond to.

For the ultimate in easy control, take a look at the FLIRC infrared remote control unit. This dinky little dongle costs £23 and plugs into a **USB** port, allowing you to use a regular domestic remote control to send commands to the Pi. It's fully configurable, so you can use any control you have lying around: it's intended primarily for people who use Raspberry Pi as a music and video centre.

Cameras and sensors

Since the Raspberry Pi uses USB, it can support all sorts of devices intended for regular PCs. A tiny wireless USB adaptor lets your Pi connect to the internet without the need for a trailing cable. Another possibility is to connect a USB webcam, to capture snaps of the world around your Pi. However, a neater option is to invest in the official Raspberry Pi camera module. This plugs into an onboard socket, so it doesn't take up a USB port, and is fully supported by the latest version of Raspbian. It captures smooth **high-definition** video and takes five-**megapixel** images – a bargain at just £25 from ***thepihut.com***.

To partner your camera, you might like to invest in Adafruit's light proximity sensor, which lets your Raspberry Pi sense and react to the world around it: for example, you could set up a program to take a photo whenever someone comes near. It works best at distances of around six inches, but for around £8 it's a fun toy. You can combine it with a microphone to capture a recording of what's going on around your Pi whenever movement is detected. The microphone costs £7 from ***www.modmypi.com***.

A last update to consider is a real-time clock: normally, if your Pi boots up without a network connection, it won't know the time or date. A battery-powered clock module solves this problem. There are several available: ***www.abelectronics.co.uk*** for example sells a simple one for £9.75. ca

▲ Catch intruders, or just take photos, with the Pi camera

▶ A proximity sensor tells your Pi when someone is close by

Troubleshooting Tips

Having problems with your Pi? Read on to find fixes for many common issues

STEP 1 SOLVE STARTUP PROBLEMS

If your Pi is completely unresponsive, turn the power off and then check whether you've properly inserted your **SD card**. The slot is quite delicate so be careful – just make sure it's the right way up and fully engaged. Have a look at the LEDs next to the USB slot(s) – the light labelled 'ACT' or 'OK' indicates SD Card activity so if you don't see it flashing, there's something wrong with the card and you should either reformat it or use a new SD card. If you do see flashing that stops before the Pi boots up, the card may be corrupted and, again you should reformat it. SD Cards usually become corrupted because you've removed the power cable before shutting down the Pi properly. The easiest way to safely end your session is to open up LXTerminal and type **sudo halt**. This will immediately begin the shutdown process – wait for the green LED to stop flashing before removing the cable. ▼

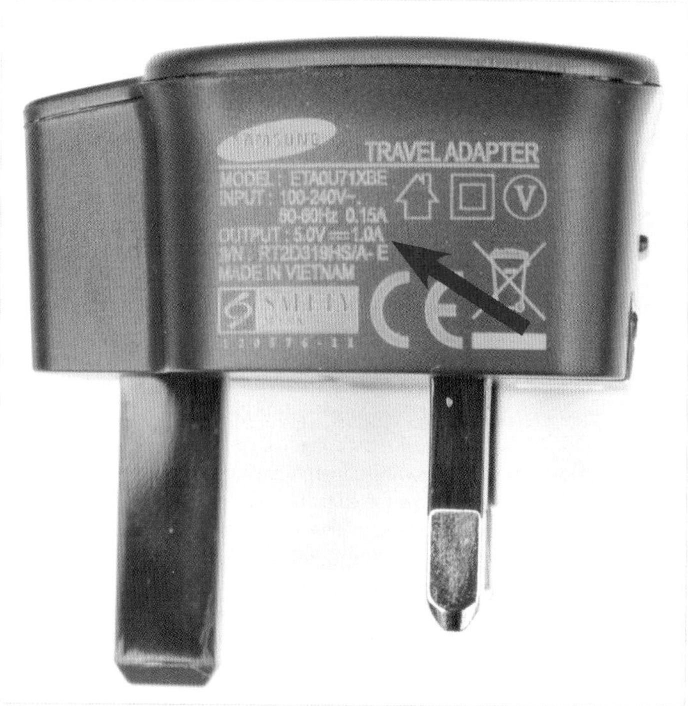

STEP 2 CURE ERRATIC BEHAVIOUR

If your Pi appears to be working properly but occasionally reboots or drops off the Wi-Fi network, it's worth checking your power supply. Whilst all micro-USB mobile chargers operate at 5v, the amount of current they supply varies. The Raspberry Pi requires a minimum of 0.7 amps (700mA) so you should look for a mobile charger of that rating or higher – 1 amp (1000mA) is ideal. You can usually find the rating of your mobile charger on the back, near the prongs – look for a section called 'Output'. You may notice that if you plug a powered USB hub into the Raspberry Pi, it'll start up – this is because the power is flowing into the Pi from the hub. However, this won't supply enough current for the Pi to operate reliably, so you should always plug in the hub after the mains cable. ▼

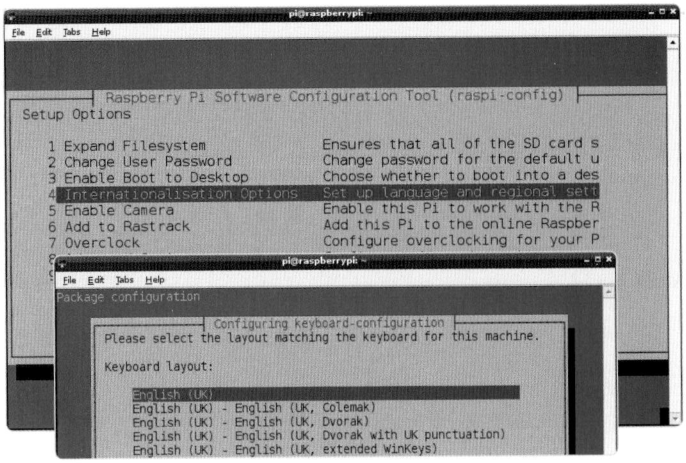

STEP 3 CURE KEYBOARD PROBLEMS

If your keyboard doesn't respond at all, whether wireless or connected via USB cable, you should check whether it's on the list of verified peripherals at *www.snipca.com/9742*. Intermittent problems are harder to track down but can often be solved by plugging it into a powered USB hub rather than directly into the Pi. If the country settings aren't right, you may find text doesn't quite match the keys pressed. To fix this, start LXTerminal and type **sudo raspi-config**. Move down to option 4 and, on the submenu, pick the third option: Change Keyboard Layout. You'll then be asked to select a keyboard model from the list and click OK. On the next screen, select your keyboard layout – usually English (UK) – you can now press Enter through the rest of the sequence. ▼

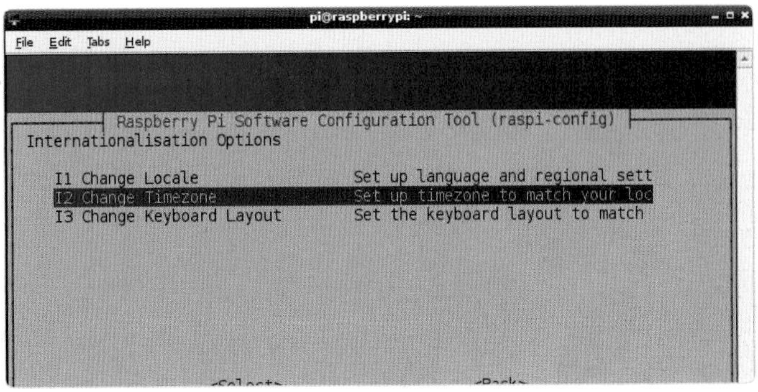

STEP 4 SET THE RIGHT TIME

The Raspberry Pi doesn't have a built-in clock so it forgets the time whenever it's turned off. When you connect the power, the Pi accesses an internet time server to set its clock but it probably won't have the correct time zone set, with the result that the minutes are correct but the hour is wrong. In LXTerminal, type **sudo raspi-config** and, in the configuration menu, choose item 4, Internationalisation Options, and then select the second option, Change Timezone. Under Geographic area, choose Europe then select the London time zone if you live in the UK. ▼

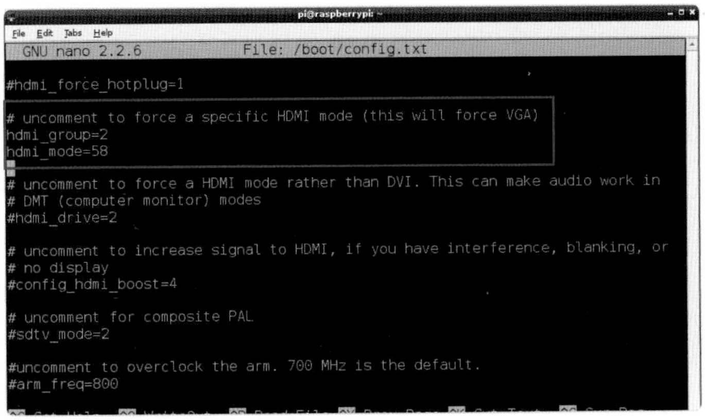

STEP 5 SET THE CORRECT MONITOR RESOLUTION

The Raspberry Pi uses a default **resolution** of 1024 x 768. This may result in a blurry picture if your display has a higher resolution. First, find out the native resolution of your monitor. Now, go to ***http://elinux.org/RPi_config.txt*** and scroll to the line saying 'These values are valid if hdmi_group=2'. In the table, find the resolution and refresh rate of your monitor and note which **HDMI** Mode it corresponds to. In LXTerminal, type **sudo nano /boot/config.txt**. Use the arrow keys to scroll down to #hdmi_group=1. Delete the hash symbol at the start of both lines and change the group to 2 and the mode to the correct value for your monitor. Press Ctrl-O and confirm to save, then type **sudo reboot**. ▼

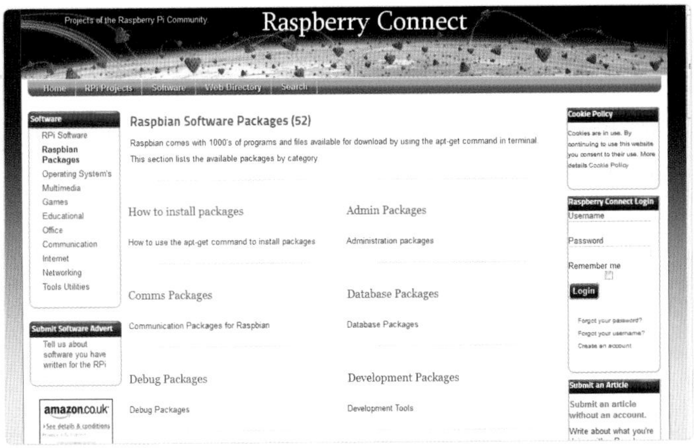

STEP 6 FIX SOFTWARE INSTALLATION PROBLEMS

You'll install most of applications using the command line utility apt-get install [software name]. This is usually a simple process, as long as you know the exact package name. Visit *www.snipca.com/9743* to browse the complete list and make a note of their exact spelling. Before installing any new software, however, run the command **sudo apt-get update** to download the latest list of packages and their locations. If you get 'mirrordirector' errors, it could well be that you haven't run 'update' and the repositories have moved. If you still get errors after establishing that the package name is correct and having run apt-get update then check your internet connection. If at all possible, connect to your **router** via wired **Ethernet** for more reliable installations. ●

Essential Raspberry Pi tricks and secrets

Uncover the Raspberry Pi's best hidden features with our expert tips

STEP 1 TRY BEFORE YOU PI

Fancy trying out some of the tips in this guide before you buy a Pi? Thanks to emulation software, you can create a 'virtual' Raspberry Pi on a Windows PC. Visit ***www.snipca.com/9823*** in your web browser and click the green 'Start Download' button. When the file arrives on your PC, right-click to extract the contents, then click the Start button, and open a command prompt by typing **cmd** and then Enter. Now type cd followed by the path to the folder where the files were extracted, eg **cd Downloads\qemu** and then type **run**. The emulator will start, and you'll see the usual Raspberry Pi boot messages. You can even run the Pi's graphical interface within Windows! It's ideal for learning the basics. ▼

STEP 2 GIVE YOUR PI A FIXED IP ADDRESS

As we'll show later, your Raspberry Pi can be used for lots of things without a monitor or keyboard attached, but you still need to be able to connect to it, and each time it's plugged into the network, it may end up with a different **IP address**. Giving it a fixed one makes it simple to connect to from other devices on your network, but if you fix the address on the Pi, and then plug it into a different network, it can be very difficult to use. So, we're going to show you how to set up the Pi so that it has a fixed address on your own network, but still works fine on any other. Turn it on, connected to a monitor and keyboard, and at the comment line type **ifconfig eth0**. Make a note of the information displayed after HWaddr, which is also known as the MAC address, then proceed to step 3. ▼

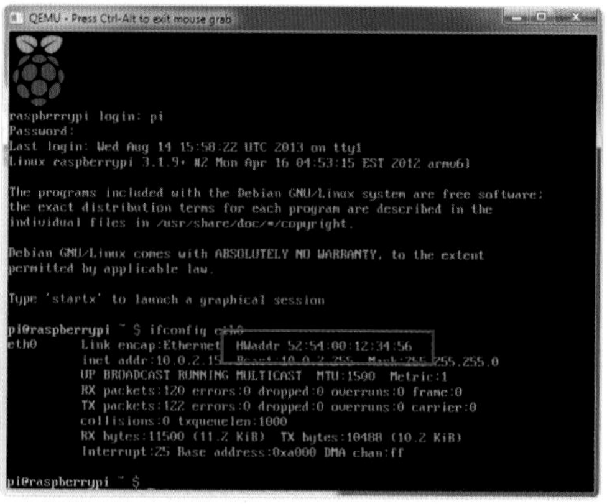

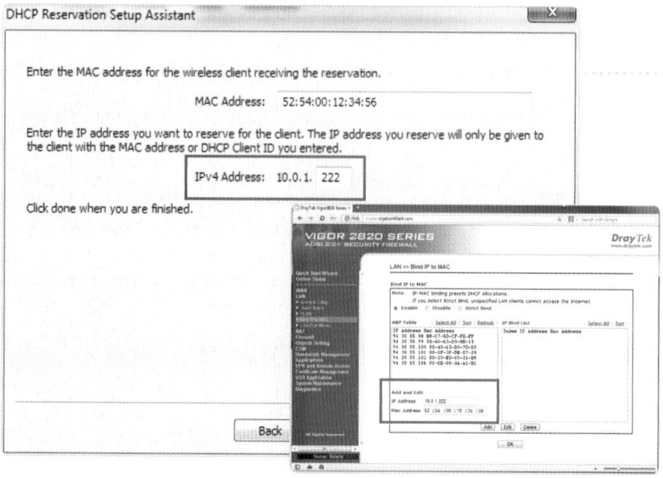

STEP 3 CONFIGURE YOUR ROUTER

Your **broadband router** is responsible for allocating IP addresses to every device on your network. Each router works slightly differently, but check the menus for **DHCP** and reservations. In the first screen here, an Apple Airport, a simple Windows **Wizard** lets you enter the MAC address for your Pi and the IP address that it should be given. In the second example, a Draytek Vigor router, the setting is under LAN (for 'local area network') and then 'Bind IP address to MAC. In the section labelled 'Add and Edit', enter the IP address and the MAC, and click Add. Before picking an IP address, take a look at the address given to your Pi automatically, and make sure the first three numbers are the same, and the last is less than 254. We picked 222, as it's easy to remember. Now, each time the Pi starts up on your network, it will have the same address. ▼

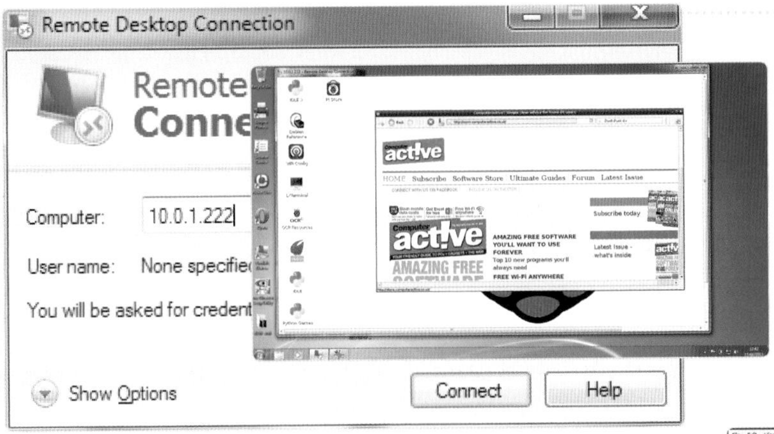

STEP 4 REMOTELY CONTROL YOUR RASBPERRY PI

The simplest way to control your Pi remotely is via Windows Remote Desktop. To do that, enter the command **sudo apt-get install xrdp** in LXTerminal or via an SSH connection to the Pi. If all is well, the message 'Starting Remote Desktop Protocol server : xrdp sesman' will appear after installation. Now, on your Windows PC, start Remote Desktop Connection (it's in All Programs, Accessories). Enter your Pi's fixed IP address (see step 2), and click Connect. Click Yes to continue if a security warning appears. You'll be asked to log in to the Pi, and then the desktop will appear. Just logout when you're done. ▼

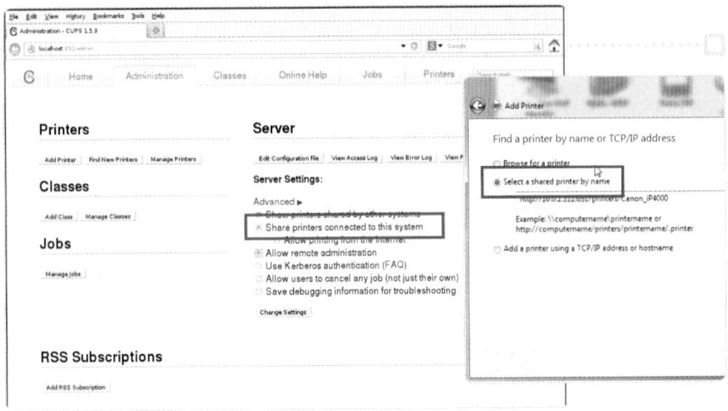

STEP 5 TURN ANY PRINTER INTO A NETWORK PRINTER

By setting up the Raspberry Pi with a fixed IP address (steps 2 and 3), you can use it to share any printer on a network. Configure the printer as explained on page 26, remembering to tick the Share box. Make sure you also tick the boxes in the Server Settings section of the CUPS web page to share printers and allow remote administration. Now, the printer will be available on your network as long as the Pi is turned on. In Windows, click to add a Network Printer, and choose the option to select a printer by name. If the Pi has the IP address 10.0.1.222 and the printer is called Canon_IP4000, type **http://10.0.1.222:631/printers/Canon_iP4000**. Click Next and select the correct Windows driver. ▼

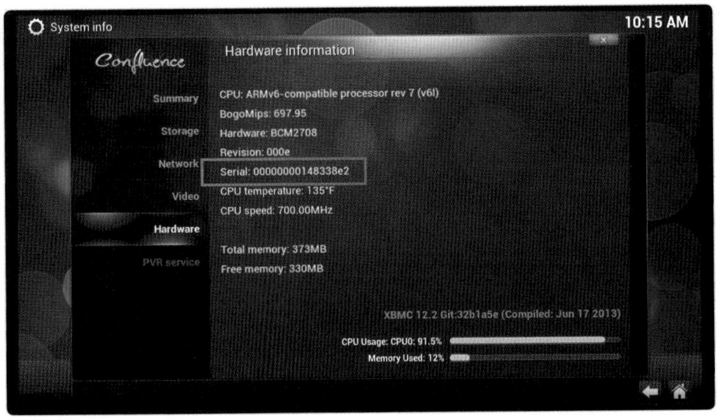

STEP 6 TURN YOUR PI INTO A DVD PLAYER

On page 32, we saw how to install OpenELEC on your Pi. With some extra work, you can make it play DVDs, too. You'll need to activate something called the **MPEG2 codec**, which costs £2.40. Go to the main menu in XMBC, click System, then System Info, and choose Hardware. Make a note of the sixteen-digit code shown as Serial. Open a web browser and go to ***www.raspberrypi.com***. Click to buy an MPEG2 license key; enter the serial number you wrote down. You'll receive an email with a licence key, like 'decode_MPG2=0x01234567'. Hold down shift as your Pi boots, press E to edit config.txt, and add the license key. Close the editor, then press Esc to reboot your Pi. ▼

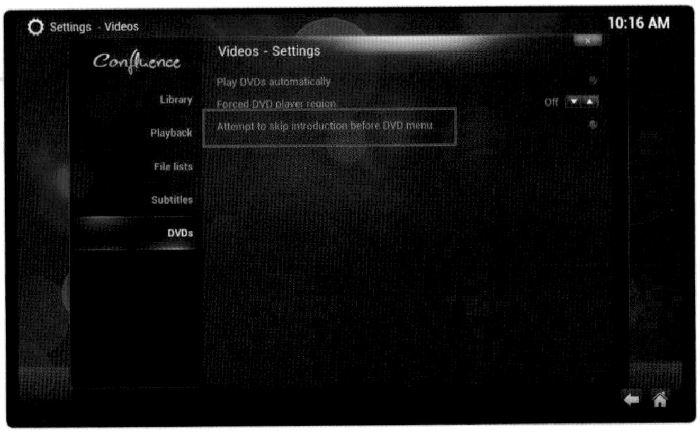

STEP 7 PLAY BACK A DVD

Connect an external DVD drive, with its own power supply – the Pi won't have enough juice to power the drive itself. The intro items on some DVDs can be problematic with XMBC, so from the main menu, choose System, Settings, then Video. Select the DVD tab and tick the box 'Attempt to skip introduction.' Now put a DVD in the drive, and after a few moments, the Play Disc option should appear on the XBMC menus. Click it and the disc's menu will appear, allowing you to select what you want to watch. If the subtitles turn on automatically, simply press the T key on the keyboard to turn them off. ●

Getting creative

Get inspired by the wild and wacky inventions other Raspberry Pi owners are coming up with

WHAT YOU'LL LEARN

- Discover great Pi projects that anyone can do
- See what's possible with a little creative thinking
- Find out how to put your Pi to practical use

Conceived as a way to encourage more software engineers, the biggest surprise for the creators of the Raspberry Pi, aside from its popularity, has been the way it has been used to create amazing hardware projects. In retrospect it's easy to see why – for less than the price of a new Playstation game you can now buy a fully working computer that you can program in a wide variety of languages. This means projects that would once have required university-level coding skills and a massive budget can now be accomplished by inventors in their sheds – the cliché has finally become reality. Throughout this guide, we have demonstrated some of the ways Pi owners can make use of their little computers but really this is just the tip of the iceberg. The possibilities are practically limitless, as some of the incredible Pi-based projects we're about to explore will prove.

By mounting a camera on a rail and moving it very slowly from left to right, taking a photo at each step, you can achieve truly breath-taking results. Sadly, the sort of rig used to create the opening credit sequence of Netflix's House of Cards costs a small fortune, but photographer David Hunt has managed to create a low-cost equivalent that's controlled by a Raspberry Pi. His setup took several months of experimentation and test shoots to put together but he's now using it to create some stunning panorama sequences of Ireland's natural and man-made landscapes. David has provided complete instructions, along with a video showing the setup in action, at his site (*www.davidhunt.ie/?p=2822*). So if you have an SLR, a Raspberry Pi and a little ambition, you could try creating your own magical compositions.

▶ Take amazing photos by using Raspberry Pi to control your camera

Grow your own with PiPlanter

Automating the care of plants is a huge growth area in agriculture and the Raspberry Pi is making it possible to achieve this in the home too. There are plenty of similar projects out there but PiPlanter (*www.esologic.com/?p=665*), created by a student called Devon, is the best documented. Devon has built a prototype system that he can then expand to a larger scale – in this case it supplies water to a crate containing tomato plants. The Raspberry Pi's GPIO ports are connected to sensors that read the light, temperature and humidity levels of the room along with how moist the soil is. Once the moisture reading falls below a pre-set level, the Pi turns on a small pump which delivers water to the crate.

Build an instant ice cream maker

On a recent episode of The Gadget Show (*www.snipca.com/9747*), presenters Jason Bradbury and Rachel Riley built an ice cream machine that used

CREATING YOUR OWN PROJECTS – HOW TO GET STARTED

You've made a good start by buying this guide; you now understand how the Raspberry Pi works, how to program it and what other people have used it for. The great thing about building your own projects is that you can start very simple and work your way up. If you break down the inventions we've listed here, you'll see that they're made up of lots of small projects, whether that's controlling a motor, reading in a barcode or taking a photo. So, the best plan is to learn how to achieve these small tasks and then put them together into a complete invention.

Exam board OCR has worked with the Raspberry Pi Foundation to put together a series of 'recipe cards' that you can use to build these micro-projects (***www.snipca.com/9744***) along with plenty of resources designed to be used in and out of the classroom. It may not seem like it at first, but, having understood the basics from this guide, learning how to use your Raspberry Pi to turn on an LED is the next step to your big idea, whether that's a roving robot, an aerial photography setup or a security system for your bedroom or snack cupboard.

◀ Make the perfect ice cream cornet, with raspberry sauce

▶ Make your microwave smarter, with Raspberry Pi

a Raspberry Pi to control the flow of the mixture through the nozzle and into the ice cream cone. A Pi-Face (***www.snipca.com/9748***) add-on board was used to turn the motor on and off – a task that draws more power than the Pi can deliver unaided. The contraption was then wheeled onto the streets but failed to produce a single 99 because the mixture wasn't cooled enough. The Raspberry Pi and Pi-Face performed perfectly however, flawlessly delivering soggy goo into the waiting cone. Do you think you could do better?

Thief Catcher

The Pi-Face add-on board was designed at the University of Manchester by Dr Andrew Robinson. It's designed to make it easy to connect to sensors and control other devices such as motors and switches. One of the first projects he built using the Pi-Face was designed to catch people trying to nab a cheeky biscuit from a cupboard. It's very simple – a standard magnetic switch from a burglar alarm system is mounted on the door and connected to the Pi-Face so that the Raspberry Pi knows when the cupboard has been opened. The Pi-Face is also wired to a battery-operated chicken with a speaker inside it. When the door is opened, a voice synthesiser plays a message telling the miscreant to get out of the cupboard. You can see how he did it, including all the code, at ***www.snipca.com/9749***.

The Intelligent Microwave

Why don't microwave ovens include barcode readers so they can automatically set the correct temperature and cooking time? Nathan Broadbent, frustrated that no such device exists, set out to create one. By working out how the keypad on the front of the microwave worked he was able to control it from his Raspberry Pi. He created his own microwave cooking database and even made the oven voice controlled. Whilst this might seem a little over the top for your average reheated curry, it makes for a lovely, integrated project. Each aspect of the project is carefully documented so you can pull out parts such as, for example, the barcode scanner, and incorporate them in your own inventions – watch the video here at ***www.snipca.com/9750***.

▼ The Pi-Face board makes it easy to attach sensors

A Pi-powered Wi-Fi Access Point

Are there parts of your home where you can't easily get a Wi-Fi signal? Guy Eastwood has created the Pi-Point project as a cheap, easy way to extend your network or, indeed, create a wireless router. Once set up, you can plug the Pi-Point directly into your **broadband router** or use a **HomePlug** adaptor to allow you to site the Pi-Point in a weak Wi-Fi area and connect to the router via the mains.

Guy has thoughtfully provided very detailed instructions and the good news is that if you have a Raspberry Pi and Wi-Fi dongle, you already have all the hardware you need. Not only is this an easy project to put together but you'll also learn a lot about networking – information that will come in very handy as you come up with your own inventions. Find out more and download the software at ***www.pi-point.co.uk***. ca

Computer active

Subscription order form

☑ **YES!** Please start my subscription to Computeractive and send me my **FREE 26-piece PC repair kit.**

YOUR DETAILS

Mr/Mrs/Ms ______ Forename ______

Surname ______

Address ______

______

______

Country ______ Postcode ______

Daytime phone ______ Year of Birth ______

Mobile No. ______

Email ______

2 EASY WAYS TO PAY

1 DIRECT DEBIT

☐ **Print Edition** – £17.50 for 6 months (13 issues) saving 32% on the shop price

☐ **Digital Edition** – £13.99 for 6 months (13 issues) saving 46% on the shop price

☐ **Print + Digital Bundle** – £22.50 for 6 months (13 issues) saving 57% on the shop price

Dennis **Instruction to your Bank or Building Society to pay by Direct Debit** DIRECT Debit

Name and full postal address of your Bank or Building Society

To the manager: Bank name ______

Address ______

Postcode ______

Account in the name(s) of ______

Branch sort code

Bank/Building Society account number

Originator's Identification Number

7	2	4	6	8	0

Instructions to your Bank or Building Society
Please pay Dennis Publishing Ltd. Direct Debits from the account detailed in this instruction subject to the safeguards assured by the Direct Debit Guarantee. I understand that this instruction may remain with Dennis Publishing Ltd. and, if so, details will be passed electronically to my Bank/Building Society.

Signature(s) ______

Date ______

Banks and building societies may not accept Direct Debit instructions for some types of account

2 CREDIT CARD – Select one option below

☐ **Print Edition** – £37.50 annually (26 issues) saving 28% on the shop price

☐ **Digital Edition** – £28.99 annually (26 issues) saving 44% on the shop price

☐ **Print + Digital Bundle** – £47.50 annually (26 issues) saving 54% on the shop price

Please charge my:

☐ Visa ☐ MasterCard ☐ AMEX ☐ Debit/Maestro (Issue No. ______)

CARD NUMBER ______ START DATE ______ EXPIRY DATE ______

SIGNED ______ TODAY'S DATE ______

RETURN TO: FREEPOST RLZS-ETGT-BCZR, Computeractive Subscriptions, 800 Guillat Avenue, Kent Science Park, Sittingbourne ME9 8JU

(This address can be used on an envelope – no stamp required)

Gift limited to 200 subscribers. Please allow 28 days for delivery. UK only.
Dennis Publishing reserves the right to limit offers of this kind to one per household.

Print Edition code: G1307P Digital Edition code: G1307D Print + Digital Bundle code: G1307B

AVAILABLE IN...

PRINT

SAVE 32%

Quote offer code G1307P
when you call or order online

Continue your subscription for **just £17.50** every 13 issues

DIGITAL

SAVE 46%

Quote offer code G1307D
when you call or order online

Continue your subscription for **just £13.99** every 13 issues

PRINT + DIGITAL

SAVE 57%

Quote offer code G1307B
when you call or order online

Continue your subscription for **just £22.50** every 13 issues

Digital Edition available on iPad, iPhone and Kindle Fire.

JARGON

8-bit
A measure of how much data makes up a picture. An 8-bit image can have 256 colours.

ADSL
Asynchronous Digital Subscriber Line. The most common type of broadband connection.

Broadband
A high-speed internet connection that is always available and provided via a modem or router.

Burn
The process of saving data to an optical disc, such as a recordable DVD or CD.

CPU
Central Processing Unit. The processor in a PC.

Codec
Coder/Decoder. A piece of software designed to process information in a specific format.

DHCP
The means by which a broadband router issues IP addresses to devices on the home network.

Dialogue box
A small window that appears to display or request information.

Dongle
A small device that plugs into a computer to provide a function like Wi-Fi access.

Drag and drop
Manipulating information by selecting it and dragging while holding the mouse button down.

Dropdown menu
A list of options displayed beneath a menu, or by clicking an option in a dialogue box.

DVI
Digital Visual Interface. A display connector.

Ethernet
A common type of wired network connection. Ethernet is often used to link PCs to routers.

FAT32
A common format for arranging information on disks and memory cards.

Flash drive
A removable disk or memory card that retains information even when unplugged.

GB, Gigabyte
1024 megabytes.

Hard disk
A high capacity storage device fitted in most PCs, made up of spinning mechanical platters.

HDMI
High Definition Multimedia Interface. A standard connector found on new TV sets and monitors.

High definition
Video pictures that have a better quality than the standard offered by DVD or broadcast TV.

HomePlug
A method of transferring computer data over the mains cabling in your home.

Icon
A small picture, often used to represent a particular application or document on a PC.

IP address
The unique identifier for a computer on a network, represented by a set of four numbers.

ISO
A common way to create images of optical discs.

JPEG
A common format used for digital photographs.

Linux
A free computer operating system.

MB, Megabyte
Normally 1024 kilobytes; occassionally 1000 kilobytes.

Megapixel
A description of the size of a digital image. A megapixel is equivalent to one million pixels.

Memory
Random access memory (RAM) is the computer's temporary working space.

Memory key
A small flash memory storage device with a USB connector that can be plugged into PCs.

MP3
A common format for storing music on a PC.

MPEG2
The codec used to store video on DVDs.

Operating system
The basic software, like Windows or Linux, that starts when your computer boots.

Pixel
Short for Picture Element. A pixel is one of the dots making up a digital image.

PNG
A format for digital pictures that allows for them to be transparent.

Ram
Random Access Memory. The working area used by the computer.

Resolution
A measure of the quality of a display, or of a digital image.

Right-click
Clicking an item with the right mouse button.

Router
A device that connects items on a computer network and links them to the internet.

SD card
The type of memory card used by the Raspberry Pi to store its operating system and data.

Server
A computer on a network or the internet that makes shared information available.

Stream
A way of playing music or video over a network without downloading it first.

TB
A terabyte is equivalent to 1024 gigabytes.

UPnP
Universal Plug and Play. A way for devices on a network to find each other automatically.

USB
Universal Serial Bus. A connector used to link peripherals such as keyboards, mice and hard disks to a PC or other computer, like the Pi.

VGA
An older way of connecting a PC to a monitor.

Wizard
An automated 'assistant' that guides you through a process step by step.